Trading Applications of Japanese Candlestick Charting

Wiley Finance Editions

Financial Statement Analysis
Martin S. Fridson

Dynamic Asset Allocation
David A. Hammer

Intermarket Technical Analysis
John J. Murphy

Investing in Intangible Assets
Russell L. Parr

Forecasting Financial Markets
Tony Plummer

Portfolio Management Formulas
Ralph Vince

Trading and Investing in Bond Options
M. Anthony Wong

The Complete Guide to Convertible Securities Worldwide
Laura A. Zubulake

Managed Futures in the Institutional Portfolio
Charles B. Epstein, Editor

Analyzing and Forecasting Futures Prices
Anthony F. Herbst

Chaos and Order in the Capital Markets
Edgar E. Peters

Inside the Financial Futures Markets, 3rd Edition
Mark J. Powers and Mark G. Castelino

Relative Dividend Yield
Anthony E. Spare

Selling Short
Joseph A. Walker

Treasury Operations and the Foreign Exchange Challenge
Dimitris N. Chorafas

The Foreign Exchange and Money Markets Guide
Julian Walmsley

Corporate Financial Risk Management
Diane B. Wunnicke, David R. Wilson, Brooke Wunnicke

Money Management Strategies for Futures Traders
Nauzer J. Balsara

The Mathematics of Money Management
Ralph Vince

The New Technology of Financial Management
Dimitris N. Chorafas

The Day Trader's Manual
William F. Eng

Option Market Making
Allen J. Baird

Trader Vic II: Principles of Market Analysis and Forecasting
Victor Sperandeo with T. Sullivan Brown

Trading for a Living
Dr. Alexander Elder

Fixed-Income Arbitrage: Analytical Techniques and Strategies
M. Anthony Wong

Trading Applications of Japanese Candlestick Charting

Gary S. Wagner and Bradley L. Matheny

John Wiley & Sons, Inc.

New York | Chichester | Brisbane | Toronto | Singapore

Publisher: K. Weber
Editor: M. Thompson
Managing Editor: J. Weisner
Composition: Impressions, a division of Edwards Brothers, Inc.

This text is printed on acid-free paper.

This publication is designed to provide accurate and authoritative information in regard to the subject matter covered. It is sold with the understanding that the publisher is not engaged in rendering legal, accounting, or other professional services. If legal advice or other expert assistance is required, the services of a competent professional person should be sought. FROM A DEC-LARATION OF PRINCIPLES JOINTLY ADOPTED BY A COMMITTEE OF THE AMERICAN BAR ASSOCIATION AND A COMMITTEE OF PUBLISHERS.

Library of Congress Cataloging-in-Publication Data:

Printed in the United States of America

10 9 8 7 6 5 4 3 2 1

Wagner, Gary S., 1954–
Trading applications of Japanese candlestick charting / Gary S. Wagner and Bradley L. Matheny.
  p.   cm. — (Wiley finance editions)
Includes index.
ISBN 0-471-58728-1 (acid-free paper)
1. Stocks—Prices—Japan—Charts, diagrams, etc. 2. Commodity exchanges—Japan—Charts, diagrams, etc. 3. Speculation. 4. Stock price forecasting. I. Matheny, Bradley L., 1963– .
II. Title. III. Title: Candlestick charting. IV. Series.
HG4638.W34   1994
332.63′222′09520223—dc20   93-25367

Contents

Foreword by John Bollinger   xi
Preface   xv
Acknowledgments   xix
Introduction   xxiii

PART ONE   **THE ART OF JAPANESE CANDLESTICK CHARTING**   1

ONE   **Candlestick Fundamentals and History**   3
Bar Charts versus Candlestick Charts   5
Identifying Single Candles   8

TWO   **Candle Location**   13
Paper Umbrellas   13
When a Small Candle or Doji Becomes a Star   13
Doji Candles   15
Flagship Candle Patterns   18

THREE   **Pattern Tables**   21
List of Candle Pattern Tables   21

FOUR   **Using Candlesticks as Leading Indicators**   39
Fibonacci Retracement Theory   40
Elliot Wave Analysis   43
Support and Resistance Trend Lines   47
Bollinger Bands   48

PART TWO   **CANDLESTICKS AND INTRACOMMODITY ANALYSIS**   51

FIVE   **Grains**   53
Soy Beans   53
Oats   58
Soy Bean Oil   60
Corn   63
Soy Meal   65
Wheat   72

SIX **Livestock** 75
  Live Cattle 75
  Feeder Cattle 81

SEVEN **Foods & Fiber** 103
  Cocoa 103
  Sugar 109
  Orange Juice 114
  Cotton 115

EIGHT **Energies** 129
  Crude Oil 129
  Heating Oil and Unleaded Gas 135

NINE **Currencies** 139
  Australian Dollar 139
  Intramarket Currency Analysis 139

TEN **Financial Interest Markets** 151
  30-Year U.S. Bonds 151
  Municipal Bonds 155

ELEVEN **Metal Markets** 159
  Gold 159
  Silver 162
  Palladium 164
  Platinum 167

PART THREE **JAPANESE CANDLESTICKS AND THE STOCK MARKET** 171

TWELVE **Cross-Market Analysis of Equities** 173
  Standard & Poor's 500 and Major Market Blue Chip Index 173
  Kansas City Value Line and New York Composite Index 177

THIRTEEN **Candlesticks and the Equities Markets** 179
  Jan Bell Marketing 179
  Kemper Corporation—Yearly Analysis for 1992 184
  Omnicom Group—Bullish Trend Analysis 195

PART FOUR **COMPUTER ANALYSIS OF CANDLESTICKS** 203

FOURTEEN **Computers and Candlesticks** 205
  Computer-aided Pattern Recognition 206
  How to Relate Japanese Candlestick Charts to a Computer 207

FIFTEEN   **Computer Filtering**
of Candlestick Patterns 213
Filtering Candlesticks with the
   Stochastic Oscillator 218
Filtering Candlesticks with Moving Averages 223
Filtering Candlesticks with William's Percent
   Retracement 228
Filtering Candlesticks with the Relative
   Strength Index 233
Filtering Candlesticks with the Relative
   Momentum Index 239
Filtering Candlesticks with Trading Bands 243

SIXTEEN   **Artificial Intelligence, Candlesticks, and**
Western Technical Indicators 249
Fundamentals of Artificially Intelligent
   Computers 249
Development of a Neural Network
   Software Program 251
Pretrained and Trainable Neural Networks 273

Conclusion 275
Bibliography 279
Glossary of Western Trading Terms 281
Index 283

Foreword

There is an old story about a group of blind men that encountered an elephant. The first blind man grasped the elephant's tail and thought the elephant was a jungle vine. The second encountered the elephant's leg and thought the elephant was a tree. The third, after he had examined the side of the elephant, declared it to be a barn. A fourth thought the ear was a giant fan. The fifth blind man declared the elephant to be a snake after encountering the trunk. Another came upon the elephant's tusk and thought the elephant to be a smooth log. Later that evening while sitting around the fire, they compared notes on their encounters with elephants. Upon learning they had all encountered but a single elephant, they wondered how each of them could have such a different impression of the same animal. We might speculate on what they agreed the elephant to be after trying to reconcile their differing impressions, but that would come to naught as they could not agree on a common "vision" of the elephant.

Most market analysts are very much like blind men examining an elephant. They see only that portion of the item they are trained to see. Most often they are unable to see beyond their narrow field of vision and reject the observations of others who, having different disciplines, will come to a differing conclusion upon examining the same item. One will look at earnings and, finding rapid earnings growth, will see a stock that should soar. Another, looking at the same stock but focusing on book value, will see overvaluation and a stock that should crash. The former's objective was to own strong growth; the latter's objective was to buy goods at a discount. Perhaps another pair of analysts comes along. One, noting the stock's increasing relative strength, would recommend a buy, while her opposite would see a severely overbought situation crying out to be sold. On one hand you have an attempt to buy performance; on the other, an attempt to pick a top. Yet another analyst might come along and reject any opinion on the stock because it was not in his "universe." The next analyst might say that the stock was too thinly traded for his volume-based methodology to apply. Here, too, we have a group of blind men who, having examined a common item, have come away with widely differing impressions.

Fortunately you do not have to suffer the same fate. The fact that you have this book in your hands suggests that you wish to see things from another point of view than that to which you are accustomed, that you wish to expand your horizons and see things in new and exciting ways. Therein lies the key to investment success.

The basic divide in the investment analysis community is between fundamentalists and technicians. Fundamentalists believe that through a careful inspection of a company's books and related factors, profitable investment decisions can be made. Technicians believe that profitable decisions can be made through a careful examination of an issue's trading activity and related factors. Further, within these camps there is endless diversity, as illustrated previously. They are both right.

There is actually a third group of market analysts that declares the analytical problems to be insoluble. Their solution is to become the market and, come what may, experience the long-haul trend of common stock returns. This group need not concern us here, as it has little impact on the analytical process.

On each side of the basic divide there is value, and within each of the subdivisions there is value as well. However, it is only through a combination of all of these factors that an analyst can hope to see the whole picture. Only by examining all of the relevant data can the analyst know the elephant. Increasingly this broad, renaissance approach is being adopted by analysts who wish to excel.

In what may be the first statement of contrarian philosophy, Henry Thoreau in *Walden* suggested that taking the less-trodden path made all the difference. I suggest that you take all the paths and see the problem from all angles to be successful in the long run. A narrow vision may work today, but it is unlikely to prevail over several market cycles.

Picture the whole of fundamental knowledge as a circle and the whole of technical knowledge as another circle. Now place them so that a portion of each circle overlaps a portion of the other. That intersection, the place where the fundamental and the technical overlap, is called the *juncture of the sets* in mathematics. I call that place the domain of rational analysis. I define a rational analyst to be one who inhabits the juncture of the sets of fundamental and technical analysis.

What you have in your hands is a book ostensibly on Japanese candlestick charting—an ancient and, for us, different way of looking at the markets. To me the value of this book is its attempt to join the sets of Eastern and Western technical knowledge. Therein, at least for me, lies the crux of the matter. This is a concept that is on the cutting edge of analysis. We no longer have a tree and a barn; now we begin to see the whole. We begin to achieve an understanding of just what the elephant is.

To go beyond the cutting edge, you have to combine this work with fundamental analysis. But that is the subject for another time and perhaps another book.

Welcome to the road(s). Good luck. It will be pleasant to have company along the way.

John Bollinger, CFA, CMT
President
Bollinger Capital Management
Manhattan Beach, California

Preface

*The future develops in accordance with fixed laws, according to calculated numbers. If these numbers are known, future events can be calculated with perfect certainty.**

—Richard Wilhelm

As a trader, commodity broker, and C.T.A., I was classically trained in the Western art of technical chart analysis. When I first began charting markets in 1980, I used a pencil rather than a keystroke and my "eye" to determine trend lines. As commercially produced, highly sophisticated software programs for charting emerged in the early 1980s, traders and technicians like myself were able to explore trading theorems at a speed and complexity never before possible. It was in this highly technical world that I would first hear about an ancient way of charting.

In the late 1980s, I was introduced to the art of candlestick charting through a data and charting service called "FutureSource." Although this service graphically displayed candlestick charts, interpretation of Japanese candlesticks was another matter. Because Japanese technical analysis was out of the realm of my Western training, I needed to gain the proper knowledge and understanding to be able to use candlestick charts.

I searched intently, asking every trader and associate I knew for knowledge of the Japanese candlestick charts. Very few had ever heard of this art form, let alone knew how to interpret them. One day I faxed a candlestick chart to one of my clients, and when I spoke to him he mentioned a candlestick pattern I had never heard of. I inquired where he had heard of this pattern, and he said it was in a book he had just bought called *The Japanese Chart of Charts* by Seiki Shimizu. "Tell me about this book!" I exclaimed. He did more than that; he ordered another copy and sent it to me.

This book was to be a pivotal point in my development as a market technician. It took some time, but after the third or fourth reading, the concepts of Japanese technical analysis and candlestick charts became clear to me. This

*Richard Wilheim, Introduction, *I Ching* (New York: New American Library, Times Mirror, 1971).

new knowledge directly affected my day-to-day market analysis. My trading performance vastly improved. The improvement was noticed first by my clients and then by the traders taking my orders on the floor. The techniques that I learned from Japanese technical analysis and candlestick charts allowed my trading to perform brilliantly with new advantages.

My clients were now extremely interested in Japanese technical analysis. They wanted to know how to recognize the patterns in a candlestick chart so that they could read them with a trained eye. Teaching myself to understand Japanese technical analysis was hard enough; teaching these concepts to others was another matter entirely. I would try to no avail to describe how to recognize and interpret candlestick charts and patterns.

Then one evening while looking at a candlestick chart, an idea came to me. If the ability to recognize patterns in the charts was achieved through a process of observation and identification and if this process could be recapitulated as a mathematical formula, then perhaps one could develop a computer program to identify and interpret Japanese candlestick patterns. Such a program would greatly benefit anyone who desired to learn about Japanese technical analysis.

Brad Matheny, a computer programmer, systems analyst, and a good friend for many years, immediately came to mind. Brad had built my first computer and taught me much of my initial computer knowledge. Over the years of our friendship, we had been exchanging ideas about technical analysis and computerized trading systems. Because of his interest in trading in the commodities market, I told him my idea. Handing him a drawing, I asked if it was possible to create a program for Japanese candlestick patterns. Brad studied the sketch, asked me a series of questions, and concluded that he could create such a program. This idea became the second pivotal point in my development as a trader and a technician.

A partnership was born, and the two of us began to develop a software program that would change both our lives. Between the two of us, we had the necessary components to design and realize our vision. From that moment, we began developing the software program that we named "The Candlestick Forecaster."

In May of 1991, while exhibiting our software product at the annual conference of the Market Technician Association, we met Steve Nison, a leading authority on Japanese technical analysis in the United States whose articles in *Futures* magazine had greatly added to our knowledge of candlestick charts. We were also eager to get a copy of his new book, *Japanese Candlestick Charting Techniques*. Curious about our program, he asked about the patterns in our library and made some suggestions. Steve Nison's book was also a pivotal point in the development of our idea, for it provided us with new knowledge and direction.

These were the important influences in our creating the computer program that led to the insights and the information found in this book. If we can share any of our enthusiasm for this project or any of the knowledge we have gained, we will have achieved our goal.

May you find the wisdom you seek,
and may that wisdom take you where you want to go.

Gary S. Wagner

Acknowledgments

Inspiration is a precious commodity. It is a state of mind that must be shared with others for fulfillment. An artist or musician without an audience is as incomplete as a mother without a child. What you achieve with inspiration is as important as where you find it. To channel it in a positive way, you must use this knowledge to acquire a better understanding and share that new idea to continue the cycle.

We would like to thank the following people for our inspiration:

Seiki Shimizu—Like the light of the candles themselves, your knowledge shines so that others might see.

Steve Nison—Although one man alone cannot move a mountain, he can make a path so that others might follow.

John Ehlers—for first suggesting that we write about our field of knowledge; Thom Hartle and *Stocks and Commodities* magazine—for allowing us to contribute; John Bollinger—for his insight and support; and Irwin Porter—a candlestick scholar from Quinter, Kansas; and to A.J.M. III, an early inspriation.

There are many people to thank, for without their help this book would not be in your hands. A market technician without data is like a chef with an empty cupboard. We would like to thank Robin Senett of Data Broadcasting Company, Tim Knight of Prophet Software, and Iverson Financial Data Service for their help in keeping our cupboard full. Special thanks to Rodney S. Allen for burning the midnight oil and providing us with his artistic talents. Thanks to John Upp and all at International Pacific Trading Company for allowing us time to write when we were needed in the office.

To Louise, Joseph Michael, and Eric Noah, my balance; and to Kitty Wagner, my beginning. G. S. W.

To Tracy, Larry, and Jeanne, and Tim Matheny. B. L. M.

Introduction

If I have all the data, I can use algebra and geometry and tell exactly by the theory of cycles when a certain thing is going to occur again..*

—W. D. Gann

You are about to embark on a journey into the fascinating world of Japanese candlestick charting. More than three centuries ago, long before W. D. Gann ever put a pencil to paper, the Japanese were creating candlestick charts to forecast price movement over time. This form of technical analysis not only predates Western analytical methodology but in many ways takes an entirely different path, which, as you will see, leads to some astounding results.

To understand candlestick charts, you must understand the way the Japanese technician thinks—you must think in Japanese. Imagine a written language composed not of letters but of a series of word pictures that reveal and describe the world. Their spoken language is created in much the same way, by linking these word pictures, or characters, together. That foundation of expressed thought is the complex matrix from which the candlestick method of technical analysis was brought into existence and conceived. The candlestick name is not just a monogram; rather, it's a complex description or picture of the meaning behind the candlestick character or pattern.

Visually, candlestick charts are an exciting means of displaying price movement over time. The images seem to bolt off the paper into a dimension of their own, revealing a fine distillation of the market they reflect. Candlestick charts and Japanese technical analysis offer insight into market movement and enhance Western technical analysis. The twentieth-century global trader who combines Eastern and Western trading techniques and concepts will possess a definitive trading methodology.

This book has been written in honor of the new global technicians and their advancements in technical analysis through the synthesis of Eastern and

---

*W. D. Gann—From an interview with Richard D. Wyckoff, "The Ticker and Investment Digest," (October 1909), New York

Western trading techniques. Our intent was not to write a guide or manual on Japanese candlesticks. Excellent manuscripts have already covered that topic. Rather, we wish to demonstrate practical trading applications by combining Western technical analysis, Japanese candlestick analysis, and computer-aided pattern recognition.

Part 1 will illustrate and explain some of the basic concepts of Japanese candle charts. Chapter 1 covers some of the fundamentals of Japanese candlesticks and compares basic differences between candlestick and bar charts as well as differences between Western and Eastern trading methodologies. Chapter 2 teaches principles necessary to create candlestick pole lines. It differentiates the three primary candle types and explains basic classifications necessary to enable one to identify the different candlestick characters. Chapter 3 introduces candlestick patterns. Advanced candlestick patterns can be defined as any grouping of two or more candles in relation to one another. Chapter 4 discusses how one can combine candlesticks with Western technical indicators to create a true leading indicator.

Part 2 applies practical candlestick trading in individual market groups. Each chapter analyzes a different commodity group. Chapter 5 illustrates trading examples in the grain markets. Chapter 6 discusses practical trading application of the cattle market. Chapter 7 gives examples of trading the "soft commodities." Chapter 8 provides trading examples in the energy markets. Chapter 9 shows candlestick trading examples in foreign currencies. Chapter 10 shows candlestick trading examples in the financial markets. Chapter 11 shows candlestick trading examples in the metals complex.

Part 3 looks at stock indexes and some of the individual equity markets that make up the Standard and Poor's 500. Chapter 12 shows candlestick trading examples in the stock indexes and an intramarket candlestick analysis using the S&P 500, New York Stock Exchange index, Major Market Index, and Kansas City Value Line. Chapter 13 looks at individual equities with detailed analysis combining Western and candlestick techniques to create proper trading methodology.

Part 4 investigates computer-aided Japanese candlesticks analysis. Chapter 14 discusses the validity of computer-aided analysis for candlestick identification. It also introduces the creation and development of computer-aided software applications specifically designed for candlestick recognition. This chapter introduces simple pattern recognition techniques, development of a knowledge base, and utilization of expert systems technologies. Chapter 15 teaches the techniques necessary to combine Western technical indicators and filter candlestick patterns. We will look at various indicators to discern appropriate usage of Western technical indicators as filters.

Chapter 16 introduces the use and development of artificially intelligent computer software applications. It discusses the fundamentals of developing an artificial intelligence software application and defines and explains the differences between a pretrained and trainable neural network. The Conclusion combines and synthesizes Western technical indicators, Japanese candlesticks, and computer-aided analyses to create a synergistic approach to trading. It will introduce a new approach or trading methodology that incorporates Eastern and Western ideology.

PART ONE

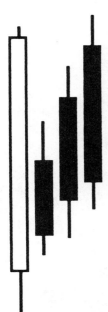

The Art of Japanese Candlestick Charting

ONE

Candlestick Chart Fundamentals and History

People have always attempted to forecast events and gain insight into what might be ahead. With the emergence of the micro-computer, exceptional effort has been expended on this quest. The statistician and technician, along with the professional trader, have continually updated the traditional method of chart analysis, which is based on open-high-low-close bars, or point and figure charts. Yet preceding these methods by over one hundred years, the Japanese were creating their own technique for analyzing markets.

Japanese rice merchants began trading "forward rice contracts" or "empty baskets" in 1654, and this practice soon evolved to become what is known to the Western technician as *candlestick charting,* because the lines that make up the charts resemble candles.

In the seventeenth century, long before the Western commodity or stock exchanges were formed, the Japanese developed the first futures exchange, the Dojima Rice Exchange, which traded "empty rice baskets" (predecessor to to-day's futures contract). Although relatively small in comparison to today's stock and futures exchanges, it provided fertile ground for the development of Japanese technical analysis, serving as price protection for the rice producers as well as a speculative tool for traders and merchants. One must realize the critical role that rice played in Japanese culture at that time; it was Japan's single most prized commodity.

The history of Japanese candlestick charting is as complex as the evolution of Japanese social culture. Sokyu Homma, who is credited with having originated this method, combined traditional Japanese folklore, military techniques, weather, seasonal tendencies, and many other factors, in his unique

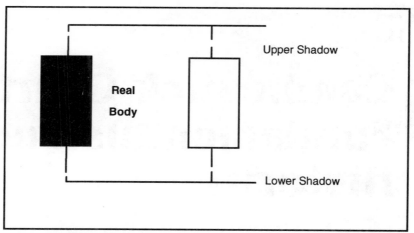

Figure 1.1 The Parts of a Candle

approach. Homma was the most prosperous and respected trader on the exchange and was even honored with the title of *Samurai* for his trading expertise in the face of his adversaries. Today his work is considered to be the foundation of modern Japanese technical analysis. Homma wrote two books, *Sakata Senho* and *Soba Sani No Den,* which explain what is now called Sakata's Five Methods, a set of patterns named for the city of his birth.

Sakata's Five Methods consist of four specific pattern types, all based on the number three, and a trading philosophy Homma employed for decision-making purposes. Because Japanese tradition held that the number three has divine power, many of the candlestick patterns are based on the number three. The four pattern types are *Sanku,* or three gaps; *Sanpei,* or three parallel lines; *Sansen,* or three rivers; and *Sanzan,* or three mountains.

Sanku forms its three-gaps pattern when four candles move in one direction, such as bullish black three-gaps or bearish white three-gaps patterns. It is considered an exhaustion signal, representing possible market consolidation or reversal.

The Sanpei pattern-type implies three parallel lines, such as in three white soldiers or three crows. It constitutes a continuation of the market trend.

The Sansen pattern-type implies three rivers, such as in three-river evening or three-river morning patterns, which indicate a top or bottom in the market. The Sanzan pattern implies three types of mountains, or top formations. The first mountain type is analogous to our head-and-shoulders formation; the second mountain type is a double top; the third is a round top.

In many ways, Japanese candlestick charts reflect the cognitive thought process of their creator and the ability of the Japanese people to convey complete messages with artistic symbols. They embody the sociological, psychological, hierarchical, and military teachings of the Japanese heritage. More than simply a colorful way to present a chart, the candles represent the interrelationships of the four price variables (open, low, high, and close), the Japanese people, and the beliefs that were held at the time of their creation.

In many cases the names given to the candles describe their shape or the relationship among them (open, high, low, or close). With titles such as rickshaw man, hangman, belt-hold line, shooting star, and many others, the Japanese have been able to use a visual image or word picture (much like their written language) to distinguish different kinds of candles. The names given to the candlestick patterns are vivid symbols and word portraits typical of Japanese culture and aesthetics: three Buddha tops, dark cloud cover, morning, evening, and three-river stars.

Bar Charts versus Candlestick Charts

Both bar and candlestick charts require four data variables: the open, low, high, and closing price for the cycle. The bar chart evolved from the simple line chart, which involves drawing a single line from one closing price to the next closing price, creating a continuous line that depicts price movement over time. The bar chart visually represents price movement over time by first drawing a single line from the high to the low price and then drawing a horizontal line to the left to show the open price and another horizontal line to the right to show the closing price. If the open and closing prices are equal, the bar chart representation and candlestick symbol are identical in shape and size. Western methodology emphasizes the relationship between the previous session's close and the current session's close.

Japanese candle charts present the same price data that other charting techniques use. The important difference is that the candle chart emphasizes the relationship between opening price and closing price rather than between closing price to prior closing price, as the Western bar chart does.

Figure 1.1 shows the parts of a candle. The thick part of the candle, known as the *real body,* represents the distance between the open and close for that cycle. The thin lines that resemble wicks, known as *shadows,* above and below the real body represent the high and low for that cycle. The location of the candle's body within the shadow indicates the high and low price range.

Visual Comparisons

Figure 1.2 shows the three candle types and their corresponding bar charts as a representation of how the same data is graphically displayed in both systems. The candle, or pole line, depicts one complete cycle with open, low, high, and

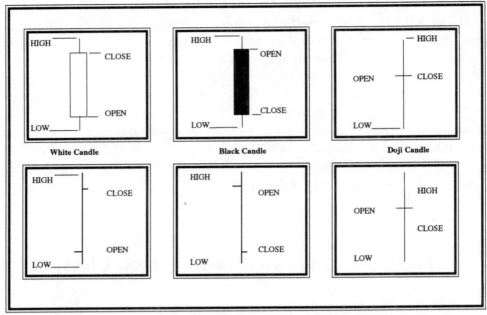

Figure 1.2 Comparison of Candlestick and Bar Charts

closing prices. A white (empty) candle indicates that the closing price is higher than the opening price for the cycle. A black (full) candle indicates the opposite: the opening price is higher than the closing price for the cycle. The *doji* occurs when the open and close prices are equal or very close to being equal. If the opening and closing prices are not equal but are very close to one another, a black or white body is formed. If the open and close are equal, a doji line is formed.

The doji candle is considered neutral, representative of a market consolidation unless it is found within a stronger pattern at the top or bottom of a trend. It is commonly found at strategic market turning points. Many of the strongest candle patterns incorporate one or more doji candles. Doji candles symbolize a clashing of heads between the bulls and the bears. Both the bulls and the bears are trying to push the market, but neither can succeed. A doji can signal major and minor reversal areas, known as support and resistance price levels. They appear more accurately during critical top and bottom formations. This seemingly uninhibited candle has a reputation of being one of the most important and should be watched for constantly.

Figures 1.3 and 1.4 are seven-minute intraday charts from Standard and Poor's 500. Figure 1.3 is a standard Western bar chart; Figure 1.4 is a Japanese candlestick chart. The most obvious difference is that Figure 1.4 uses black candles (lower closes) and white candles (higher closes) instead of a single

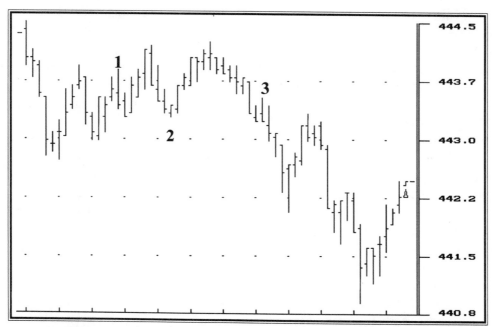

Figure 1.3 Seven-Minute Bar Chart, Standard and Poor's 500 Index (March 1993)

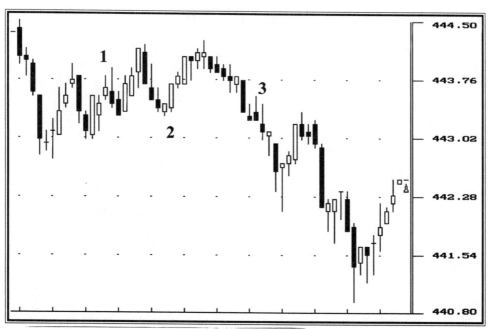

Figure 1.4 Seven-Minute Candlestick Chart, Standard and Poor's 500 Index (March 1993)

line. This visual difference allows one to discern price movement at a glance. In a congestion area (Area 1 of Figure 1.4), the candles tend to alternate from black to white and allow a more realistic visual representation by depicting congestion as a series of different colored candles. In the bar chart, the same information is not as readily revealed. In a bearish and bullish trend, the difference between a candlestick chart and a bar chart becomes even more dramatic. In Area 2 of Figure 1.4, the price advance is graphically displayed as a series of white candles moving in an upward direction. In Area 3 the price decline is shown as a series of black candles moving downward. Although both charts visually display price movement over time, the candlestick chart offers more perceptible evidence of price change, a distilled visual representation not present with a bar chart.

The candlestick chart interrelates the single candles to one another to define multiple candlestick patterns. Analyzing price data in this manner provides the trader with a more accurate depiction of market movement and trend definition. In addition, Japanese candlestick charts provide traders with predefined patterns, or groupings of candles, to predict future price movement. The Japanese candlestick charting technique is rich with descriptive patterns that are attuned to particular market scenarios.

Identifying Single Candles

The study of candlesticks is, in effect, the investigation of the relationship each time period has with the time period that preceded it. Identifying any candle or candlestick pattern and its message relies primarily upon our ability to identify each candlestick accurately.

Any candlestick chart is simply a collection of single candlesticks relating price movement over time. Each candlestick represents a given time frame's price movement, or trading session. Almost like pieces to a puzzle, the smaller pieces relate to the larger picture. Keeping this concept in mind, let's advance to the more subtle traits of the candles.

Within candlesticks, we are essentially emphasizing the different size and shape of the pole lines to determine a signal. Larger candlesticks would seem to have greater strength when predicting any price move over smaller ones, but larger candles do not upstage smaller candles in any way. A large candle is defined as one having a body that is greater than average in size. (The candle body is measured against an average of all the bodies on the chart.) Because it is considered large, it may fall into one of the special classifications for candles that are significant when found with specific continuation patterns. If not, it will be considered a common long white or black pole line. Small candlestick pole lines would have a body size that is smaller than average. These candles signify indecisiveness in the market. If a small candle gaps above or below the prior session, it becomes a *star*. A gap, as used in this context, is a price void (ie, no trading) from one price area to another.

We begin to learn how to identify a single candlestick pole line by first identifying its size. Next, we need to identify the candle's body color, size, and position within the shadows of the candle. After we have ascertained all of this information, we have identified the differentiating characteristics that make up a candle. We simply need to match the description of this candle to the possible types that are known.

Figures 1.5, 1.6, and 1.7 identify the different candle types. We shall refer to these candle types throughout the book.

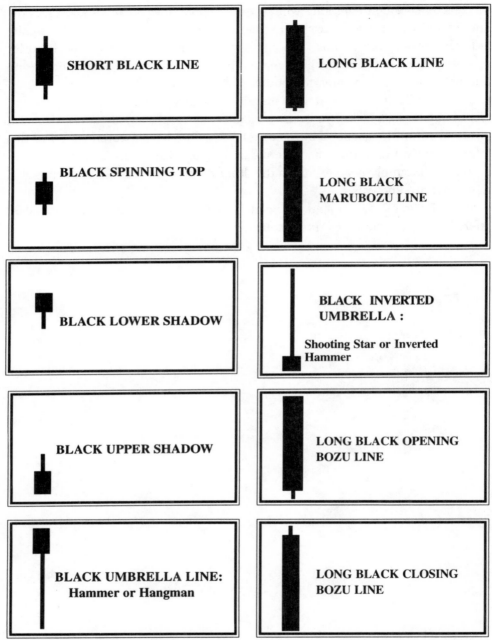

Figure 1.5 Black Candles

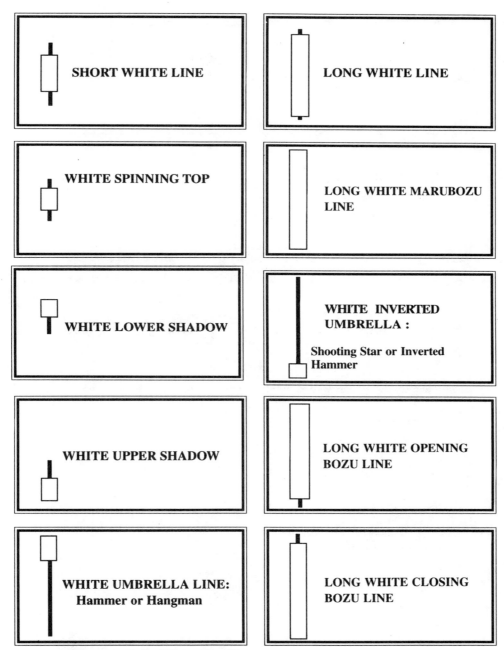

Figure 1.6 White Candles

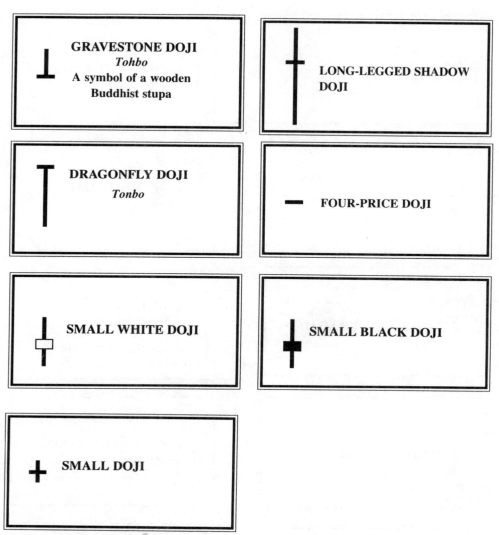

Figure 1.7 Doji Lines

TWO

Candle Location

In Chapter 1 we discussed how to recognize the different types of candles, but the significance of some candles is determined not only by their shape but also by their location within the chart. Moreover, each new candle can alter the types of candlestick patterns that may form. Two major classifications are used to determine the candle's location. They are based upon its location within a trend and its position in comparison to the prior candle. Only two candle types are affected by these two classifications: umbrellas and stars.

Paper Umbrellas

This group of candles is known in Japanese as *karakasa,* or paper umbrellas, because that is what these candles look like. The hangman, hammer, inverted hammer, and shooting star make up the umbrella group (Figure 2.1). A black hammer or hangman is created when the close is less than the open during a large daily range. The lower shadow must be twice the length of the body. A white hammer or hangman is created when the open is less than the close during a large daily range. The lower shadow also must be twice the length of the body. This candle is called a hammer if it occurs at the bottom of the market and a hangman if it occurs at the top. It can be recognized by the fairly tight opening and closing ranges. The inverted hammer and shooting star are just the opposite. The upper shadow must be at least twice the length of the body.

When a Small Candle or Doji Becomes a Star

The other types of candles that can convey different meanings depending on their location are the small and doji candles. They are significant in

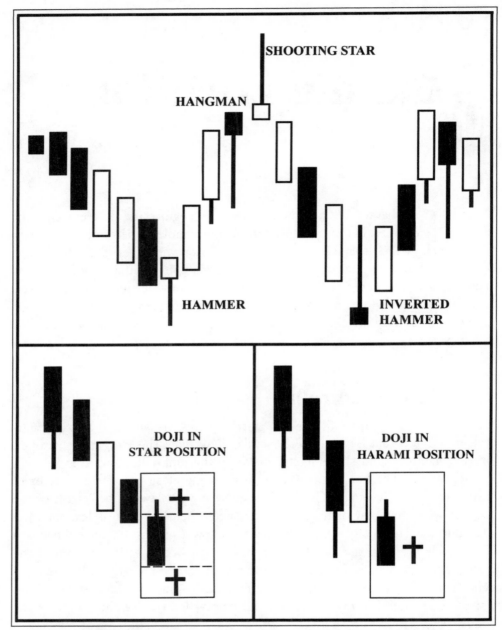

Figure 2.1 Location and Position for Stars and Umbrellas

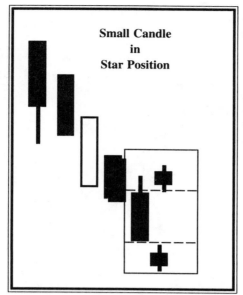

Figure 2.2 Small Candle in Star Position

that the narrow open and closing ranges depict uncertainty of direction. Neither the bears nor the bulls dominates the price activity. When found at the top or bottom of a market, these candle types can be a significant reversal indicator.

A small candle that gaps above or below the body of a prior candle is called a star (Figures 2.1 and 2.2). It can be in the form of a doji, a spinning top, any small body (black or white), or an inverted hammer. If an inverted hammer gaps above the prior candle, it becomes a shooting star. This pattern is called a *star reversal*.

The body of a small candle or doji that trades within the range of the prior candle body is called a *harami pattern. Harami* means "pregnant" in Japanese; this pattern resembles a pregnant woman, and hence the name. The harami is analogous to the Western "inside day" (Figure 2.1, Example 3, and Figure 2.3).

Doji Candles

Although both the small candle and doji candle can be significant because of the indecisiveness they depict, the doji is a much more powerful single candle. It represents the purest form of indecision; the market opens and closes exactly in the same place. The larger shadowed (the session high and low) doji are indicative of a very volatile session, whereas the small shadowed doji are indicative of a consolidating session. The doji candle represents the inability of

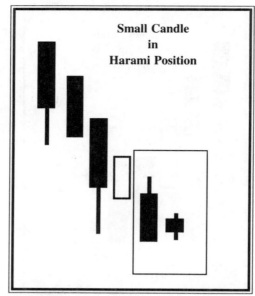

Figure 2.3 Small Candle in Harami Position

the bulls or the bears to continue the price advance or decline and has classically been viewed as signalling a major reversal in a consolidating market. Doji candles are often found at or near tops or bottoms, indicating that the market has exhausted its previous bullish or bearish trend move and should begin to reverse or stall. We need to pay close attention to the doji candle and how it forms within other patterns for early warning signs of a potential market reversal as well as the direction it is likely to take.

A doji candle or small candle can appear as a star by gapping either above or below the prior candle. The difference between evening and morning star formations involves the placement of the doji candle's body in relation to the prior candle's body. Other similar single candles can also become stars in the morning or evening position. A doji candle becomes a star reversal when it is gapped above or below the previous candle's real body. A visible window between the two candles' bodies must be apparent for the doji star formation to be correct. When a doji candle appears and a gap is also formed between the doji and the previous candle, a multitude of specific candle patterns can form from the doji star pattern and indicate the future trend of the market. Traders who have learned the importance of these particular candles have learned to constantly watch the market's activity for any doji star pattern or formation.

For a star to create and complete a three-river evening position, the candle found following the star must first gap, or open, below the body of the star. Secondly, the candle must be a long black line that closes significantly into the white candle found before the star.

For a star to create and complete a three-river morning position, the candle found following the star must first gap, or open, above the body of the star. Secondly, the candle must be a long white line that closes significantly into the black candle found before the star.

The term *morning position* refers to the location of the doji-shaped candle within the pattern that formed (Figure 2.4). When the doji, or star-shaped candle, forms below the previous and following candles with a gap or window between the real bodies of the three candles, the star is said to be in a morning position if it completes a three-river pattern. We should consider any three-river morning pattern a potential bottom or bottom reversal indicator if the other technical conditions confirm. A doji candle that appears below the surrounding candles is showing us that the star is setting and that the symbolic upcoming sunrise, or daybreak, will continue to push the market price upward and may initiate a bullish price move.

The term *evening position* refers to the opposite pattern formation (Figure 2.5). When the doji forms above the previous and following candles with a gap, or window, between the real bodies of the three candles, this doji, or star, is said to be in an evening position if it completes a three-river pattern. Any three-river evening pattern should be considered a potential top or top reversal indicator. A doji that appears above the surrounding candles is showing us that the star is rising and that the symbolic end of daylight, or nightfall, will continue to push the market price downward and may initiate a bearish price move.

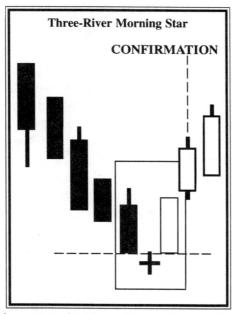

Figure 2.4 Three-River Morning Star

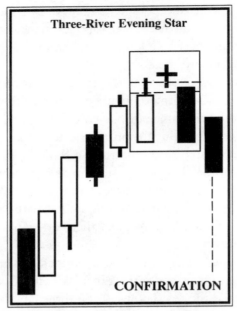

Figure 2.5 Three-River Evening Star

Flagship Candle Patterns

Just as a flagship leads a fleet of ships to its new destination, a *flagship pattern* is the first pattern to initiate a market move, or reversal. Other patterns most certainly will follow and provide additional support, but it will have been the flagship pattern that led the way. Therefore, flagship patterns are always found at the most significant market tops and bottoms.

A critical distinction between Japanese candlesticks and Western bar charts or other Western technical indicators is that the Japanese candlestick charting technique, when interpreted properly, returns more illuminating evidence and information of a market move than indicators based upon equations that use averages to obtain a value. Because most of the Western technical indicators are lagging indicators, they react after a market begins to make a move up or down. The delayed reaction time of these indicators and oscillators is necessary for determining the market trend, trend strength, direction of momentum, and most current market conditions when they are applied properly to a chart.

The Japanese candlestick charting technique, bit by bit, identifies the intermarket relationship of one market session (represented by a candle) to others that have appeared earlier and has an advanced predeveloped weighting system that applies to each specific candle and candlestick formation. To help identify a flagship candle or candlestick formation, we must first learn the basic single candle and candlestick formations as individual pieces of a much larger structure. We need to be concerned with more than just a single candle or a single candlestick patterns. To increase our understanding of Japanese candlestick charts and to begin to apply the knowledge we learn from the candlestick symbols and pattern formations, we must be aware of the larger structure and of each individual candle as a part of it.

Almost like characters in a play, the candles appear, one after another, to produce a legible, colorful, and accurate depiction of the market's advance, decline, or stagnation. Each individual candle that appears will provide us with more information about current market conditions and trends. A candlestick pattern is simply a combination of two or more candles which have been found to contain significant meaning. The pre-defined order of single candles together which make up a pattern, is information which has been obtained through centuries of research and technical observation. Candlestick patterns are created as different combinations of single candles are built upon one another. The color, size, shape and location are the variables that will determine what type of pattern has formed.

Flagship candles are often specific candle types such as a hammer, hangman, or a bozu line that form into other candlestick patterns and initiate a market move upward or downward. Even though a candlestick pattern may have actually issued a buy or sell signal, the actual candle that initiated or led the market move would be considered a flagship candle, not the candlestick pattern. Any candlestick pattern that includes the flagship candle is a product of the flagship candle and its surrounding candles. When a flagship candle and a candlestick pattern predict a similar potential market move, we are seeing a confluence of candlestick patterns, and we look to the market for movement in that direction. When a flagship candle and a candlestick pattern predict different potential market moves, the advanced candlestick pattern and any others immediately prior to it have a better probability of accurately predicting the market move.

Because candles, just like any other representation of a trading session, are fixed once the trading session has passed, a flagship candle is always found at the top or bottom of a chart. Remember, flagship candles lead or initiate a market move. The current candle may be continuing, confirming, or indicating a market's particular strength or weakness and not necessarily initiating a market move. These additional candles would either support the current market move or forewarn that the current market trend is weakening or about to stall. Eventually, a new flagship candle will form, possibly forming a candlestick pattern that may indicate a potential market trend reversal and initiate a new market trend.

This new flagship candle would stimulate the others because it is more likely to initiate a particular market move or trend direction. However, the older flagship candles and the advanced patterns that they create are still very important to the market technician. They provide us with defined information about the market's past price movement and identify important support and resistance price levels as well. They also provide historical evidence of the types of flagship candles that have formed and initiated a market move so that we can watch for them to form in the future.

THREE
Pattern Tables

Candlestick patterns consist of groups of single candles that are significant not only within themselves but also in their relationship to each other. The time period described by the patterns ranges from 2 to as many as 60 days.

The interaction of single candles with each other is analogous to the bulls and bears. Each candlestick pattern was inherently defined and distilled over the last 300 years to depict different market traits. As these traits were, over time, weighted and tested by Japanese technicians, a refined collage of accurate candle patterns evolved and was handed down to our generation. When combined with Western oscillators and trade analysis, these candlestick patterns can generate reliable buy and sell signals.

Because the number of possible candlestick patterns is immense, learning the Japanese candlestick charting technique takes time. The following lists and illustrations of candlestick patterns are in no way meant to be complete; rather, we have included them as templates to be used as a comprehensive reference guide. These samples are not actual charts; they are intended to serve solely as examples. We recommend that you refer back to this section during the course of reading this book.

List of Candle Pattern Tables
Bearish Reversal Patterns

Figure 3.1a
- Bearish Harami
- Dark Cloud Cover
- Engulfing Bearish
- Upside Gap Two-Crows

Figure 3.1b
- Hangman
- Shooting Star
- Doji Star Reversal
- Star Reversal

Figure 3.1c
- Tweezers Tops
- Tower Tops
- Bearish Harami Cross
- Bearish Meeting Lines

Figure 3.1d
- Breakaway Three–New Price Top
- Bearish White Three-Gaps
- Bearish Window
- Three-River Evening Star

Figure 3.1e
- Two-Mountain Top
- Southern Evening Cross
- Abandoned Baby

Figure 3.1f
- Gapping Play (Bullish and Bearish)
- Eight to Ten–New Price High

Bullish Reversal Patterns

Figure 3.2a
- Bullish Harami
- Piercing Line
- Engulfing Bullish
- Double Thrusting Pattern

Figure 3.2b
- Hammer
- Inverted Hammer
- Doji Star Reversal
- Star Reversal

Figure 3.2c
- Tweezers Bottoms
- Tower Bottom
- Bullish Harami Cross
- Bullish Meeting Lines

Figure 3.2d
- Breakaway Three–New Price Bottom
- Bullish Black Three-Gaps
- Bullish Window
- Three-River Morning Star

Figure 3.2e
- Two-Mountain Bottom
- Abandoned Baby

Figure 3.2f
- Eight to Ten–New Price Low

Gap, Continuation, Multiple, And Exhaustion Patterns

Figure 3.3a

▌ Simultaneous Three Wings: Bearish Continuation Signal

▌ Unique Three-River Bottom: Exhaustion Signal

▌ Tasuki Upside Gap: Bullish Continuation Signal

▌ Three-Winged Top: Exhaustion Signal

▌ Three-Line Strike: Bearish Reversal Signal

Figure 3.3b

▌ Tasuki Downside Gap: Bearish Continuation Signal

▌ Engulfing Bullish and Hammer: Multiple Pattern Group

▌ Upside Gap Side-by-Side White Lines: Bullish Continuation Signal

▌ Falling Three Method: Bearish Continuation Signal

Figure 3.3c

▌ Bullish Three-Line Breakaway and Close-in Line (Doji in Harami Position): Exhaustion Signal

▌ Bearish Three-Line Breakaway and Close-in Line (Doji in Harami Position): Exhaustion Signal

▌ Mountain Gap: Bullish Continuation And Sell Signal

Figure 3.3d

▌ Bozu Three Wings: Bearish Continuation Signal

▌ Tri-Star Bottom: Exhaustion Signal

▌ Rising Three Methods: Bullish Continuation Signal

▌ Tri-Star Top: Exhaustion Signal

▌ Advance Block with Hangman: Exhaustion Signal

Figure 3.3e

▌ Multiple Patterns: Piercing Line and Tweezers Bottoms

▌ Multiple Patterns: Ananume, Inverted Hammer, Doji, Engulfing Bullish, Hammer and Tower Bottoms

Figure 3.3f

▌ Three Crows: Bearish Continuation Signal

▌ Anaume: Exhaustion Signal

▌ Three White Soldiers: Bullish Continuation Signal

▌ Three-Line Star in Deliberation: Exhaustion Signal

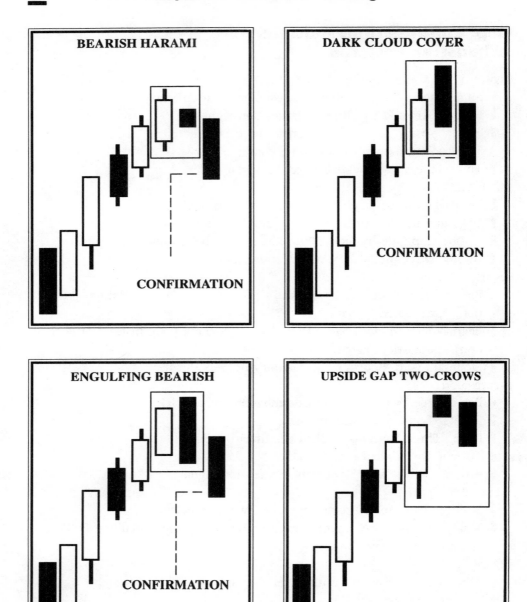

Figure 3.1a Bearish Reversal Patterns: Bearish Harami, Dark Cloud Cover, Engulfing Bearish, and Upside Gap Two-Crows

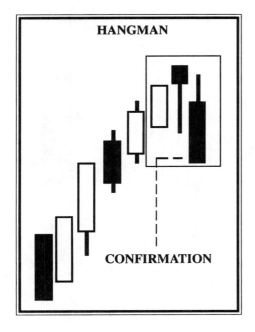

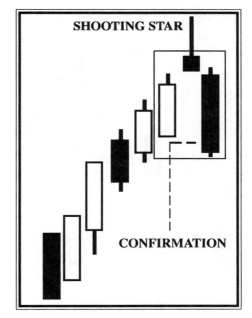

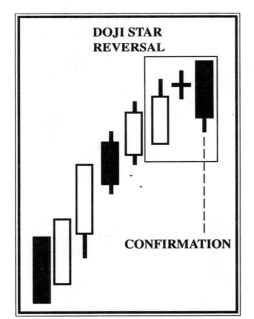

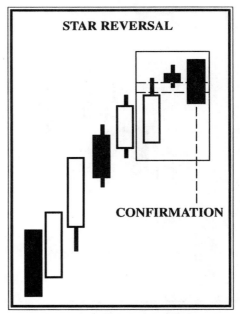

Figure 3.1b Bearish Reversal Patterns: Hangman, Shooting Star, Doji Star Reversal, and Star Reversal

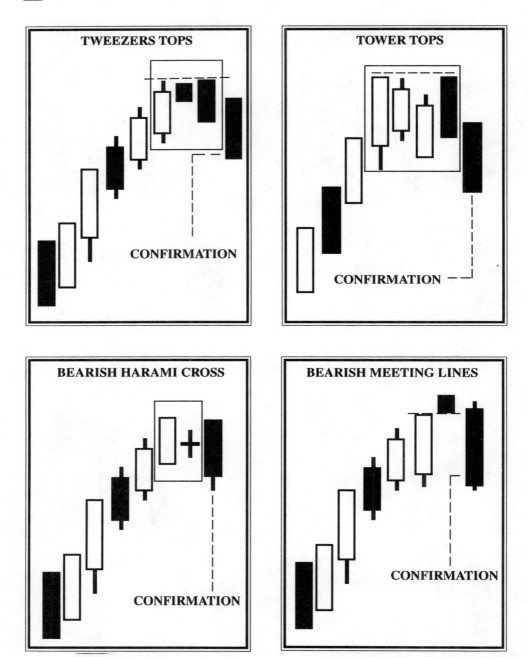

Figure 3.1c Bearish Reversal Patterns: Tweezers Tops, Tower Tops, Bearish Harami Cross, and Bearish Meeting Lines

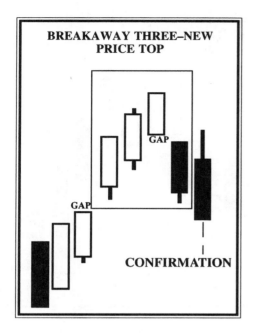

BREAKAWAY THREE–NEW PRICE TOP

GAP

GAP

CONFIRMATION

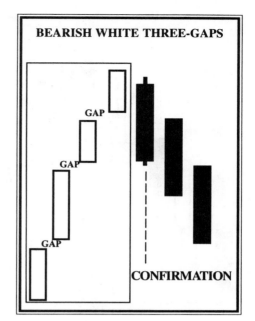

BEARISH WHITE THREE-GAPS

GAP

GAP

GAP

CONFIRMATION

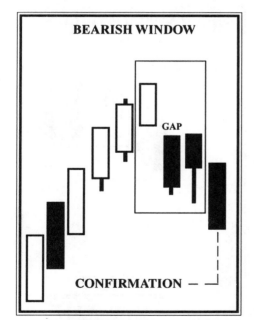

BEARISH WINDOW

GAP

CONFIRMATION —

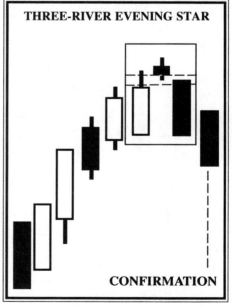

THREE-RIVER EVENING STAR

CONFIRMATION

Figure 3.1d Bearish Reversal Patterns: Breakaway Three–New Price Top, Bearish White Three-Gaps, Bearish Window, and Three River Evening Star

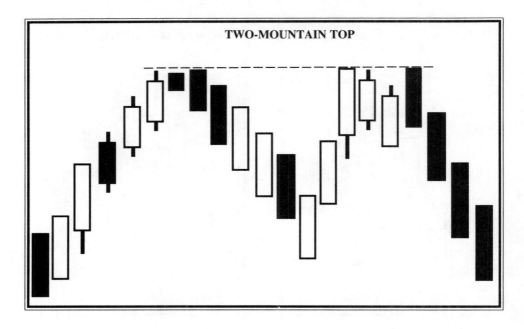

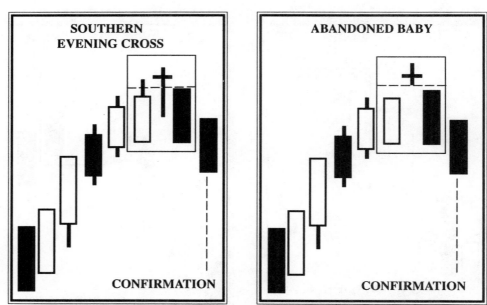

Figure 3.1e Bearish Reversal Patterns: Two-Mountain Top, Southern Evening Cross, and Abandoned Baby

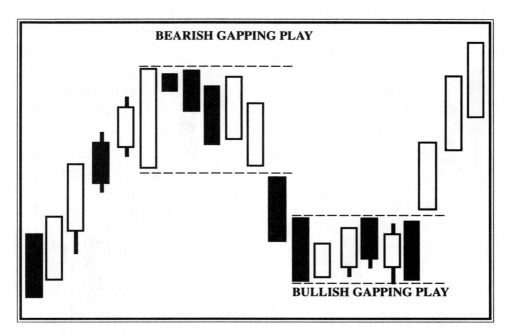

Figure 3.1f Bearish Reversal Patterns: Gapping Play (Bullish and Bearish) and Eight to Ten–New Price High

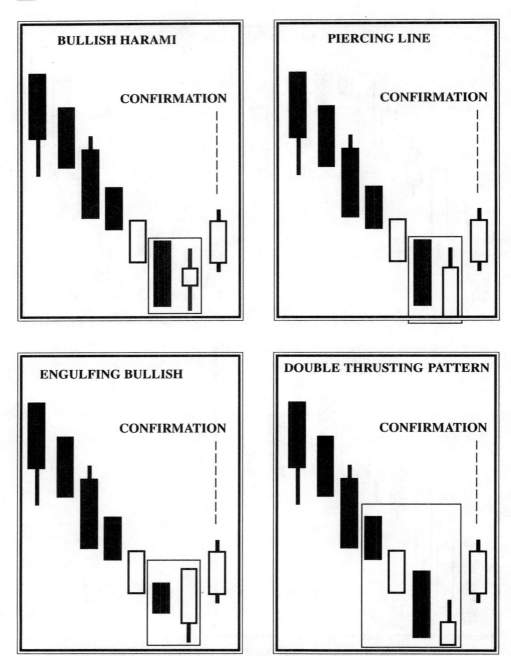

Figure 3.2a Bullish Reversal Patterns: Bullish Harami, Piercing Line, Engulfing Bullish, and Double Thrusting Pattern

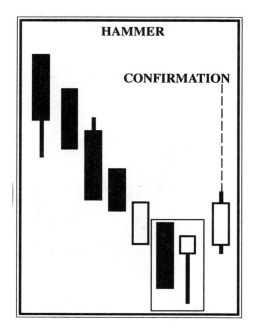

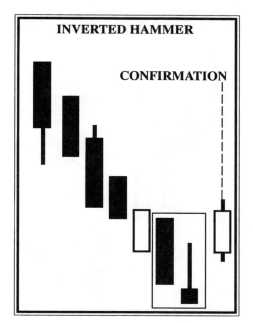

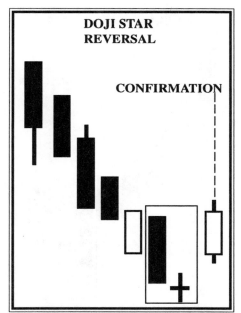

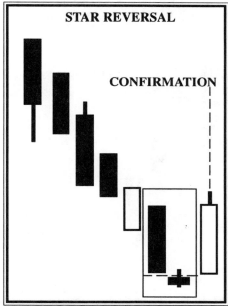

Figure 3.2b Bullish Reversal Patterns: Hammer, Inverted Hammer, Doji Star Reversal, and Star Reversal

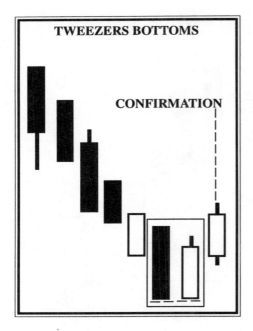

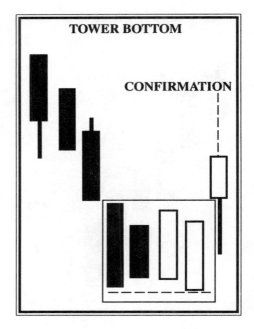

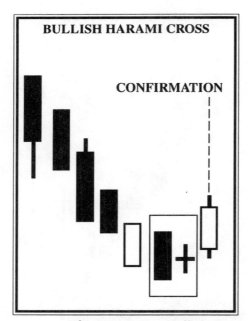

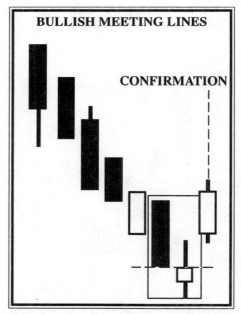

Figure 3.2c Bullish Reversal Patterns: Tweezers Bottoms, Tower Bottom, Bullish Harami Cross, and Bullish Meeting Lines

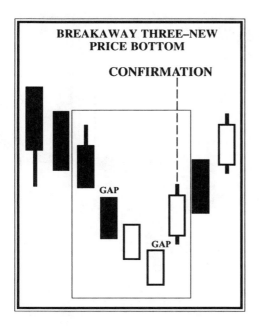

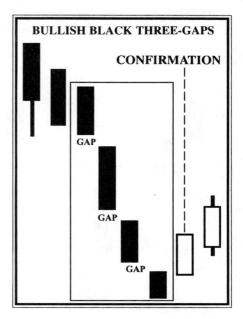

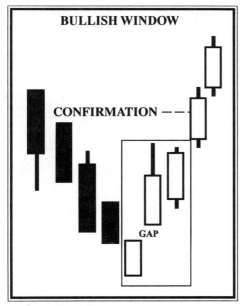

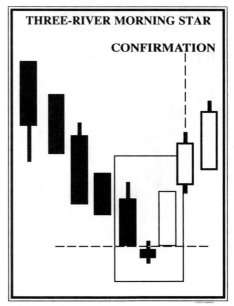

Figure 3.2d Bullish Reversal Patterns: Breakaway Three–New Price Bottom, Bullish Black Three-Gaps, Bullish Window, and Three-River Morning Star

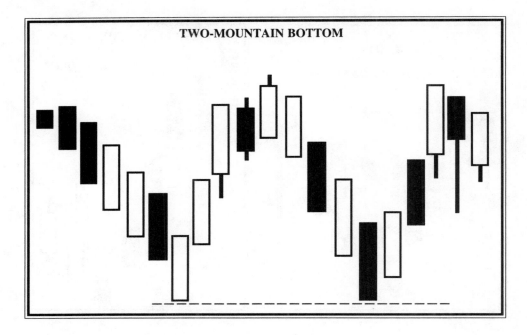

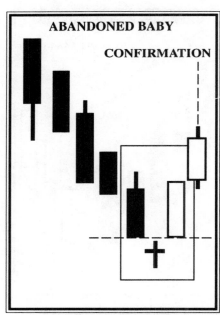

Figure 3.2e Bullish Reversal Patterns: Two-Mountain Bottom and Abandoned Baby

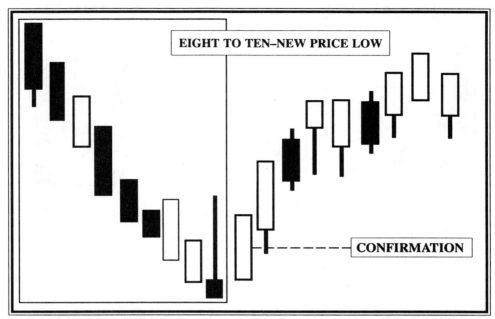

Figure 3.2f Bullish Reversal Pattern: Eight to Ten–New Price Low

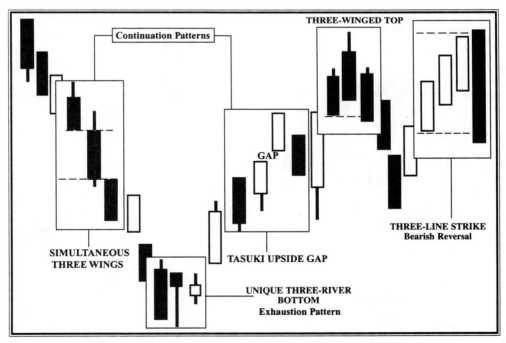

Figure 3.3a Gap, Continuation, Multiple, and Exhaustion Patterns: Simultaneous Three Wings, Unique Three-River Bottom, Tasuki Upside Gap, Three-Winged Top, and Three-Line Strike

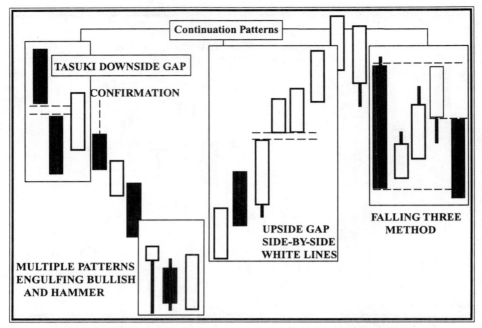

Figure 3.3b Gap, Continuation, Multiple, and Exhaustion Patterns: Tasuki Downside Gap, Engulfing Bullish and Hammer, Upside Gap Side-by-Side White Lines, and Falling Three Method

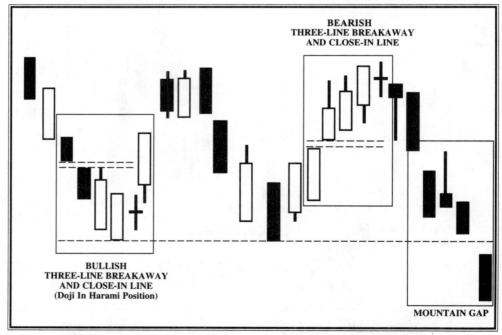

Figure 3.3c Gap, Continuation, Multiple, and Exhaustion Patterns: Bullish Three-Line Breakaway and Close-in Line (Doji in Harami Position), Bearish Three-Line Breakaway and Close-in Line (Doji in Harami Position), and Mountain Gap

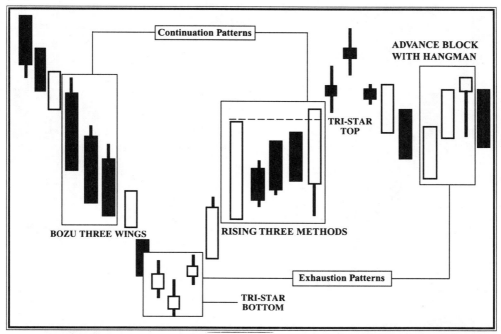

Figure 3.3d Gap, Continuation, Multiple, and Exhaustion
Patterns: Bozu Three Wings, Tri-Star Bottom, Rising Three Methods,
Tri-Star Top, and Advance Block with Hangman

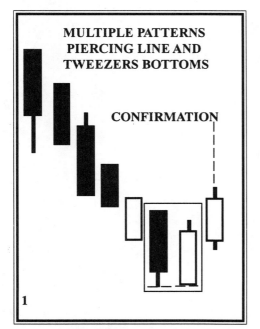
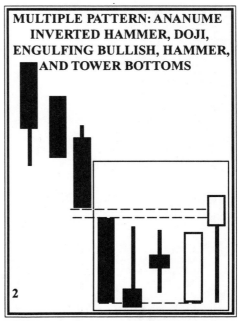

Figure 3.3e Multiple Patterns: Piercing Line, Tweezers Bottoms,
and Confirmation. Ananume, Inverted Hammer Doji, Engulfing
Bullish, Hammer and Tower Bottoms

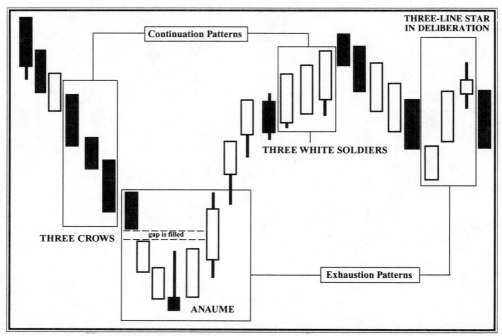

Figure 3.3f Gap, Continuation, Multiple, and Exhaustion Patterns: Three Crows, Anaume, Three White Soldiers, and Three-Line Star in Deliberation

FOUR

Using Candlesticks As Leading Indicators

Although Western technical analysis brings together many different theories and methodologies, most are mathematically based calculations using an average to obtain a value. Relying on a value that is based on averages of previous prices and comparing that value to a current value results in a lagging indicator. The best it can do is to tell you what a market is doing in comparison to where it has been, not where it is likely to go. A lagging indicator can predict market moves only after a turning point. A leading indicator, on the other hand, can predict market moves before they happen.

This is not to say that Western technical analysis is completely void of leading indicators or that Japanese technical analysis provides the only leading indicator available to the technician. In fact, to use candlesticks correctly as a leading indicator, one must fuse them with Western technical indicators to ascertain the market's trend and momentum. In this way the trader will have the necessary information to "filter" the candlestick pattern, to correctly know when and when not to use a particular candlestick pattern. Steve Nison is a prominent advocate of the utilization of multiple indicators as filters for candlesticks to ascertain the probability of success for candlestick patterns that are found. This style of candlestick analysis is called "the Rule of Multiple Technical Techniques."[1] It is based on the theory that when Western technical indicators agree with each other or with candlestick charts, there is an increased probability that trade will be successful. When applied to candlesticks, it acts as a primary filter to increase the probability of success. A bearish reversal pattern should only be considered if the market is in an overbought condition; likewise, a bullish reversal pattern is only relevant at the bottom of a market or during an oversold market condition. This is why we need to combine Western technical indicators with candlesticks, to determine if it is technically correct to act on information suggested by a candlestick pattern.

Western fundamental market analysis is based upon assumptions of cause and effect—a price change in the bond market will affect the stock market, a change in the price of grains will affect the livestock market, and so on. Fundamental analysis is based upon a predefined set of rules that predict price change based upon information and the effect of that information on a market's price. Fundamental market analysis is the inverse of technical market analysis. Whereas technical analysis obtains its values from market activity, fundamental analysis uses economic information about supply and demand to investigate market movement.

Fibonacci Retracement Theory

Fibonacci retracement theory is a Western indicator that has some of the qualities of a leading indicator. Though it relies on a market top or bottom to already be in place, it predicts levels of support and resistance before the market trades at that price. The retracement numbers developed by Fibonacci are 38 and 62 percent. They are derived from the Fibonacci number sequence of 1, 1, 2, 3, 5, 8, 13, 21, 34, 55, 89, 144. Fibonacci arrived at this series by adding the previous two numbers to obtain the third.[2] The ratio between any two of these numbers is always 62 percent, hence the calculation to determine a Fibonacci retracement level is basically the same in both bullish and bearish markets. Tables 4.1 and 4.2 show the basic formula used to return a Fibonacci retracement value (FRV).

Bearish Retracement Formula for gold example	
1. CP - PP = PD	1. 350.00 - 300.00 = 50.00
2. PD x 38 % = FRV 38	2. 50.00 x 38 % = 19.00
3. PD x 62 % = FRV 62	3. 50.00 x 62 % = 31.00
4. CP - FRV 38 = FRL 38	4. 350.00 - 19.00 = 331.00
5. CP - FRV 62 = FRL 62	5. 350.00 - 31.00 = 319.00

Table 4.1 Bearish Fibonacci Retracement Formula

Bearish Retracement Formula	Bullish Retracement Formula
1. CP - PP = PD	1. PP - CP = PD
2. PD x 38 % = FRV 38	2. PD x 38 % = FRV 38
3. PD x 62 % = FRV 62	3. PD x 62 % = FRV 62
4. CP - FRV 38 = FRL 38	4. CP + FRV 38 = FRL 38
5. CP - FRV 62 = FRL 62	5. CP + FRV 62 = FRL 62

PP = Previous Price
CP = Current Price
PD = Price difference
FRV 38 = 38 % Fibonacci Retracement Value
FRV 62 = 62 % Fibonacci Retracement Value

FRL 38 = 38 % Fibonacci Retracement Level
FRL 62 = 62 % Fibonacci Retracement Level

Table 4.2 Fibonacci Retracement Formula

First calculate the difference between the last market move and the current price and divide that number by 38 and 62 percent. Now take those two numbers (FRV 38 and FRV 62) and subtract (for a bearish retracement value) or add (for a bullish retracement value) to the current price. For example, if gold recently moved up $50 (say, from $300 to $350 an ounce), closing above its moving averages, and now begins to trade below the moving average, Fibonacci retracement theory would predict that the first level of support would be at $331, followed by a support level at $319. One shortcoming is that this model will only predict where a market is headed after a key reversal. It is a leading indicator only for trend definition, not for key reversal prediction.

Figure 4.1 is a daily British pound chart. On October 13, 1992, the market formed a high at 1.68 British pounds (168.00) to the U.S. dollar (A). Following this high, the bears gained control and pushed the market substantially lower. During a four-week selling spree from the middle of October to November 13, 1992, the British pound dropped to a low of 149.00 (B), a 9 percent price decline.

Using the formula in Figure 4.1, we were able to produce the following Fibonacci retracement numbers. The first target was the 38 percent retracement of point A to B, which created horizontal line 3. This put the first level of resistance at 156.22. Line 1 is the 62 percent retracement target of 160.78. Line 4 is the

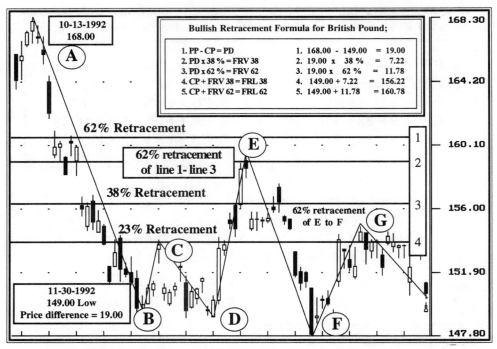

Figure 4.1 Fibonacci Retracement: British Pound, March 1993

23 percent level, which was calculated by multiplying the 38 percent retracement line by Fibonacci's 62 percent retracement line. Targets are calculated using the ratio of 1.62 percent, the ratio of any number to the next smaller number. In this example we can see that Fibonacci levels correctly predicted support and resistance levels following the price decline. After falling to a low of 149.00 (B), the British pound traded to a high of 153.00 (C) on December 3, 1992. This was a 23 percent retracement from point A to point B. Twenty-three is 62 percent of 38, falling perfectly into the guideline of Fibonacci retracement theory. After failing to take this resistance area, the British pound once again traded lower. The price finally stabilized after forming a double bottom (D). This double bottom was significant; a doji formed at the bottom and was then engulfed by a white candle on the following day. In seven days the market rose to a high of 159.36 (E), just below the 62 percent retracement level, to fall on line 2. Line 2 is a secondary line, which is a 62 percent retracement of line 1 (64 percent) to line 3 (38 percent).

This resistance level held, and the price began to drop once again. Twenty days later the British pound had broken the previous low of 149.00 (B) and created a new contract low on December 28, 1993, of 147.80 (F). This was a price drop of 11.76, almost the same number as the first 62 percent retracement level (11.78). The market traded higher and, just as predicted by Fibonacci theory, did not find any resistance until it reached a 62 percent retracement (E to F) of the previous drop (G) at 154.89.

Elliot Wave Analysis

Fibonacci retracement theory relies on a market top or bottom to be already in place before it will predict levels of support and resistance. The logical evolution of this technical approach was created by R. N. Elliot, who took Fibonacci's theories and saw that these retracement laws were a part of a much larger cycle.[3] According to his theory, known as Elliot wave analysis, price variation moves in waves, and these waves repeat themselves over time. This continuous defined sequence, known as the *wave principle,* is based upon a wave pattern containing a five-wave advance, followed by a three-wave decline, for a total of eight waves that repeat over time.

With a predefined numeric sequence to rely upon, the Elliot wave theorist is able to calculate target price areas and projected reversal points. The numeric sequence for the wave placement is based upon Fibonacci's retracement theory combined with two other primary components: wave identification and time. Elliot waves are classified into two categories: *impulse waves,* which move in the direction of the trend, and *corrective waves,* which are Fibonacci retracement waves of the prior impulse waves. In either a bullish or bearish cycle the wave count is always identical. Waves 1, 3, and 5 are impulse waves, and waves 2 and 4 are corrective waves. In a perfect bullish wave formation each corrective wave will have a higher low than the last corrective wave, and each impulse wave will contain a higher high than the last impulse wave. The opposite is true for a bearish wave formation; each corrective wave will have a lower high than the last corrective wave, and each impulse wave will contain a lower low than the last impulse wave.

Figure 4.2 gives an example of an Elliot wave pattern during a bearish cycle in wheat. Wave 1 occurred as a bearish impulse wave carrying the market from $3.80 ½ down to $3.49 ¾ per bushel on May 21, 1992. This impulse wave was followed by the first corrective wave (wave 2) on June 10, 1992, which forced the market to a new high of $3.87 per bushel. Impulse wave 3 was short-lived and ended three days later on June 15, 1992. In that short time, however, it managed to gain back about 62 percent of the price of the previous corrective wave.

Wave 4 was a slow corrective wave ending on June 29, 1992, that came to completion on June 29, 1992, with a high of $3.67. The bearish force of impulse wave 5 dominated the markets as it pushed the market below wave 3 ($3.59) and wave 1 ($3.49 ¾) to a new contract low of $3.43 ½, on July 13, 1993. The A wave was a corrective wave and took back 13 ½ cents, almost the

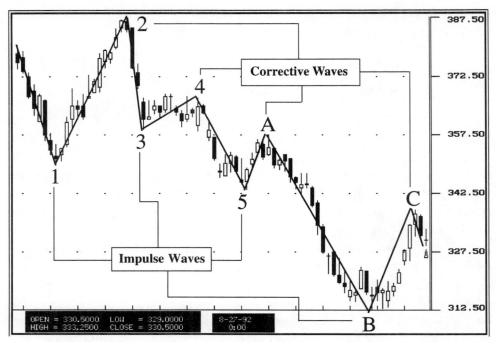

Figure 4.2 Bearish Cycle Elliot Wave: Daily Wheat, December 1992

perfect 62 percent retracement of 14 ½ cents that Fibonacci's theory would predict. The floor dropped out of the wheat market, and the final and most powerful of the impulse waves (wave B) began. In a little less than a month, from July 17, 1992, until August 13, 1992, the B wave, with the strength of a typhoon, forced the market down 44 ½ cents. The B wave ended on August 13, 1992, with a doji at a new contract low of $3.12 ½. The B wave was the last impulse wave of this bearish cycle that started on May 21, 1992. The wheat market, which was trading above $3.80 then, was now 67 ½ cents lower, with 62 percent of the total price decline (44 ½ cents) occurring in this final impulse wave. The last wave (C) retraced 38 percent, and on August 27, 1992, a doji marked the end to this Elliot wave.

Figure 4.3 shows a bullish Elliot wave cycle at the end of the last corrective wave (C) in Figure 4.2. As you will see later in this chapter, both cycles, each containing eight waves, are a part of a much larger picture. We begin viewing this chart on the first wave count. Wave 1 occurred as a bullish impulse wave carrying the market from $3.25 ¼ per bushel to $3.48 ¼ on September 2, 1992. The market dropped to its first corrective wave, wave 2, on September 23, 1992, where it reached a low of $3.54 ¼. The next impulse wave, wave 3, occurred on October 1, 1992. Wave 3 was strong enough to carry

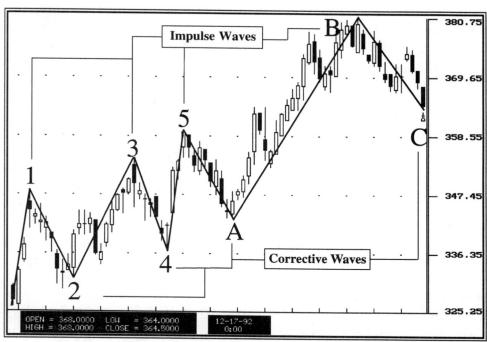

Figure 4.3 Bullish Cycle Elliot Wave: Daily Wheat, December 1992

the market to a new high of $3.54 per bushel, above the previous high of impulse wave 1. Wave 4, the corrective wave of wave 3, pushed the market down to the 62 percent retracement level, as predicted by Fibonacci's theory. On October 9, 1992, the corrective wave 4 came to rest at $3.37 per bushel. Most importantly, corrective wave 4 contained a higher low ($3.37) than corrective wave 2 ($3.34 ½).

Impulse wave 5 accelerated the market's upward drive to an almost 90-degree rally. In three short days the market was driven up more than 22 cents per bushel and traded at a high of $3.59 ½ on October 14, 1993. Over the next two weeks the market entered a corrective wave (A) until a small doji was formed on October 26, 1992. The A wave was completed when the prior doji line was engulfed the following day, and impulse wave B commenced. This final bullish wave, which started on October 27, 1992, lasted well over a month and propelled the market to a new contract high of $3.80 ¾ on November 30, 1992. With a price move of 37 ¾ cents, this was certainly the strongest of all the prior impulse waves. Wave 8, the final corrective wave of this cycle, retraced 2 cents below the Fibonacci 38 percent level of $3.66 ¹⁄₁₀, with a low on December 17, 1992, of $3.64 per bushel.

As in fractal geometry, each Elliot wave is but a small segment of a single period that forms one complete cycle, and that complete cycle is a single wave in a yet larger cycle. The Elliot waves for that larger time value will then be a smaller part of a wave on another larger time scale. Figures 4.2–4.5 illustrate that point. The weekly wheat chart in Figure 4.4 contains all the price activity found in the other three figures. The price activity in Figure 4.2 can be condensed to a single wave on Figure 4.4. This single Elliot wave begins on May 8, 1992 (Figure 4.4, wave 4), and ends on August 14, 1992 (Figure 4.4, wave 5). As you can see, this condensed wave, when viewed on the daily chart (Figure 4.2), actually contains a full cycle of eight waves. Also the price activity in Figure 4.3 can be condensed to a single wave in Figure 4.4, where this single Elliot wave begins in the middle of August (wave 5) and ends on December 11, 1992 (B wave).

As in the last example, you can see that this condensed wave, when viewed on the daily chart (Figure 4.3), also contains a full cycle of eight waves, but in this case it is bullish. Just as in fractal geometry, a wave will always be a diminutive part of a larger cycle or a condensation of a cycle of a lesser time value. Each wave is a microcosm of the next level. Figure 4.5, which combines Figure 4.2 and Figure 4.3, contains all the price activity of the daily charts. In

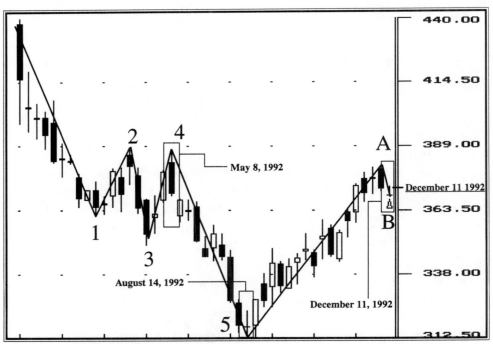

Figure 4.4 Elliot Wave and Candlesticks: Weekly Wheat, December 1992

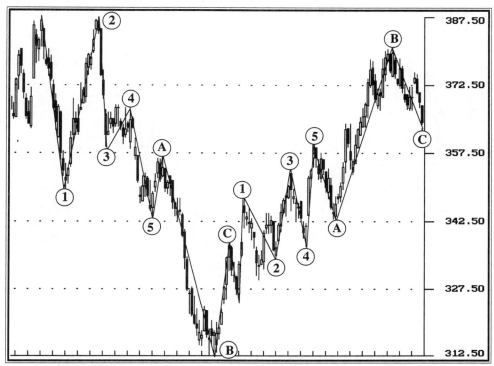

Figure 4.5 Elliot Wave and Candlesticks: Daily Wheat, December 1992

this way we can see that the bearish Elliot waves found in Figure 4.2 ran a full cycle and the bullish Elliot waves found in Figure 4.3 actually began after the bearish Elliot wave had completed its eight cycles.

Support and resistance lines, trading bands, and Bollinger bands (a variation of trading bands) are excellent technical tools that allow candlestick patterns to act as leading indicators for key reversals.

Support and Resistance Trend Lines

Support and resistance trend lines show where the current price is in relation to the trading range (Figure 4.6). By searching for critical clusters of highs and lows, support and resistance areas can be obtained, and trend lines can be drawn. This type of analysis will determine logical and mathematical targets for future price movement. These indicators will in turn create an envelope, or line, surrounding the trading range. When the current price approaches the edge of this envelope, the potential for a key reversal increases.

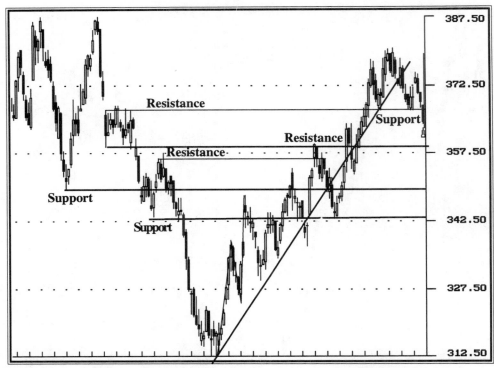

Figure 4.6 Trend Lines and Candlesticks: Daily Wheat, December 1992

Bollinger Bands

Trading bands and Bollinger Bands,[4] a variation of these, are excellent technical tools that allow candlestick patterns to act as leading indicators for key reversals (Figure 4.7). Candlestick technical analysts have discovered and labeled certain types of formations and created a defined set of rules that predict price changes. However, candlestick analysis requires that you use certain patterns at specific points in a market to accurately use them. One must still determine if the market is at that specific point to correctly utilize the information gained from any candlestick pattern found. Knowledge of the current market trend is necessary to correctly analyze Japanese candlestick patterns. Patterns that issue a reversal signal are more significant when found at market tops and bottoms than when found in the middle of a trading range. Support and resistance levels will allow the trader to determine the trading range.

According to John Bollinger, rapid price changes tend to occur after the bands tighten; in this scenario, tightening bands would lend confluence to any candlestick reversal pattern found. If a market is trading near but not above the upper Bollinger band, look for candlestick patterns such as tweezers tops,

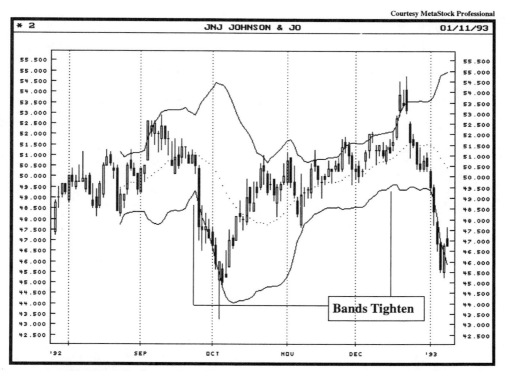

Figure 4.7 Daily Johnson & Johnson with Bollinger Bands

an anaume, advance block, eight to ten–new price high, bearish meeting lines, bearish harami (especially a harami cross), doji stars, three-river evening formations, three-winged top, three-line star, three-line strike, dumpling top, bearish three black gaps, or a low-price gapping play. Also look for candles such as hangman, shooting star, or belt-hold line to add additional confluence to any pattern found.

If a market is trading near but not below the lower Bollinger band, look for candlestick patterns such as bullish harami, three-winged bottom, 8 to 10– new price low, bullish meeting lines, doji stars, three-river morning stars, fry pan bottom, or a high-price gapping play. Hammers, inverted hammers, and belt-hold lines add additional confluence to any pattern found. If a market is trading above the upper Bollinger band, look for candlestick continuation patterns, such as three white soldiers, bullish meeting lines, window patterns, or any long white bozu line (Marubozu, opening bozu, and closing bozu). If a market is trading below the lower Bollinger band, look for candlestick continuation patterns such as three crows, bearish meeting lines, or any long black bozu line (Marubozu, opening bozu, and closing bozu). See examples of all these patterns in the preceding chapter.

Notes

1. Arthur Sklarew, *Techniques of a Professional Chart Analyst*, (New York: Commodity Research Bureau, 1980).
2. Considered to be one of the finest mathematicians, Leonardo Fibonacci da Pisa was born in Italy in the twelfth century. In Egypt he studied the great pyramids of Gizeh and observed that the pyramids' design incorporated the Golden Ratio into its architecture. Through his studies he discovered the sequence of numbers now known as Fibonacci Numbers. This number set begins with 1 and 1. The numbers are derived by adding the last two numbers to obtain the next. The Fibonacci numbers are 1, 1, 2, 3, 5, 13, 21, 34, 55, 89, 144, 233, 377, 610, 987, and so on to infinity.
3. R.N. Elliot was a market technician and theoretician who in the early 1900s developed the wave principle from his studies of Fibonacci numbers.
4. Named for their creator, John Bollinger, who created them to account for changes in market volatility and momentum.

PART TWO

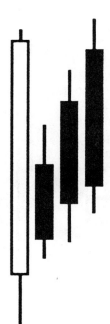

Candlesticks and Intra-commodity Analysis

P arts 2 and 3 present the results of research achieved using both subjective and computer-aided investigation. Many of the examples contained here are the interpretive output of our software application called the Candlestick Forecaster. This trading application integrates its copyrighted library of over 1,000 candlestick patterns with an expert system, artificial intelligence, and Western technical indicators to issue text-sensitive information about the data it is analyzing. We used this application to historically back-test both the equities and commodities markets. When viewing examples created through computer analysis, you will notice that the candles being reviewed are highlighted in a box, with a descriptive window, known as the *forecast window*, explaining the computer's findings. This window is composed of four basic sections. On the top line is the title of the candlestick that was selected for interpretation. The graphic window is on the left-hand side of the forecast window. In this area you will see the candlestick drawn again. The largest component of the forecast window is the text block, which contains a brief description of the candlestick, displays any relevant technical indicators, and in many cases displays its name in Japanese. Frequently you will see a suggested stop placement. On the bottom line is the signal window, which contains information about the

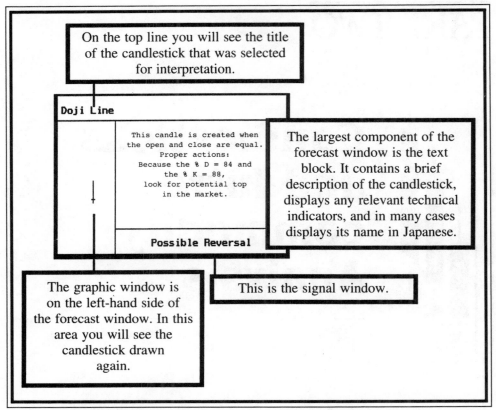

Figure 5.0 Example of the forecast window from the Candlestick Forecaster

strength and trend indications the candle and technical studies may contain. Figure 5.0 is an example of a forecast window.

Within the text block of the forecast window, many references to Western technical indicators are made. They are used primarily to filter the Japanese candlestick patterns. We used five Western technical indicators to filter the patterns found: moving averages, William's percent retracement, the relative strength index (RSI), stochastic oscillators, and trading bands. These are discussed in detail in Chapter 16.

References to Steve Nison in the text block of forecast windows depicted on the following pages indicate that the material therein is from his book *Japanese Candlestick Charting Techniques* (New York: New York Institute of Finance, Simon & Schuster, 1991).

FIVE

Grains

S ound technical approaches work equally well in related and nonrelated markets and convey valid insights when used for intramarket comparison. Grains are very well suited for interpretation with Japanese candlestick charts, as you will see in our examination of the markets for soy beans, soy meal, soy oil, corn, wheat, and oats.

Research has shown that there is a direct correlation between the prices of different grains. The economics of supply and demand dictate that to be the case. Therefore, if candlestick charts are truly reliable, they will reflect the same correlation. When markets move in unison, we should find candlestick patterns reflecting that market sentiment.

During mid-June 1992, the entire grain complex was under tremendous selling pressure. Within days of each other, all the grains began to trade aggressively lower. Analyzing the data, we found that every grain chart except wheat issued strong sell signals on June 11, 1992. In each case a significant bearish reversal pattern was found on or about the same day.

Soy Beans

Figures 5.1 through 5.8 are daily soy bean charts for November 1992. Figure 5.1 is an overview of many of the patterns found during this time period. Examples 1, 4, and 5 are engulfing bearish patterns, which seemed to predominate this market during a two-month selling spree. Of special interest is a tristar bottom (example 7). Figure 5.2 begins on June 9, 1992. A black hangman gapped above a large white candle to become the flagship candle of an advanced pattern that would take three more days to develop. The following day, June 10, 1992, a white doji star gapped below the hangman (Figure 5.3).

The combination of the doji and the hangman candlesticks together, as on June 10, 1992, in Figure 5.4, created a very strong reversal indicator. This was the first signal of the bearish sentiment that was about to enter the market.

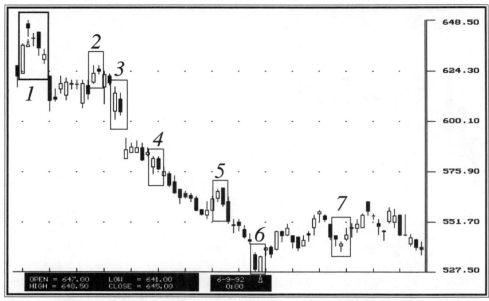

Figure 5.1   Soy Beans—November 1992 (6/3/92)

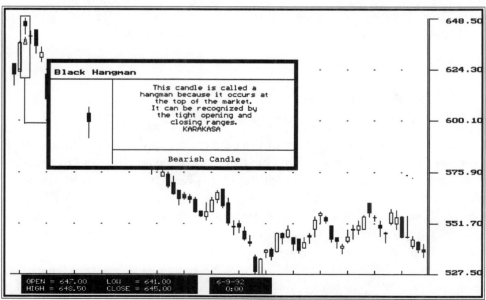

Figure 5.2   Soy Beans, November 1992—Black Hangman (6/9/92)

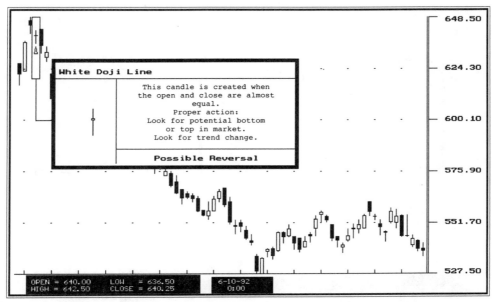

Figure 5.3 Soy Beans, November 1992—White Doji Line
(6/10/92)

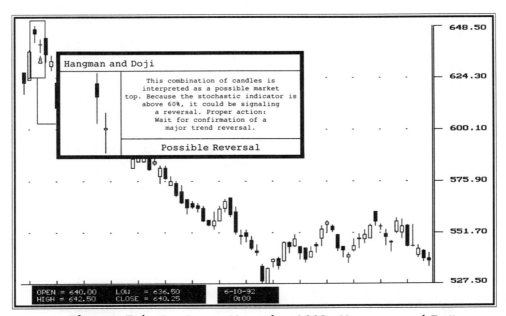

Figure 5.4 Soy Beans, November 1992—Hangman and Doji
(6/10/92)

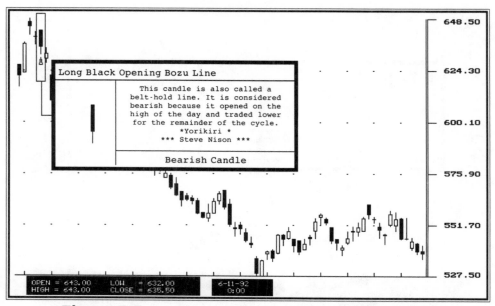

Figure 5.5 Soy Beans, November 1992—Long Black Opening Bozu Line (6/11/92)

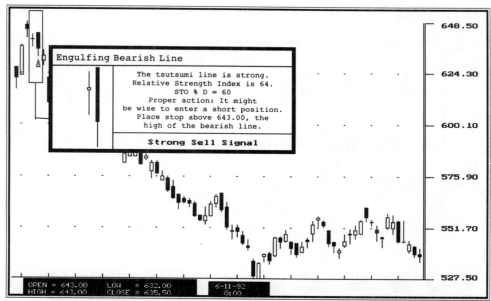

Figure 5.6 Soy Beans, November 1992—Engulfing Bearish Line (6/11/92)

The conservative trader would wait until this combination pattern is confirmed. Figure 5.5 shows that on the following day, June 11, a long black opening bozu candle was created. This candle is very bearish. It has a greater than average daily range and is never traded at a price higher than its open. By itself it gives no definitive signals, but it is very significant within the patterns of which it is a part.

The candles in Figures 5.5, 5.6, and 5.7 form a set of advanced patterns all clustered together. Figure 5.4 shows a doji and a hangman, a classic example of two candlestick types that are much more powerful in combination than separately. An engulfing bearish pattern formed when the opening black bozu line seen previously engulfed a doji (Figure 5.6). The combination of all of the patterns appears in Figure 5.7. This cluster of candles predicted a price decrease in soy beans that would last almost two months; as soy beans drifted lower, it was to have one final drop before finding a bottom. Example 5 in Figure 5.1 is the engulfing bearish pattern that was to be the last pattern in this downtrend.

On August 10, 1992, a piercing line signaled the completion of the bear's reign and the potential for a rise in price (Figure 5.8). Also on that day, the stochastic oscillators crossed, offering confluence and additional validity to this signal. The tumble in soy bean prices had finally come to an end, and the analysis provided through candlestick charts allowed us to see its direction clearly.

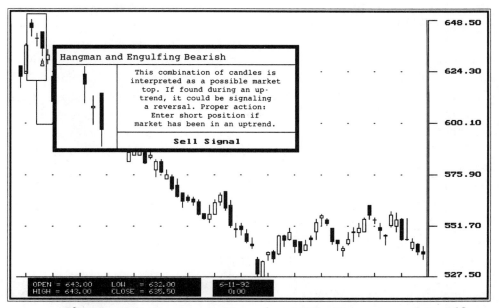

Figure 5.7 Soy Beans, November 1992—Hangman and Engulfing Bearish (6/11/92)

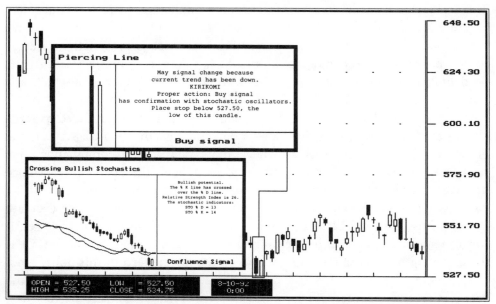

Figure 5.8 Soy Beans, November 1992—Piercing Line and Crossing Bullish Stochastics (8/10/92)

Oats

On June 9, 1992, the same day that the hangman formed in November soy beans, bearish white gaps were found in the December contract of oats (Figure 5.9). In this refined candlestick pattern, which is composed of three large white candles, each white candle must gap completely away from the prior candlestick body and shadow. This pattern shows that the bulls had run out of steam; confirmation of this pattern was needed to complete this signal. The following day, June 10, a large white closing bozu candle's body gapped above the prior session. Because the shadows of each of the white candles were within the other candle's bodies, no gap was formed, and no confirmation was given.

A sell signal confirmed the prior exhaustion signal when an engulfing bearish pattern was formed in December oats on June 10, 1992 (Figure 5.10), the same day that November soy beans had a cluster of sell signals. After four concurrent bullish white candles, an opening black bozu surrounded the last white closing bozu. The engulfing pattern was created and confirmed with Western technical indicators. The Williams percent retracement was at 15 percent, and a rise above 20 percent would confirm this sell signal.

Just as in soy beans, oats prices drifted lower and were going to have one final drop before finding a bottom. In Figure 5.11, the bullish black gaps were to be the last pattern in this downtrend. As in the soy bean market, an engulfing bearish pattern formed during the last drop but developed into a bullish

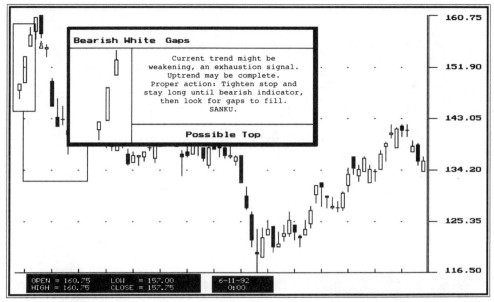

Figure 5.9 Oats, December 1992—Bearish White Gaps (6/11/92)

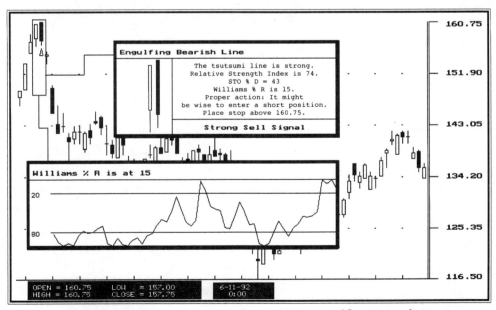

Figure 5.10 Oats, December 1992—Engulfing Bearish Line (6/11/92)

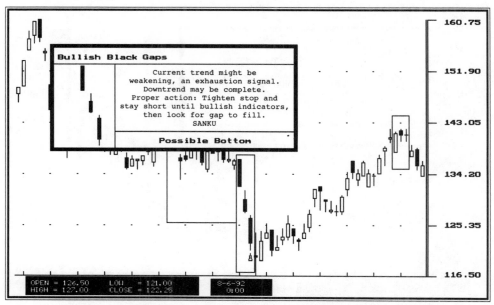

Figure 5.11 Oats, December 1992—Bullish Black Gaps (8/6/92)

black gaps pattern. Just as the bearish white gaps found at the top of this market (Figure 5.9) signaled an exhaustion to the preceding bullish price move, this mirror pattern signaled an exhaustion of the bearish price decline. A doji star, in the morning position, followed on August 12, 1992. The bulls finally lost their domination of the market on August 13, 1992. A white belt-hold line engulfed the prior doji, signaling an end to the price decline within days of a bottom in the soy bean market.

Soy Bean Oil

Unlike soy beans and oats, soy bean oil exhibited no hints of its impending price crash on June 10, 1992. On June 11, however, it was to begin a price decline that would also last well into August. Just as in oats and soy beans, an engulfing bearish line (Figure 5.12) was found on June 11, predicting lower prices and issuing a sell signal. This market reflected the moves in both soy beans and oats.

As in soy beans and oats, soy bean oil prices drifted lower and were going to have one final drop before finding a bottom. Example 1 in Figure 5.13 shows the dark cloud cover pattern that was to be the last pattern in this downtrend. On August 11, a thrusting line confirmation (Figure 5.13) signaled the completion of the bears' reign and the potential for a rise in the price of soy

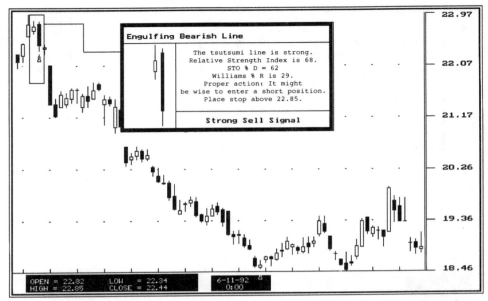

Figure 5.12 Soy Bean Oil, December 1992—Engulfing Bearish
Line (6/11/92)

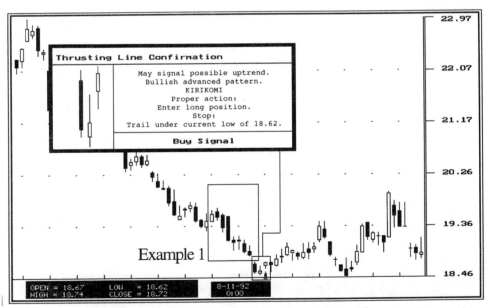

Figure 5.13 Soy Bean Oil, December 1992—Thrusting Line
Confirmation (8/11/92)

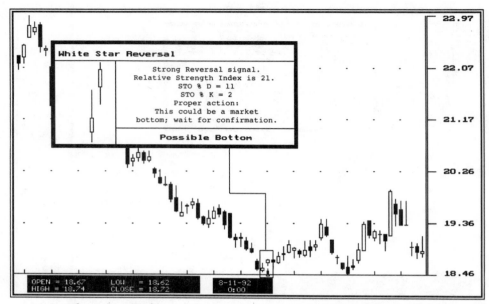

Figure 5.14 Soy Bean Oil, December 1992—White Star Reversal (8/11/92)

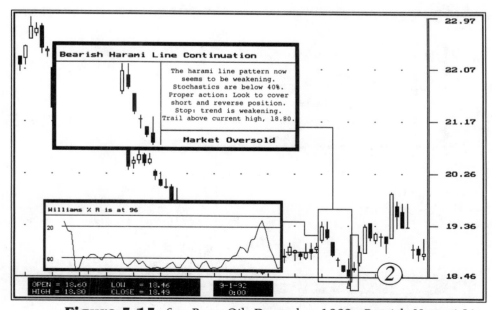

Figure 5.15 Soy Bean Oil, December 1992—Bearish Harami Line Continuation (9/1/92)

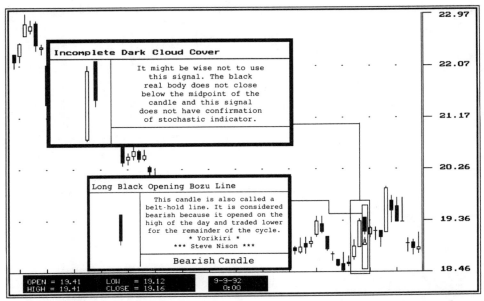

Figure 5.16 Soy Bean Oil, December 1992—Incomplete Dark Cloud Cover and Long Black Opening Bozu Line (9/9/92)

bean oil. Figure 5.14 shows a white star that also formed at the bottom of this market, adding credibility to the thrusting pattern issued a day ago.

After a slight rise in price, soy bean oil came under tremendous selling pressure about two weeks later. A bearish harami line signaled a fall back to the bottom of the channel (Figure 5.15). This was to end when an inverted hammer and a doji star formed a bottom (Figure 5.15, Example 2). The market continued higher only for about four days until a long opening bozu line created an incomplete dark cloud cover (Figure 5.16).

Corn

Figure 5.17 is a daily December corn chart for June 11, 1992. Just as in the soy bean, oat, and soy bean oil markets, an engulfing bearish pattern formed. This pattern issued a sell signal for the corn market. As in the other markets, a strong sell signal was issued on the very same day. Although this seems to be textbook example, the point being made is very valid. Comparable markets that move in unison will have candlestick patterns form that confirm this trend and issue analogous signals.

Just as in soy beans, oats, and soy meal, corn prices drifted lower and were going to have one final drop before finding a bottom. On August 7, 1992, a doji line signaled the completion of the bears' reign and the potential for a

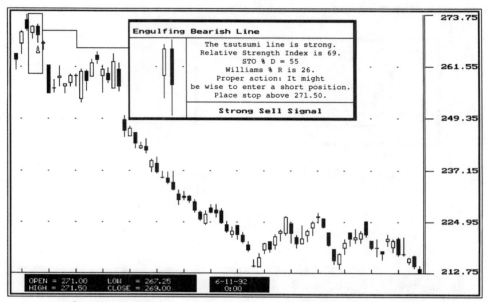

Figure 5.17   Corn, December 1992—Engulfing Bearish Line (6/11/92)

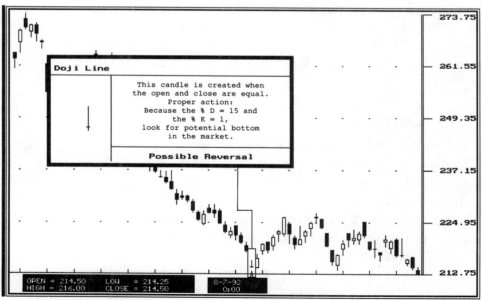

Figure 5.18   Corn, December 1992—Doji Line (8/7/92)

rise in the price of corn (Figure 5.18). This doji line had gapped below the prior black candle, creating a doji star (Figure 5.19). This candle signaled a potential reversal and possible trend change. The bottom was confirmed when an open bozu line engulfed the doji, signaling a bullish reversal in corn. Figure 5.20 shows the engulfing bearish pattern that was to be the last pattern found in this down-trend.

Another pattern found to be decisive and reliable in its ability to predict price changes within the grain markets is the bearish three-line strike (Figure 5.21). This formation contains a grouping of four candles. The first three are white lines, all having increasingly higher closes but each trading within the bodies of the prior candle. Next, a large black candle will engulf the prior three candles. Confirmation is necessary to complete this signal.

A lower open is required for confirmation, and a black candle should form before one takes this call. The bearish three-line strike can be found at market tops issuing a sell signal or within a bearish trend as a continuation signal. An engulfing bearish pattern is always going to be found at the end of a bearish three-line strike (Figure 5.22). The engulfing formations in corn seem to dom-inate in each wave of a market decline (Figure 5.23). An engulfing bullish pattern in corn signals the end of this selling pressure (Figure 5.24).

Soy Meal

On June 9, 1992, a white doji gapped above a large white candle (Figure 5.25, Example 1) and was followed as in soy beans with a black hangman on June 10, 1992 (Figure 5.25, Example 2). A doji and a hangman (Figure 5.26), when found together at the top of a market, can signal a very volatile market move. This combination pattern was followed by yet another hangman (Figure 5.27), which engulfed the previous hangman, confirming the reversal indicator.

Almost identical to November soy beans, December soy meal on August 10, 1992, formed a piercing line (Figure 5.28). Figure 5.29 shows a piercing line confirmation. To confirm a piercing line, the subsequent candle should first open higher then the previous candle's low and close higher than its open, creating a white candle.

Figure 5.30 is a daily December soy meal chart. Its time frame encom-passes three months from the beginning of 1992 to May of that year. Examples 1 (thrusting pattern), 3 (bullish harami), and 6 (bullish harami) are bottom reversal patterns. Examples 2, 4, 5 (engulfing bearish), 7 (incomplete dark cloud cover), and 8 (bearish harami) are top reversal indicators. The fascinating thing about this chart is that each major top and bottom is accompanied by appropriate reversal candlestick patterns.

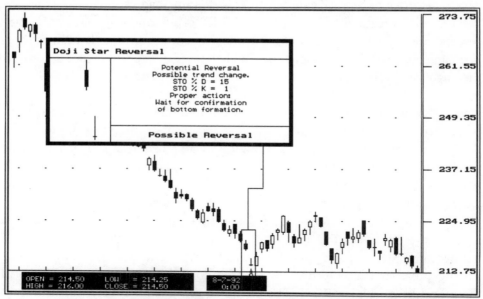

Figure 5.19 Corn, December 1992—Doji Star Reversal (8/7/92)

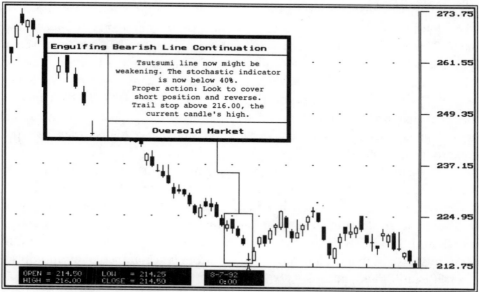

Figure 5.20 Corn, December 1992—Engulfing Bearish Line Continuation (8/7/92)

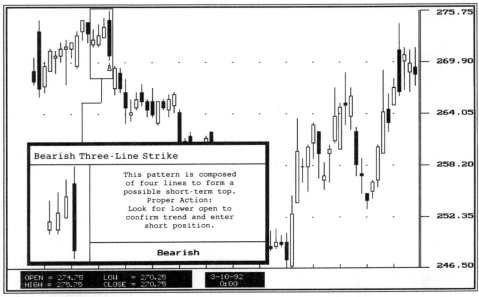

Figure 5.21 Corn, December 1992—Bearish Three-Line Strike
(3/10/92)

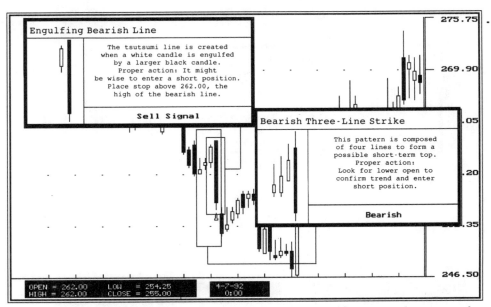

Figure 5.22 Corn, December 1992—Engulfing Bearish Line and
Bearish Three-Line Strike (4/7/92)

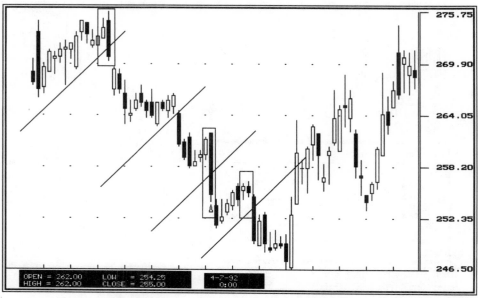

Figure 5.23 Corn, December 1992—Engulfing Formations and Market Decline (4/7/92)

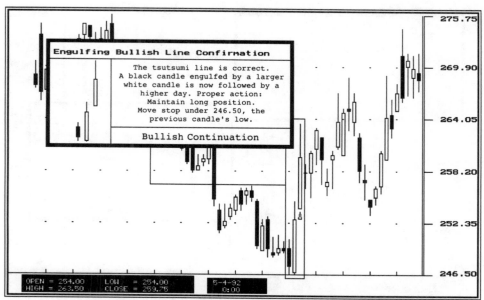

Figure 5.24 Corn, December 1992—Engulfing Bullish Line Confirmation (5/4/92)

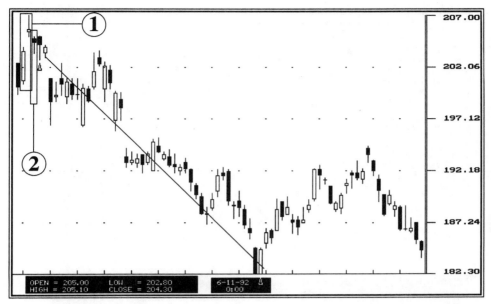

Figure 5.25 Soy Meal, December 1992—White Doji above White Candle (6/11/92)

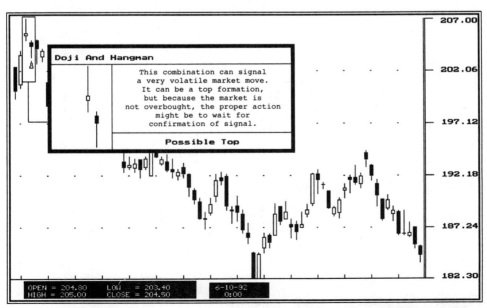

Figure 5.26 Soy Meal, December 1992—White Doji and Black Hangman (6/10/92)

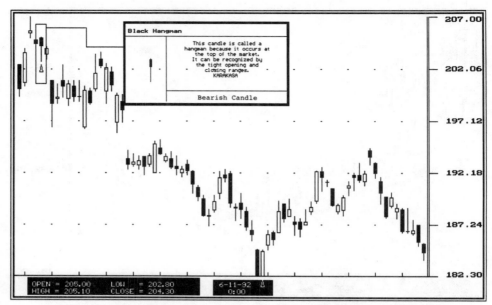

Figure 5.27 Soy Meal, December 1992—Black Hangman (6/11/92)

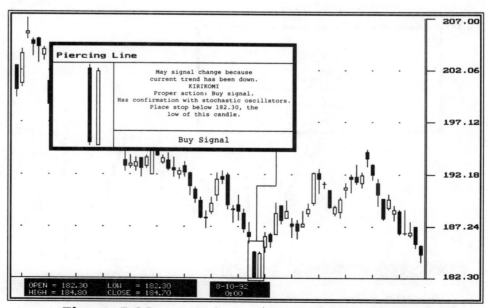

Figure 5.28 Soy Meal, December 1992—Piercing Line (8/10/92)

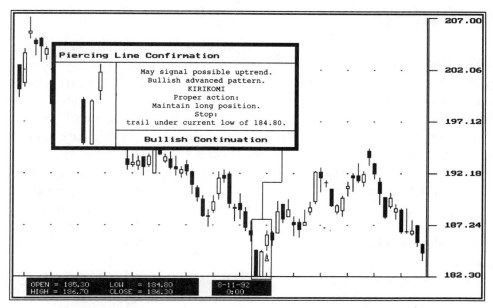

Figure 5.29 Soy Meal, December 1992—Piercing Line Confirmation (8/11/92)

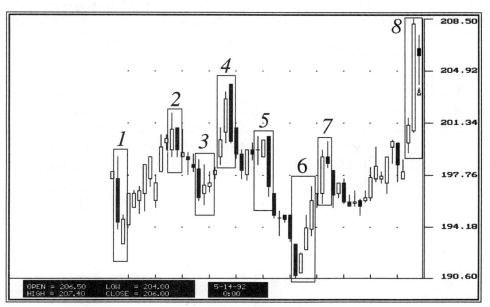

Figure 5.30 Soy Meal, December 1992—(8/14/92)

Wheat

Unlike all of the grains looked at previously, wheat was the only market not to issue a direct sell signal on June 11, 1992. Figure 5.31 is a daily December wheat chart. Example 1 is a highlighted box of June 11, 1992, when a black candle formed. Because it opened within the body of the prior white candle, however, it could become neither a dark cloud nor an engulfing bullish pattern. To become either of these bearish patterns, the black candle would have to open above the body (open and close) of the previous white candle.

This illustrates a key point. With the knowledge and information gained from the other patterns found on the same day in the grain complex, one could determine a trading strategy in wheat based upon candlestick patterns found in the other grains and the incomplete pattern found in wheat. Wheat was not completely void of candlestick patterns (see Figure 5.32). To understand the patterns found during this period, we first have to go back five days.

Example 1 in Figure 5.32 is a harami line continuation pattern. To meet the criteria of a bullish continuation pattern, it must have a higher high or a higher low than the last candle. If there is a lower close than the previous candle, it is pointing to a weakening trend but does not necessarily mean a termination of the trend. In this case the candle does make a new high; however, it closes lower on the day, creating a black candle that almost engulfed the previous candle. The stochastic oscillator is now above 65 percent and the RSI (relative strength index) has just moved above 80 percent (Figure 5.32, Example 2). Another pattern found is tweezers bottoms (Figure 5.32, Example 3). This pattern is most significant when found following a new low or in an established down-trend. Because this pattern is found on a new high, it may point to short-term support. Once this area is taken out and the area of support is broken, it is safe to assume the market will move to the next support area.

In August 1992 a doji line and a hammer (Figure 5.31, Example 2) signaled the completion of the bears' reign and the potential for a rise in the price of wheat. As in the other market viewed, there was an indication of the end of this bearish market; however, one can see that the candlestick patterns found in this market were less defined than in corn, soy, and oats. Clearly the added input from other grains during this period was critical in properly identifying market direction.

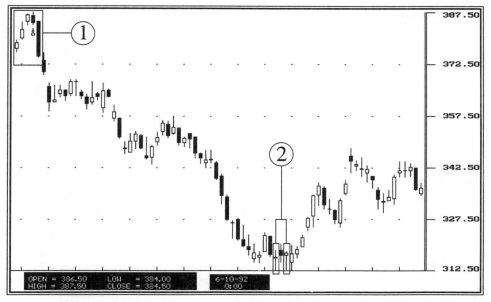

Figure 5.31 Wheat, December 1992—(6/10/92)

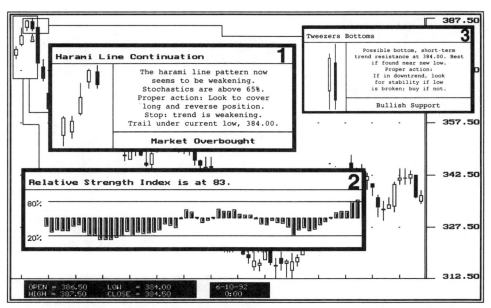

Figure 5.32 Wheat, December 1992—Harami Line Continuation and Tweezers Bottoms (6/10/92)

SIX

Livestock

Live Cattle

Figure 6.1, a daily December 1992 live cattle candlestick chart from March of 1992 to June 4, 1992, illustrates the tightly consolidated range at which live cattle was trading before entering a bullish rally (Figure 6.2). These charts should be used for overview during this analysis.

The first two candles of this chart (Figure 6.2), a black line and a black doji line, form a harami line pattern—a common reversal pattern (Figure 6.3). On the third day we got a confirmation of the harami line with a short white line, and on the fourth day, June 10, 1992, we got a continuation pattern. Notice that by using candlesticks and Western technical studies as confirming indicators, we can easily determine that the market, at this time, was indicating an oversold condition and had stronger bullish potential. The same confirming indicator technique shows us that the engulfing bearish pattern formation on June 10, 1992, was still bearish, although it did not confirm with the Western technical indicators (Figure 6.4). This was not the time to enter a position; it was the time to wait for other signals.

On June 11, 1992 (Figure 6.2), a single small doji line candle was formed, indicating a reversal or consolidating market, and could have been forming a top or bottom in the market. The Western technical indicators showed that the market was oversold; one might have thought that a bottom was forming, with a doji as the lead candle. The doji also had the same low price as the previous long black candle, supplying a tweezers bottoms formation and suggesting we might have seen a bullish support level at or near the low price. Although these pattern formations did not indicate anything strong enough to enter a position, they were showing the potential for reversal and a stronger chance that the reversal would be to the up side. Aggressive traders might have entered a long position. Conservative traders would have looked for confirmation of the bullish trend reversal before entering a position.

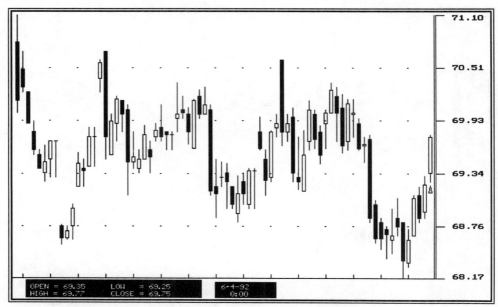

Figure 6.1 Live Cattle, December 1992 (6/4/92)

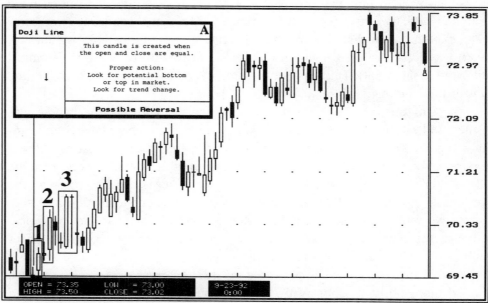

Figure 6.2 Live Cattle, December 1992—Doji Line (9/23/92)

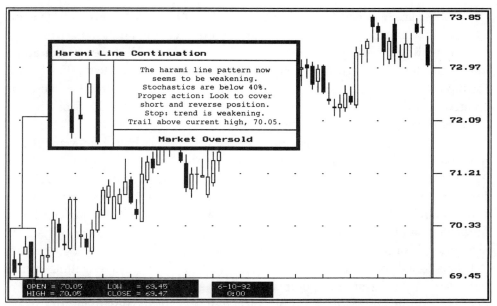

Figure 6.3 Live Cattle, December 1992—Harami Line Continuation (6/10/92)

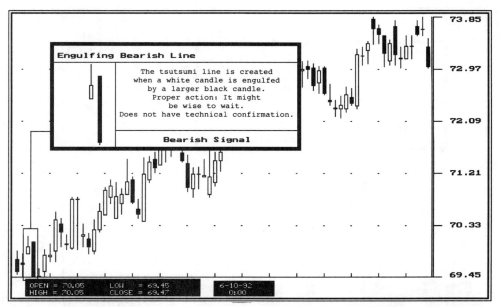

Figure 6.4 Live Cattle, December 1992—Engulfing Bearish Line (6/10/92)

Again, between June 15 and June 25, 1992, we find three of the same tweezers bottoms patterns. First, a white doji line candle and a long white line formed with the same low prices (Figure 6.2, Example 1). Next, a doji and a long white line appeared one after another, all with the same lows (Figure 6.2, Example 2). Then, another small doji line, a long white line, and a second doji created a third tweezers bottoms. Of course, all of these tweezers bottoms showed even more support for a future bullish move.

After nearly two weeks of trading, we see some bullish movement and moderately strong bearish resistance pushing the price down to near 70.00. Again, we see a tweezers bottoms pattern showing more support at 69.86 on June 25, 1992 (Figure 6.5). If the aggressive trader and the conservative trader had not already entered a long position, they were at this point seeing continued predictions and should have been looking for a pattern that issued a buy signal. Sure enough, an engulfing bullish pattern formed with the same two candles that had issued the tweezers bottoms pattern (Figure 6.6). The engulfing bullish pattern was strong at this point and issued a buy signal. The prevalence of tweezers bottoms formations was our early indicator for the potential price move. After nearly two weeks of continued bullish support and upward price movement, we had overwhelming evidence that the market was moving up. The engulfing bullish pattern was the clincher. It was time to enter a long position.

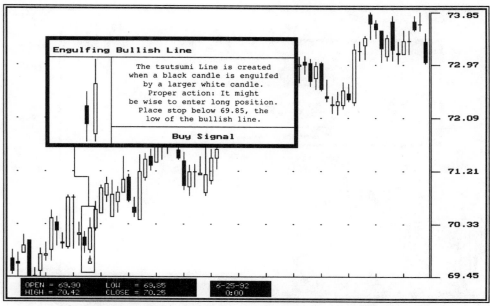

Figure 6.5 Live Cattle, December 1992—Tweezers Bottoms (6/25/92)

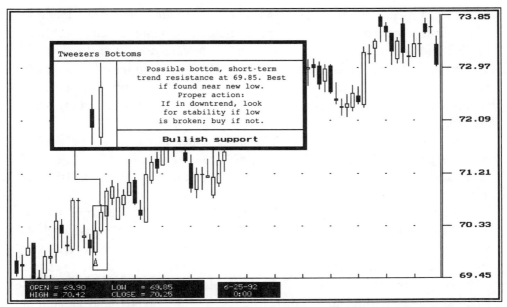

Figure 6.6 Live Cattle, December 1992—Engulfing Bullish Line (6/25/92)

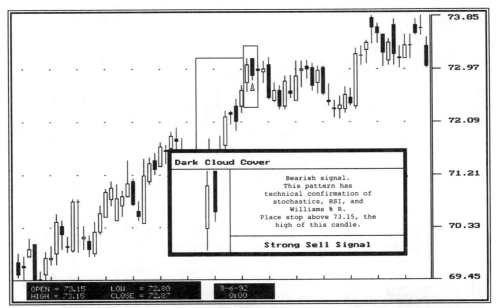

Figure 6.7 Live Cattle, December 1992—Dark Cloud Cover (8/6/92)

On August 6, 1992 (Figures 6.7 and 6.8), after almost two months of solid bullish price movement with a price increase of nearly 3 cents per pound, a dark cloud cover pattern formed, confirmed the forecast of the Western technical indicators, and issued a strong sell signal. This could have been signaling the top of the market or just a short-term correction. The same two candles also had the same high price and formed a tweezers tops pattern, establishing bearish resistance at 73.15.

A trading strategy would have been either to exit any long positions and take profit or to tighten the stop price just below support. An aggressive trader might have entered a short position with a stop price above the resistance price level. Notice that the following two candles were doji and predicted even stronger potential for a reversal. The market had consolidated over the next month and offered little chance for any profitable short- or long-term trades. In fact, it eventually reconfirmed support and resistance with multiple tweezers tops and tweezers bottoms patterns (Figure 6.8, Examples A, B, C, and D) at various price levels between 72.80 and 73.50. Each of the individual short-term rallies ended at either interim support or resistance, and the market consolidated into a tight trading channel. Figure 6.9 illustrates specific candlestick pattern formations that will be discussed within our analysis. Please refer to this figure for reference.

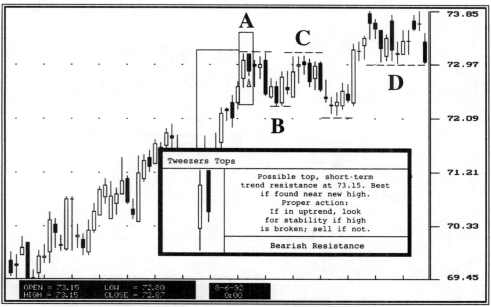

Figure 6.8 Live Cattle, December 1992—Tweezers Tops (8/6/92)

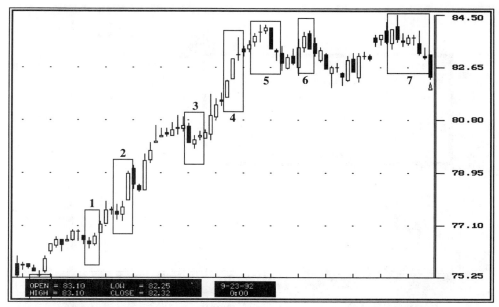

Figure 6.9 Feeder Cattle, November 1992 (9/23/92)

Feeder Cattle

On June 11, 1992, a very small doji line candle appeared, predicting a potential reversal (Figure 6.10). Remember, doji candles often form at tops or bottoms of markets. The doji, in relation to the previous black candle, appeared in the morning position (Figure 6.11), providing strong evidence that a bottom could be forming. In this case, our Western technical indicators were all showing oversold conditions with a stronger potential for a bullish move. We even got a four-candle engulfing bearish line continuation pattern (Figure 6.12), which showed that the bears had driven the price down and the market had become oversold.

A long white line (Figure 6.12) formed after the small doji line that completed the engulfing bearish line continuation (Figure 6.10). This candle completed a three-river morning star pattern (Figure 6.13), a reliable bottom reversal indicator. The next candle, found on June 15, 1992 (Figure 6.14), was another white line that continued the bullish price movement and formed a white window, showing increased energy in the bullish price advance. Most importantly, it confirmed the three-river morning star pattern and provided a solid candle foundation for the bottom reversal with a high-price gapping play pattern that issued a buy signal (Figure 6.15). Notice how both the high-price gapping play and the three-river morning pattern confirmed and continued the bullish price movement (Figure 6.16). Conservative traders should have entered a long

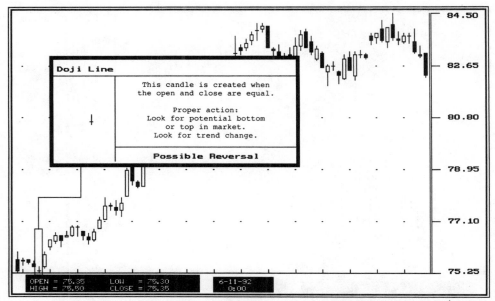

Figure 6.10 Feeder Cattle, November 1992—Doji Line (6/11/92)

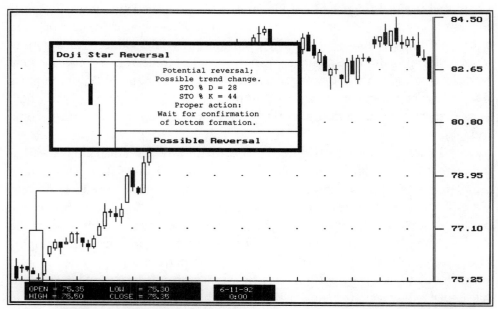

Figure 6.11 Feeder Cattle, November 1992—Doji Star Reversal (6/11/92)

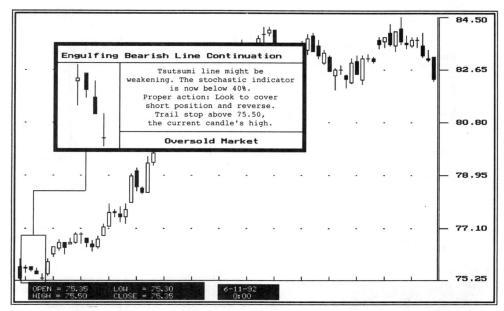

Figure 6.12 Feeder Cattle, November 1992—Engulfing Bearish Line Continuation (6/11/92)

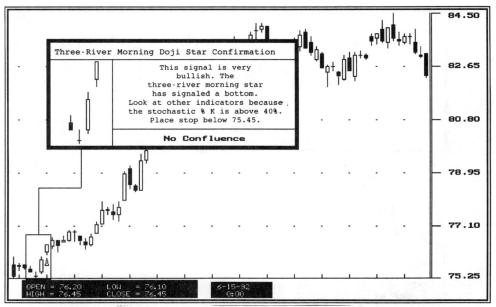

Figure 6.13 Feeder Cattle, November 1992—Three-River Morning Doji Star Confirmation (6/15/92)

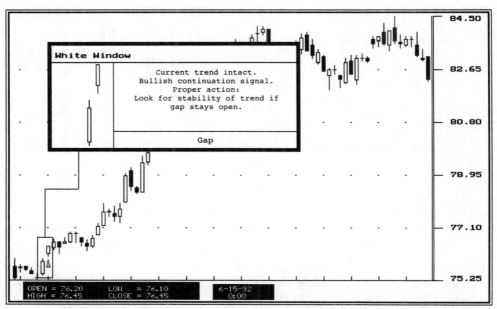

Figure 6.14 Feeder Cattle, November 1992—White Window (6/15/92)

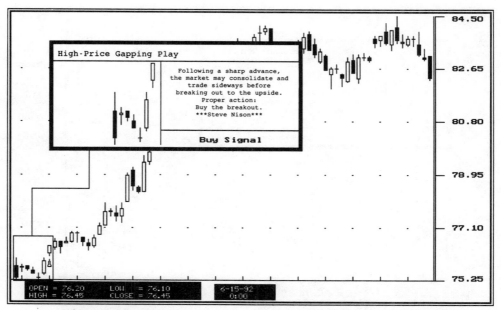

Figure 6.15 Feeder Cattle, November 1992—High-Price Gapping Play (6/15/92)

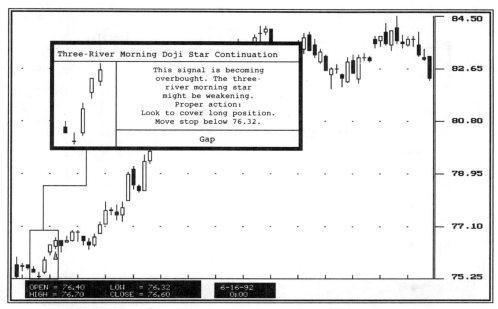

Figure 6.16 Feeder Cattle, November 1992—Three-River Morning Doji Star Continuation (6/16/92)

position when the three-river morning pattern confirmed and placed a stop price at a comfortable price level below the low of the confirming candle.

Aggressive traders might have entered when the three-river morning pattern formed. On June 16, 1992, a third white line candle appeared to continue the three-river doji star pattern (Figure 6.13). A window (gap) is noticeable within the continuation pattern, showing the intensity of this bullish move. This three-river star pattern grouping initiated a long position that continued for nearly two months. We should also notice that the RSI indicator had climbed substantially to 80 and was now indicating that the bullish rally had strengthened and might continue (Figure 6.17).

An engulfing bullish pattern formed on June 25, 1992 (Figure 6.9, Example 1), issuing another buy signal. It confirmed and continued for three days before a short-term correction started. Then, one day after the market started to correct, another engulfing bullish pattern formed and confirmed (Figure 6.9, Example 2), again showing a strong bullish push to the upside. When multiple patterns appear predicting the same price move and the price moves in that direction, the patterns are viewed as support of the original pattern. Sometimes it helps to view these patterns as separate minor support or resistance levels. After a long price move, however, remember that the market should try to retrace, reverse, or consolidate at some point.

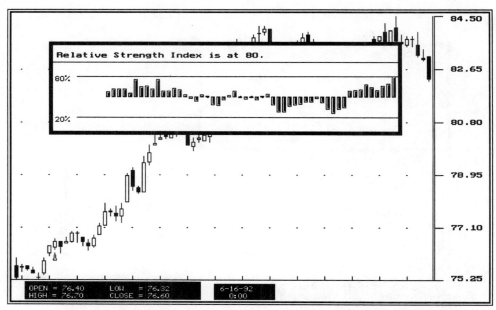

Figure 6.17 Feeder Cattle, November 1992—Relative Strength Index at 80 (6/16/92)

Proper stop price placement is essential to maintain equity (profit) during any trade. Be sure that your stops are not too tight or loose. It can mean the difference between staying with a profitable trade and getting stopped out too early. Continuation patterns are used to monitor the length of a trend and can be used to refine your short-term trading techniques.

On July 13, 1992, a white inverted hammer formed (Figure 6.9, Example 3), followed by four separate doji. The inverted hammer was showing support to a potential bullish move, but the doji indicated the potential for a reversal, top, or bottom. We indeed did see a correction after the fourth doji, although the bearish price correction stopped at the low of the inverted hammer, indicating that the support as 79.85 is still intact. A thrusting pattern (Figure 6.9, Example 4) made up of the correction candle (long black line) and a short white line appeared next. The thrusting pattern can be interpreted as bullish or bearish. If the thrusting line pattern were found in a defined bearish trend, it would be considered bearish. If two of these patterns are found within a bearish trend, look for a bullish confirmation pattern to form near the low of the white candle. In this case, we found the thrusting pattern in a bullish trend with a third confirming candle at a support level indicated by a previous white inverted hammer, predicting future bullish price movement.

On August 2, 1992, a long white opening bozu line (Figure 6.9, Example 5) showed that the bulls were making a solid attempt to drive the price up. A long white marubozu candle followed, the single strongest bullish candle that formed with a white window (gap). This is an excellent indicator that the bulls intended to drive the price up and, if found after a bottom formation, were showing strong potential for future bullish price movement. After the marubozu candle, a long-legged doji line candle appeared. The doji appeared in a star formation and accurately predicted a potential top. The actual pattern that formed with these three candles is a variation of a three-line star in deliberation (Figure 3.3f, Example 4). In a classic example, the second candle would be much larger. At this time, we should be looking for a top to form in this market.

A second doji star pattern formed on August 10, 1992 (Figure 6.18), four days after the first potential top warning. This second star formation was actually a market top. It's interesting that two similar patterns would be found within six trading days to accurately predict the market top. Remember, multiple candlestick patterns can appear and predict the same potential price move. These patterns often confirm one another and are useful for identifying support or resistance, in this case a market top (resistance).

After this second doji star pattern, a white spinning top candle appeared with the same high as the doji line, forming a tweezers tops pattern (Figure 6.19). This pattern also predicted a possible market top and identified resistance

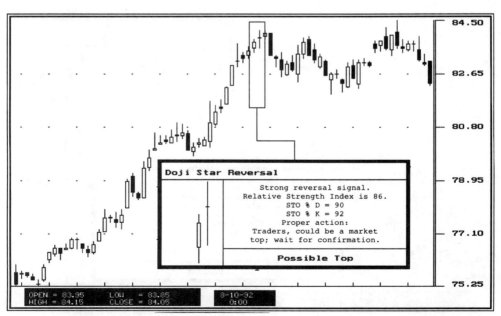

Figure 6.18 Feeder Cattle, November 1992—Doji Star Reversal (8/10/92)

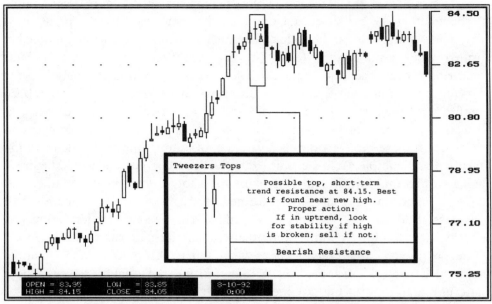

Figure 6.19 Feeder Cattle, November 1992—Tweezers Tops (8/10/92)

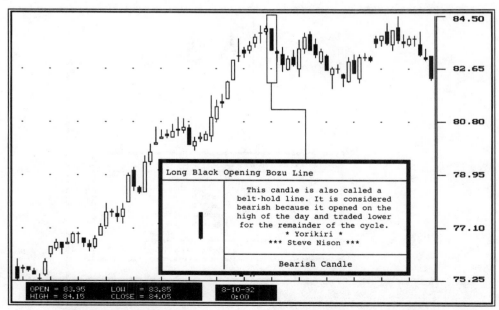

Figure 6.20 Feeder Cattle, November 1992—Long Black Opening Bozu Line (8/10/92)

at 84.15. The next candle after the spinning top was a long black opening bozu line (Figure 6.20), one of the strongest bearish candles of the single candle types. It and the spinning top formed an engulfing bearish pattern (Figure 6.21), issuing a strong sell signal.

The stochastic indicator crossed in a bearish formation at the same time, showing stronger potential for the future bearish price move (Figure 6.22). Conservative traders would need to look for confirmation of the engulfing bearish pattern before entering a short position, but aggressive traders could have entered a short position when the engulfing bearish pattern formed after the appearance of three separate top formations. We did receive a confirmation of the engulfing bearish pattern with a black hangman (Figure 6.23). Hangman candles appear at the top of a market and are excellent in showing the market's intention to continue dropping (Figure 6.24). A four-day continuation of the engulfing bearish pattern is formed by a long black line showing the market's intent to continue pushing the price down (Figure 6.25).

Ending the prior engulfing bearish continuation pattern, an engulfing bullish pattern formed—in this case, a last engulfing bullish pattern, which has more bearish potential than bullish (Figure 6.26). If an engulfing bullish pattern is found at or near a top, it appears as a last engulfing bullish pattern. The opposite is true for the engulfing bearish; if it is found at or near a bottom, it is considered a last engulfing bearish pattern. The last engulfing pattern's lack of

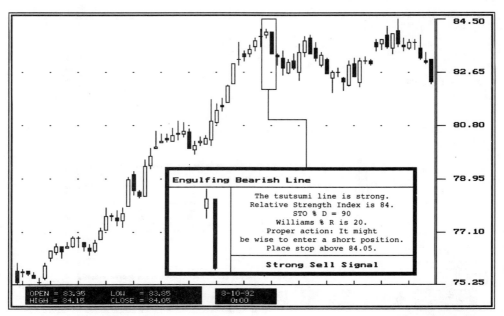

Figure 6.21 Feeder Cattle, November 1992—Engulfing Bearish Line (8/10/92)

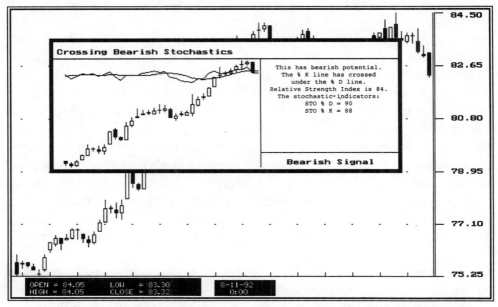

Figure 6.22 Feeder Cattle, November 1992—Crossing Bearish Stochastics (8/11/92)

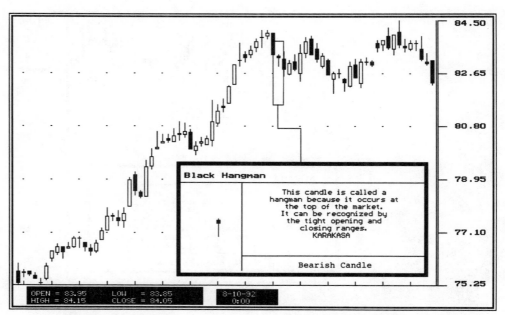

Figure 6.23 Feeder Cattle, November 1992—Black Hangman (8/10/92)

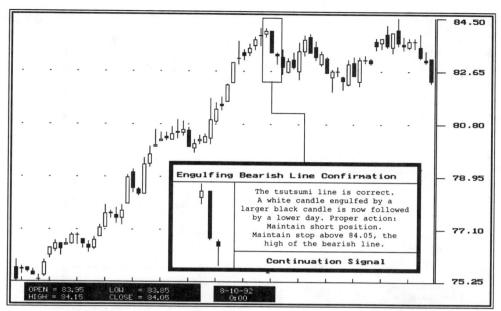

Figure 6.24 Feeder Cattle, November 1992—Engulfing Bearish Line Confirmation (8/10/92)

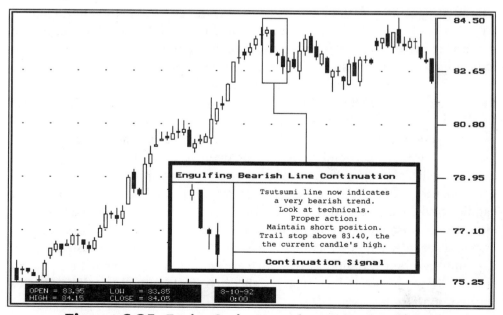

Figure 6.25 Feeder Cattle, November 1992—Engulfing Bearish Line Continuation (8/10/92)

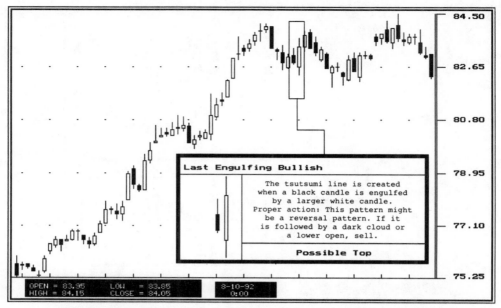

Figure 6.26 Feeder Cattle, November 1992—Last Engulfing Bullish (8/10/92)

other confirming indicators and rather out-of-place appearance actually shows an attempt by the bulls to form support near the top. This last engulfing pattern will often become a dark cloud, engulfing bearish, or bearish harami line and will possibly be part of the actual sell signal pattern. The last engulfing bullish pattern confirmed with the next candle. Still, the prior candlesticks and technical indicators were telling us that the market should sell off.

A second engulfing bearish pattern formed on August 15, 1992, below the resistance level of 84.15, indicating a strong bearish reversal in the market (Figure 6.27). The engulfing bearish pattern confirmed and continued with bearish price movement (Figure 6.28). It was apparent that the market was consolidating at this time. Consolidation areas are often very difficult to trade, although an accomplished short-term or intraday trader can take profits during a market consolidation. This engulfing bearish pattern confirmed with a second black candle and issued a second sell signal for conservative traders. Notice that now, after the top formation, we begin to find classic candlestick sell patterns. This engulfing bearish pattern initiated a downward price move that lasted for six days until reaching the support level formed by the last engulfing bullish pattern and the long-legged doji line, which stalled the market's bullish rally and forewarned of a topping formation.

The indication that support had formed came from the double thrusting pattern on August 26, 1992, during this last downtrend (Figure 6.29). You might

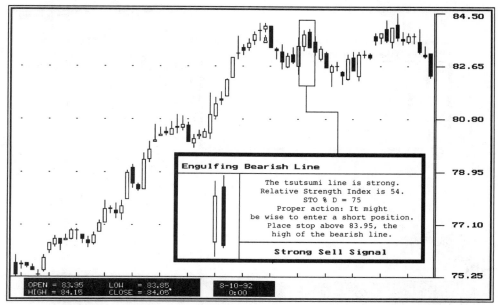

Figure 6.27 Feeder Cattle, November 1992—Engulfing Bearish Line (8/10/92)

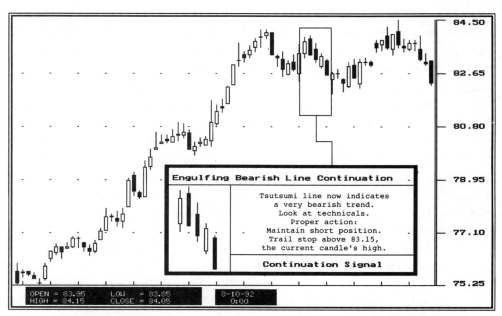

Figure 6.28 Feeder Cattle, November 1992—Engulfing Bearish Line Continuation (8/10/92)

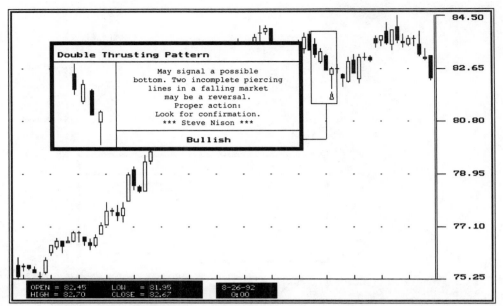

Figure 6.29 Feeder Cattle, November 1992—Double Thrusting Pattern (8/26/92)

remember that a single thrusting pattern found in a downtrend is a bearish pattern as long as it does not confirm; two thrusting patterns found in a downtrend show that the current trend may be approaching completion. We also see that our long-term moving average values had crossed with a bearish dead cross pattern on August 25, 1992 (Figure 6.30), showing that the market was consolidating and topping with bearish intent.

On August 28, 1992 (Figure 6.31), a black hammer formed after a small doji line. Both of these candles appeared directly after the double thrusting pattern. The doji emphasized the strong potential for a reversal at this time, and the black hammer predicted the direction—up. Hammers are considered bullish because they are often found at the bottom of a market. In this instance the hammer correctly identified the end of a retracement period that followed a two-month bullish drive. The bullish hammer confirmed with a long white line and formed an engulfing bullish pattern, issuing a buy signal (Figures 6.32 and 6.33).

The engulfing bullish pattern in Figure 6.32 was not a last engulfing pattern because it had other confirming candle patterns that predicted the same bullish price move or short-term bottom. Notice how the doji candle plays an important role when the hammer confirms (Figure 6.34), issues a buy signal, and continues (Figures 6.35 and 6.39). In this case, the doji and the black hammer actually showed support and formed right at the short-term bottom.

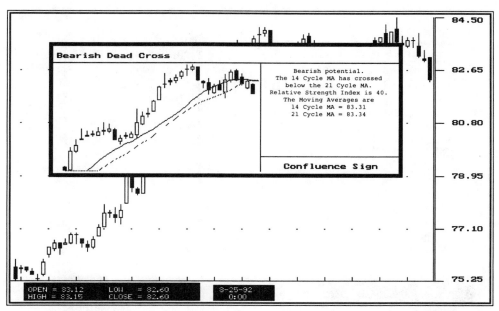

Figure 6.30 Feeder Cattle, November 1992—Bearish Dead Cross (8/25/92)

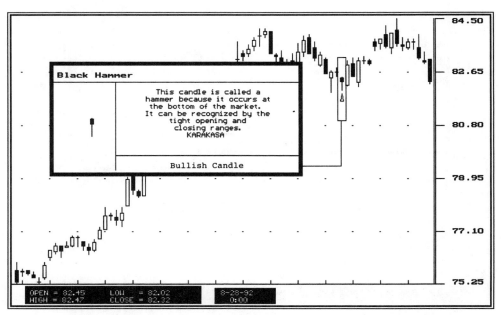

Figure 6.31 Feeder Cattle, November 1992—Black Hammer (8/28/92)

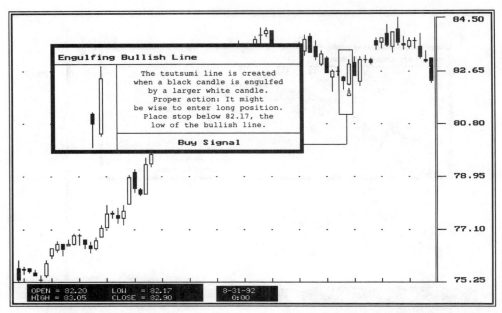

Figure 6.32 Feeder Cattle, November 1992—Engulfing Bullish Line (8/31/92)

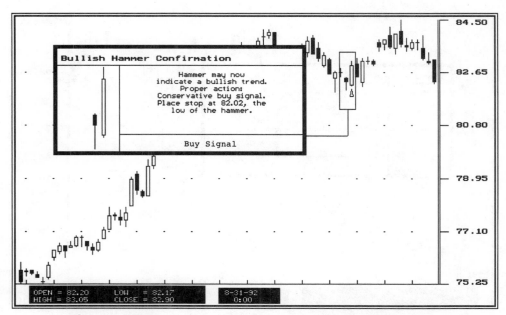

Figure 6.33 Feeder Cattle, November 1992—Bullish Hammer Confirmation (8/31/92)

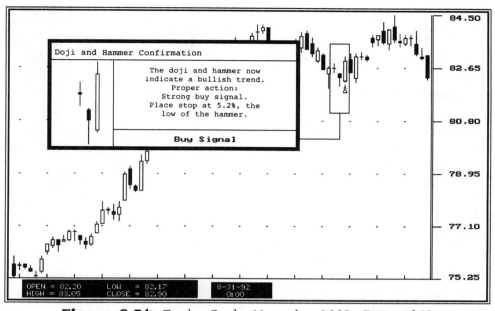

Figure 6.34 Feeder Cattle, November 1992—Doji and Hammer Confirmation (8/31/92)

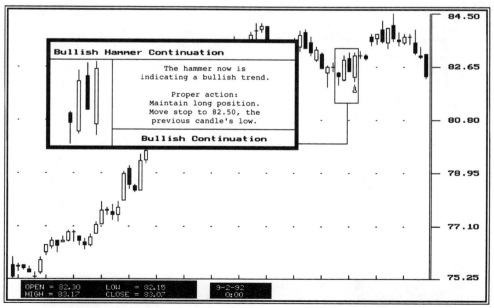

Figure 6.35 Feeder Cattle, November 1992—Bullish Hammer Continuation (9/2/92)

The next candle was a black line that formed a dark cloud cover pattern (Figure 6.36). It did not issue a sell signal because it did not confirm with the other technical indicators, and other candlestick patterns indicated that the bulls are gaining strength. This black line forms a doji and hammer continuation pattern, showing gained strength for the bulls (Figures 6.37 and 6.38).

Next, a long white line appeared and engulfed the prior black line, forming another engulfing bullish pattern and continuing the bullish hammer pattern (Figures 6.39 and 6.40). Despite the lack of much upward price movement, the engulfing bullish pattern issued another buy signal and initiated an attempt by the bulls to drive the price up. This particular pattern grouping is an excellent example of the clarity and simplicity of the Japanese candlesticks. All of these bullish patterns appeared at or near the defined support level, providing further evidence of the upcoming bullish price movement.

On September 11, 1992, an engulfing bearish line pattern appeared after a bullish window (the actual upward price move predicted earlier), showing some bearish intent (Figure 6.41). This pattern did not have the confirmation of the other technical indicators, so it would not issue a sell signal unless it confirmed with a following black candle having a lower low. Two days later, on September 15, 1992, a dark cloud cover pattern formed with a new high (Figure 6.42) issuing a sell signal. We had been forewarned of the initial bearish intent

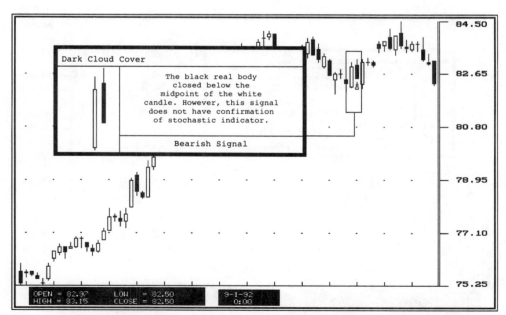

Figure 6.36 Feeder Cattle, November 1992—Dark Cloud Cover (9/1/92)

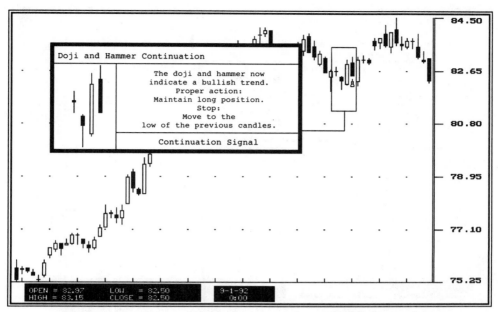

Figure 6.37 Feeder Cattle, November 1992—Doji and Hammer Continuation: 9/1/92

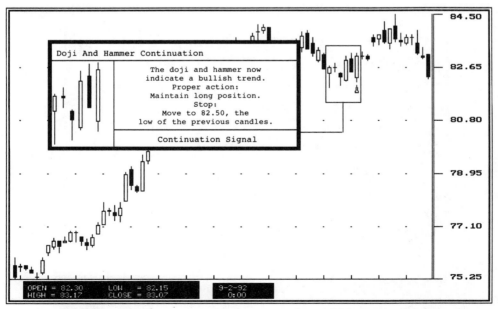

Figure 6.38 Feeder Cattle, November 1992—Doji and Hammer Continuation: 9/2/92

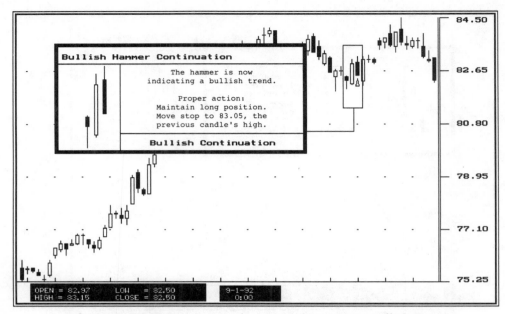

Figure 6.39 Feeder Cattle, November 1992—Bullish Hammer
Continuation (9/1/92)

Figure 6.40 Feeder Cattle, November 1992—Engulfing Bullish
Line (9/2/92)

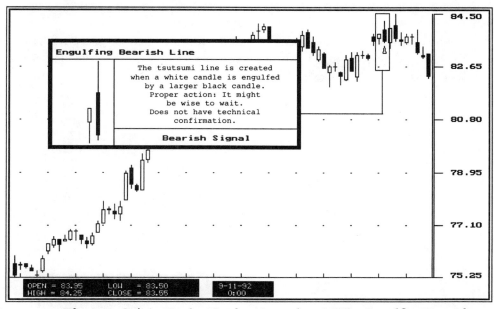

Figure 6.41 Feeder Cattle, November 1992—Engulfing Bearish Line (9/11/92)

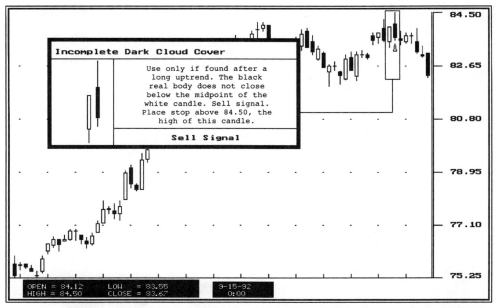

Figure 6.42 Feeder Cattle, November 1992—Incomplete Dark Cloud Cover (9/15/92)

with the engulfing bearish pattern. Now the dark cloud pattern became a flagship pattern and reversed the market. A confirmation candle appeared the following day as the conservative trader's entry point. Continued bearish price movement in the future, with potential for finding support at or near one of our defined support levels, would be likely.

SEVEN

Foods and Fiber

In Chapter 6, we looked at the relationship between candlestick patterns and different grain types. We found that if a group of commodities moves in unison, similar candlestick patterns will form. We can refine and articulate our trading strategy on the basis of this information. Because no counterpart for cocoa exists in grains, we compare different contract months of the same market to gain information. The most thinly traded month should be given the least amount of weight when analyzing the data. Additional confirmation through this type of market analysis will reinforce our findings and knowledge.

Cocoa

Figure 7.1 contains daily cocoa charts for three months in 1993; July (cc____93n.fnn) is shown at the top, May (cc____93k.fnn) is in the middle, and March (cc____93h.fnn) is on the bottom. Each of the charts is enlarged in Figures 7.2 (March), 7.3 (May), and July (7.4). Examples 1 through 9 highlight patterns that were similar or the same in each contract month. Commodity contracts are traded based on active contract months, which change with the months of the year. Different commodity markets are traded in different contract months. We should first analyze the most current, or active, contract month for candlestick patterns, then confirm or deny our findings by comparing these results with the next two most active contract months ("outer months") of the same commodity market. Because the prices of the outer contract months are based upon the most active or current contract month plus *contango* (costs of carrying this contract longer), you will find that the prices usually move in unison. However, a pattern might form in an outer month that reveals a missed signal in the most active contract. In Example 1 of Figures 7.1–7.4, we see the price of cocoa test a support level after a bearish price decline, with the May contract testing the $1,000 benchmark ($1,000 per metric ton).

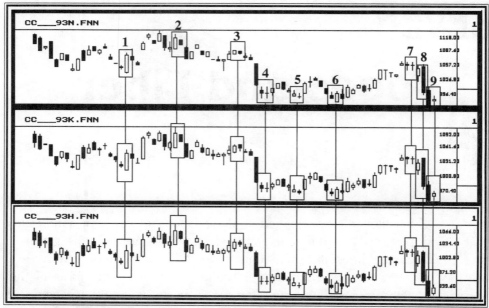

Figure 7.1 Daily Cocoa—July, May, and March 1993

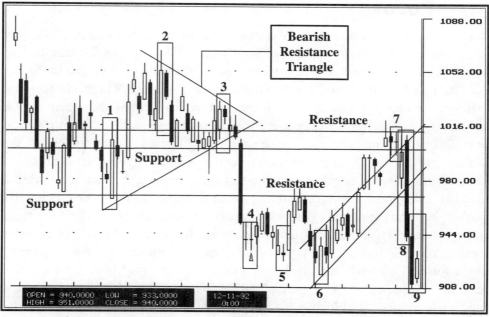

Figure 7.2 Daily Cocoa—March 1993 (12/11/92)

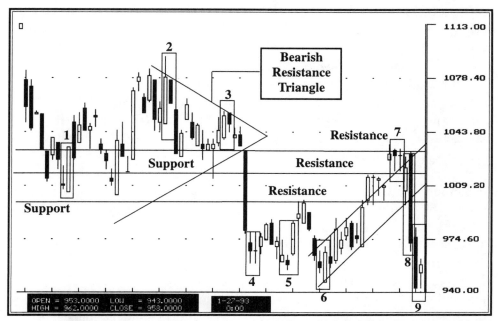

Figure 7.3 Daily Cocoa, May 1993—Bearish Resistance Triangle (1/27/93)

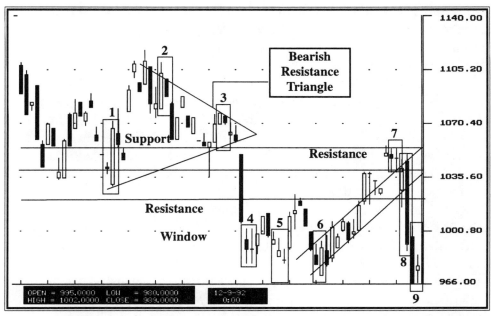

Figure 7.4 Daily Cocoa, July 1993—Bearish Resistance Triangle (12/9/92)

In all three contract months an engulfing bullish pattern was created, issuing a buy signal. In fact, the March and May charts almost formed a pattern called rising three method, a five-candle pattern that is significant as a bullish continuation signal (see Figure 3.1a). It is composed of a large white candle followed by three small candles all trading within its range. The last candle in this pattern is a large white that closes above the previous highs. The significance of this move is that the engulfing bullish lines in Figures 7.2 and 7.3 (Example 1) engulfed the three prior candles, the same composition as the last four candles in the rising three-method.

The following two trading sessions were uneventful for the bulls. Although inverted hammers were present in all three contract months, which are typically bullish during an oversold market, they formed bearish harami patterns. Since the market is technically oversold, confirmation would be necessary to use this call to exit the buy signal issued by the previous engulfing bullish pattern. The inverted hammer was followed by gravestone doji in both the May and March charts, revealing that neither the bulls nor bears had absolute control. The doji were followed by a strong white candle breaking to new highs three days after the engulfing bullish patterns issued a buy signal and signaling a bullish market move.

The market traded within a narrow range for the next five trading days, on three sessions trading at new highs. The last of these new highs was the white candle in Example 2 of Figures 7.2–7.4. This white candle was followed by a small black candle, creating a bearish harami. This harami pattern was confirmed with a strong move down on the next day. The overall range of the market was decreasing, and for the next nine trading days the market traded within an ever-lessening range. This decreasing range formed a bearish resistance triangle, or flag formation.

A flag formation formed in all three contract months of cocoa. The trading range narrowed the apex of this bearish resistance triangle (Example 3 of Figures 7.2, 7.3, and 7.4). In May and March cocoa, dark cloud cover patterns appeared; in July a bearish harami formed. For two days after the dark cloud cover issued a sell, the market trades nominally lowered. On the third day after the dark cloud, the market broke support, gapping below it, and fell almost $50 per metric ton in one day.

The market moved lower on the following day. Figure 7.5 shows that a bullish black gap pattern formed on December 9, 1992, in July cocoa. No patterns are found in either of the other two charts that might reveal a reversal. This is our first hint that a potential bottom might be at hand. A significant bottom was formed on December 11, 1992. In all three charts almost identical patterns were formed (Example 4 in Figures 7.2–7.4). Twin doji candles formed in the March cocoa contract with the same high and low, which created a tweezers pattern (Figure 7.6). If two sessions (they do not have to be concurrent) have

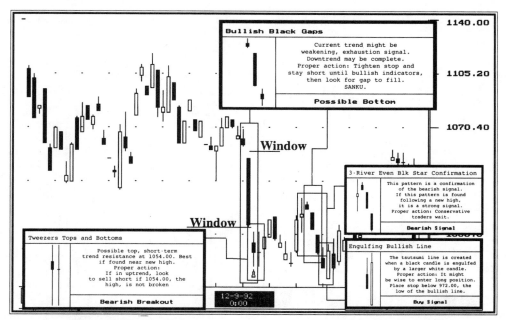

Figure 7.5 Daily Cocoa, July 1993—Tweezers Tops and Bottoms, Bullish Black Gaps, Three-River Evening Black Star Confirmation, and Engulfing Bullish Line (12/9/92)

equal highs, tweezers tops are formed. If two sessions have equal lows, tweezers bottoms are formed. When two sessions have an equal high and low, a significant breakout may occur.

By placing the formation within its trading range, one can determine if a market is more likely to break out to the upside or downside. All three charts create tweezers bottoms and tops (Figures 7.5, 7.6, and 7.7). All three tweezers tops and bottoms patterns formed after the market broke support and fell considerably. Their placement implies that they were showing strong support to the upside. Along with the bullish black gaps pattern, we have a stronger indication of the market bottom.

After a short bullish reversal, the market retested the support formed by the intermarket tweezers top and bottom patterns and was met by another doji (Figure 7.2 and 7.4, Example 5). The placement of the single doji reconfirmed the support level, and another attempt to rally the market upward began. Market price moved upward for two trading sessions and ended with a three-river black evening star pattern on December 25, 1992, in the July contract (Figure 7.5), issuing a bearish signal. This candlestick-topping formation formed at a 50 percent retracement of the major bearish price move, indicating more continued resistance. The three-river black evening star pattern confirmed the

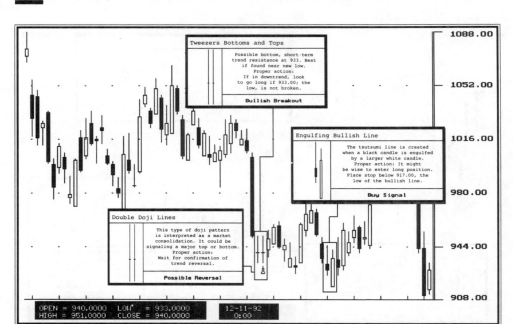

Figure 7.6 Daily Cocoa, March 1993—Double Doji Lines, Tweezers Bottoms and Tops, and Engulfing Bullish Line (12/11/92)

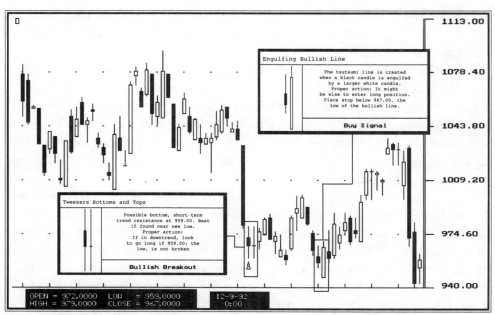

Figure 7.7 Daily Cocoa, May 1993—Tweezers Bottoms and Tops and Engulfing Bullish Line (12/9/92)

following trading session and continued a bearish price decline to the original support level.

At this point in all three markets, an engulfing bullish pattern formed on December 28, 1992, at the preexisting bullish support price level, signaling to buy (Figures 7.5, 7.6, and 7.7). The support price level had withstood three bearish price declines and should indicate a major support level. The ability of each of these candle patterns and markets to have independently predicted the support level and a buy signal lies within the individual price movement of the market and the candles themselves.

Sugar

The sugar market entered a bullish trend and was attempting to form support above 8.6 cents per pound. Near the end of the bullish price advance, a bearish white gaps pattern formed on October 14, 1992, forewarning that the bullish move was weakening (Figure 7.8, Example 1). On October 16, 1992, after a strong bullish price advance, a bearish harami line pattern formed at the market top (Figure 7.8, Example 2). The last candle of the bullish rally was a long white opening bozu line. It was actually a strongly bullish candle. Its placement indicated that it represented a strong effort to push the market price up and may have exhausted the strength of the bulls. The following candle was a

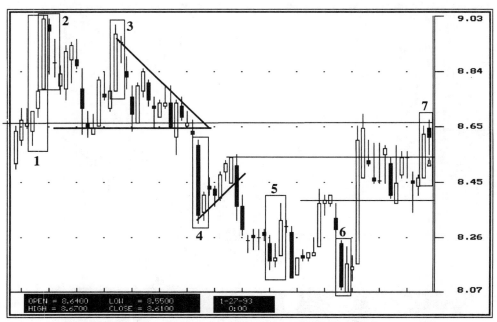

Figure 7.8 Sugar—March 1993 (1/27/93)

black hangman, which indicated a top and even stronger bearish price activity. Together, they formed the bearish harami line, which was a bearish reversal pattern.

Individually, these two candles were opposites and contradicted each other. In this case, a strong bullish price advance ended with an opening white bozu line and reversed with a black hangman and an engulfing bearish pattern. The doji that followed the bearish harami line (Figure 7.8, Example 2, and Figure 7.9) is a sign of a consolidating market and often promotes a market reversal. The doji line also confirmed the bearish harami line pattern to issue a sell signal. It would have been wise to wait and not enter a short position because the doji line is not a very strong confirmation candle. It is often found at major market tops or bottoms, although its placement here indicated that the market was likely to consolidate. If it had been a long black line, we would have entered a short position.

After more market consolidation, the price activity rebounded from a support level at 8.65 cents, with a bullish meeting lines pattern on October 27, 1992 (Figure 7.10, Example 1), indicating a potential change in market direction. The recommended action would be to wait for a confirming candle. The bullish meeting lines pattern showed interim support level at about 8.5 cents. Had this session closed higher than the previous black candle's close, the bullish meeting lines would have developed into a thrusting pattern or a piercing line to show

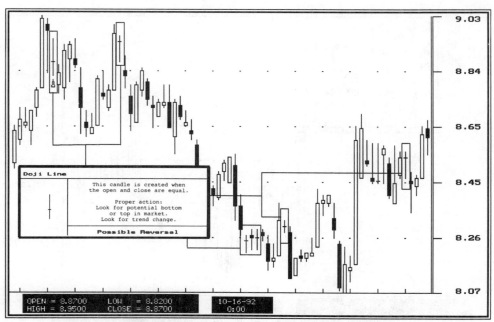

Figure 7.9 Sugar, March 1993—Doji Line (10/16/92)

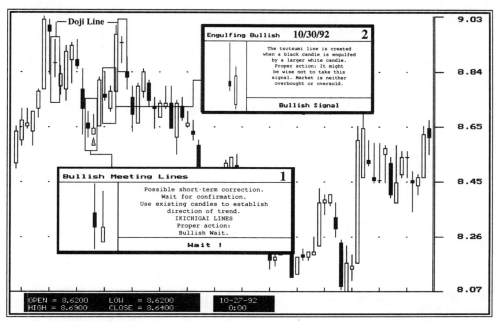

Figure 7.10 Sugar, March 1993—Bullish Meeting Lines and Engulfing Bullish (10/27/92)

more strength. A belt-hold line on the following session confirmed the bullish meeting lines and moved the market higher.

Two days later, on October 30, 1992, an engulfing bullish pattern formed (Figure 7.10, Example 2). This pattern appeared during overbought market conditions, indicating a short-term signal at best. The following day bullish price action continued with another opening white bozu line similar to the candle at the first market top (the last candle in Example 1 of Figure 7.8). Unable to break major resistance at 9 cents, a single doji line formed on November 3, 1992, and completed a harami white cross (Figures 7.9 and 7.11). The doji lines (Figure 7.9) indicated resistance above 9 cents.

On November 4 and November 5, 1992 (Figures 7.12 and 7.13), the harami white cross confirmed and continued with black candles, and the market began to form a bearish resistance triangle between existing support at 8.5 cents and resistance at 9 cents (Figure 7.8). A second bearish harami line pattern formed at the apex of the bearish resistance triangle, breaking out to the downside. This pattern broke at a pivotal support level and did not find support until 8.3 cents. A bullish harami line pattern developed on the following day, indicating a possible short-term bottom (Figure 7.8, Example 4). The retracement provided little price advance and proved to be a retracement of the bearish trend.

After rising only .2 cents, the market broke its momentum and fell to a new contract low indicated by another bullish harami line (Figure 7.8, Example

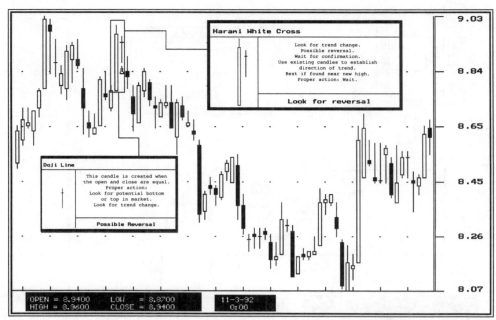

Figure 7.11 Sugar, March 1993—Doji Line and Harami White Cross (11/3/92)

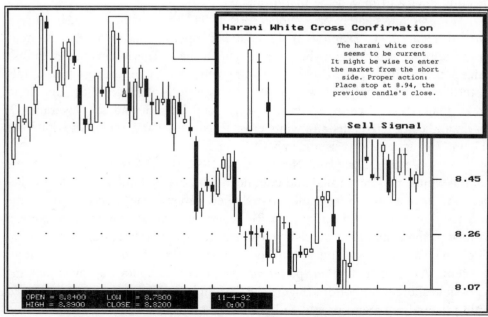

Figure 7.12 Sugar, March 1993—Harami White Cross Confirmation (11/4/92)

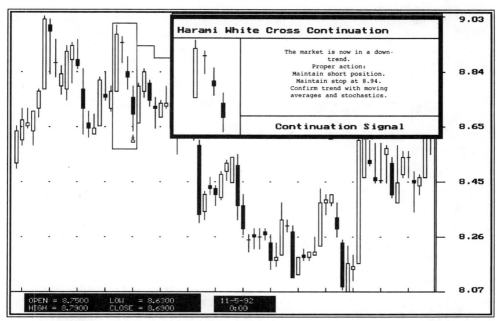

Figure 7.13 Sugar, March 1993—Harami White Cross
Continuation (11/5/92)

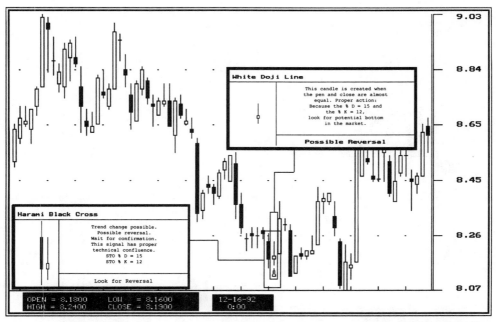

Figure 7.14 Daily Sugar, March 1993—Harami Black Cross and
White Doji Line (12/16/92)

5, and Figure 7.14). The abundance of harami patterns found in this sugar chart should be considered significant, as this pattern appears at many key reversal areas.

Orange Juice

Figure 7.15 is a daily orange juice chart of the November 1992 contract that illustrates the market's price movement from March 10, 1992, to September 23, 1992. At the beginning of this chart, the market entered a downtrend after the formation of a gravestone doji line at 133.00 (Figure 7.15, Example 1). The gravestone doji line is often found at market tops. It is not a common doji. It opens on the low of the day, trades higher throughout the day, and closes exactly where the market opened. The gravestone doji represents strong resistance capable of holding the market price at its current low, and its placement indicated resistance at 133.00.

The market dropped sharply after the gravestone doji and formed a large window in the process. After a gravestone doji line at the market top, we should expect a market price drop. The bearish window indicated continuation of the trend. The market fell to support at 120.25 and then began to consolidate. The following seven trading sessions propelled the market to a low of 120. Notice the number of tweezers top or bottom patterns that formed during the market's

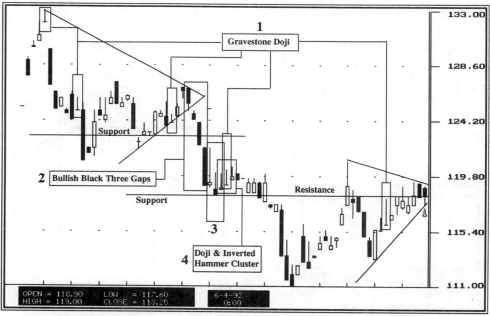

Figure 7.15 Daily Orange Juice—November 1992 (6/4/92)

consolidation. Each new tweezers bottoms pattern had a higher low, and each new tweezers tops pattern had a lower high, tightening the trading range. On the other hand, the tweezers bottom patterns that formed were unable to promote a major price advance, and eventually the market price activity tightened to points within the support and resistance levels. This type of market consolidation often promotes a market breakout. The market price is being channeled into a tighter and tighter price range with a flag formation. At the pinnacle of a flag formation, the market should break out to one side or the other. The patterns found indicate that the market sentiment was still bearish. Logically, the price should have dropped to the next support level.

At the pinnacle of the flag formation, the market began a strong bearish price decline and dropped nearly 10 points in four days. Each time a new black candle formed, a bearish window also formed, indicating a continuation of a trend (Figure 7.15, Example 2).

A four-day bullish black three-gaps pattern (Figure 3.2d) formed at the end of the bearish price move (Figure 7.15, Example 2). The bullish black three-gaps pattern is an exhaustion signal. It can indicate a weakening trend, and with confirmation this pattern can be an excellent reversal indicator. The new support price level formed at 118.25 with three inverted hammers after the bullish black three-gaps pattern formed (Figure 7.15, Example 3). The inverted hammers are market bottom indicators and while they indicated support, no rally followed. Instead, the market began to consolidate. The bears, in essence, had not lost control of the market. The formation of the doji and inverted hammer cluster were a prelude to the impending price decline (Figure 7.15, Example 4). When the support level was broken, the market decline continued to a new contract low of 111.00.

Almost immediately after the market found support at 111.00, the bulls reentered the market and reversed the trend. After this bottom, the market began trade, once again, into a narrowly defined range.

Cotton

The candlestick charts in Figures 7.16 and 7.17 are daily December 1992 cotton charts. They illustrate the market's price movement from March 15, 1992, to September 23, 1992. During the early trading of this cotton market, the price movement and trend had begun to consolidate near 60.00. A thrusting pattern formed with a white inverted hammer candle (Figure 7.16, Example 1), indicating that a support level had formed and the bulls were attempting to drive the market price upward. We would normally watch for a second thrusting pattern to form before we expected the market to reverse to the upside.

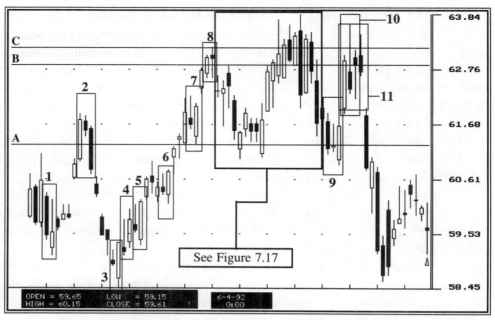

Figure 7.16 Daily Cotton—December 1992 (6/4/92). See also figure 7.17.

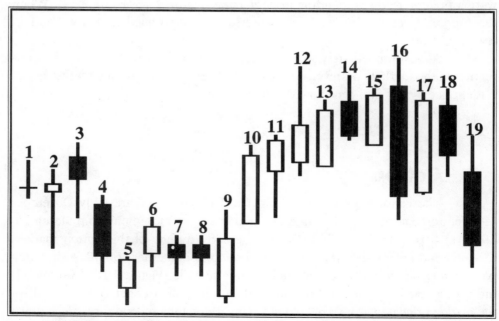

Figure 7.17 Close up of figure 7.16, Daily Cotton—December 1992 (6/4/92)

The white inverted hammer is a common bottom reversal indicator and should promote a bullish price reversal. Both the thrusting pattern and the white inverted hammer confirmed with a small black candle on the next trading session, indicating that the bullish price rally had started. To end the bullish rally, a bearish harami line pattern formed (Figure 7.16, Example 2) and confirmed to reverse the market into a bearish trend. The bearish harami line pattern was found above our support/resistance level, which indicated that the bears would attempt to push the market price below the defined resistance level. After finding new support at 58.45, the bulls reentered the market with an engulfing bullish line pattern (Figure 7.16, Example 3) at the market bottom. Notice the prevalence of the engulfing bullish line pattern throughout this market (Figure 7.16, Examples 3, 5, 6, and 7).

This engulfing bullish candlestick pattern should be considered a flagship candlestick pattern because it formed repetitively to accurately predict the market's future price movement. Confirming our initial engulfing bullish pattern (Figure 7.16, Example 3), a black inverted hammer formed (Figure 7.16, Example 4), also predicting a market bottom. With this confirmation, we should have entered a long position and watched for the market price to continue upward.

Again, reissuing an earlier buy signal, three separate engulfing bullish line patterns formed (Figure 7.16, Examples 5, 6, and 7), giving us further evidence that the market was in an uptrend; we should have continued to watch for upward price movement.

Each time the market consolidated during the long-term bullish trend, the engulfing bullish patterns formed to reinitiate the bullish price advance. Forming the first major market top, an incomplete dark cloud cover pattern formed with a black doji line as its flagship candle (Figure 7.16, Example 8). This candlestick pattern predicted a bearish reversal. It issued a sell signal because it had confirmation of Western technical indicators. A fall in the market price was likely. Another doji line followed the incomplete dark cloud cover and confirmed the bearish reversal with a hint of market consolidation in the future. The next series of candles was critical to the market's future price direction— pay attention!

In Figure 7.17, a long white doji line formed (Example 1) that engulfed the prior doji line (Example 2) to produce a last engulfing bullish doji line, warning of more topping action and possibly a support/resistance level. Next, a black candle formed (Example 3) and created a gap between its body and the prior candle's body, meaning that it was placed in an evening formation. We should have expected this next candle. Now, a long black line formed (Example 4) to complete a three-river evening top formation (Examples 2, 3, and 4 combined). These candlestick patterns were predicting strong bearish resistance at or near 63.00. We should have looked for continued bearish movement or consolidation in the future. A small white line formed next (Example 5), and the gap between its body and the body of the prior long black line indicated a morning formation (Examples 4 and 5). Bullish support would be likely to form if the market price were to move up.

Next, in Figure 7.17, another small white line formed (Example 6), this time with a gap between its body and the prior white candle's body. It completes the three-river morning bottom pattern (Examples 4, 5, and 6), showing that we are finding strong support at or near 61.00 (Figure 7.16, Line A). All of this indicated that the market would continue to consolidate within the defined support and resistance levels and eventually break out to one side or the other.

At this point in Figure 7.17, a tweezers tops and bottoms pattern formed (Examples 7 and 8). Because it formed closer to our support level, a bullish price breakout was probable. If it had formed closer to our resistance level, a bearish price move might have been expected. Next, a long white line formed (Example 9), and its body engulfed the prior candle's black body (Example 8), forming an engulfing bullish line pattern that issued a buy signal to end the market consolidation and start a bullish price rally. It's easy to identify support and resistance levels. The market should consolidate, because the candlestick patterns accurately identified each individual market trait. The engulfing bullish line pattern confirmed with a long white opening bozu line (Example 10).

The market continued its bullish price rally until it reached the resistance level. Then, a dark cloud cover pattern formed (Example 9), predicting bearish price movement. If the dark cloud cover pattern had confirmed, we should have looked for strong bearish price movement. But instead a long white line formed (Example 10) as a last engulfing bullish line, signifying the end of the second bullish price rally and the start of a market top. Next, an engulfing bearish line pattern formed (Example 11) out of the prior engulfing bullish pattern, and the market price dropped considerably. The bulls pushed the market price back up with a long white line (Example 12), forming a bullish harami line pattern.

This represented a push-and-shove match between the bulls and the bears, each pushing as hard as possible to move the market price. Eventually, only one would win. This type of price action is considered a market consolidation. Then a black candle formed (Example 13) and created a bearish harami line pattern to initiate another bearish price move. This harami line confirmed, and the market price fell back to our defined support level.

A bullish harami line pattern (Example 14), caused by a strategic doji line, ended the bearish price move at our support level. The bullish harami line pattern was predicting a bullish reversal in the market. It confirmed with a long white line, and the market continued to advance to the defined resistance levels (Figure 7.16, Lines B and C). This type of market provides excellent profit taking for the experienced short-term trader. After the short bullish rally back to the resistance level, a bearish harami line pattern formed, predicting a bearish price reversal (Example 15). It was followed with a black hangman that presaged of a third top in the market, strongly warning of a bearish price move in the future. This third top completed a three-Buddha top candlestick formation (Figure 17.16), or head-and-shoulders formation, providing further evidence that a short position in this market would have been advantageous. With a large window, the market price broke sharply downward until it reached its initial support at 58.45.

Weekly Cotton Chart Comparison

In Figure 7.18, a weekly chart comparison of the cotton market we just completed, the top of the chart represents the previously noted three-Buddha top formation. The third top in the market moved very quickly, however, and was represented as an engulfing bullish line. The weekly candlestick chart displays more current data than the daily chart, so the long-term bearish trend initiated by the three-Buddha top formation is more obvious. Let's start at the top.

On June 19, 1992, after a bullish market move that established a new high and bearish resistance level, a black hangman candle formed (Figure 7.18 and Figure 7.19, Example 1), indicating that the market was topping and that a bearish market move was imminent. The black hangman's body was placed within the prior white line's body, creating a bearish harami line pattern (Figure

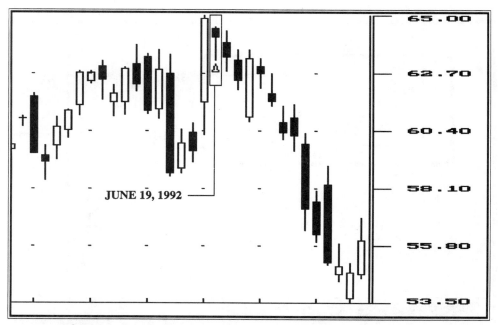

Figure 7.18 Weekly Cotton, December 1992—Hangman in Harami Position

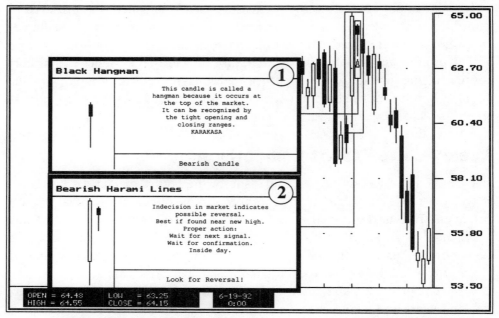

Figure 7.19 Weekly Cotton, December 1992—Black Hangman and Bearish Harami Lines (6/19/92)

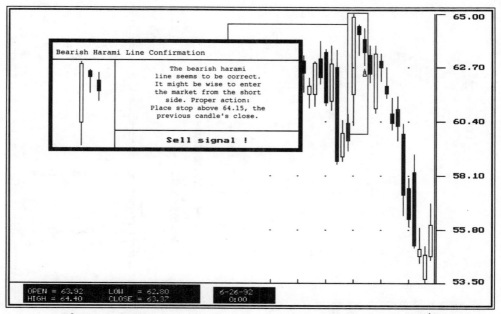

Figure 7.20 Weekly Cotton, December 1992—Bearish Harami Line Confirmation (6/26/92)

7.19, Example 2), also forewarning of a bearish market reversal. When the bearish harami line pattern confirmed on June 26, 1992 (Figure 7.20), a sell signal was issued, and we entered a short position. The black hangman itself confirmed on the same day, issuing a second sell signal in the market (Figure 7.21).

Notice how, independently, the bearish harami line and the black hangman combined to drive the market price downward (Figures 7.22, 7.23, 7.24, and 7.25). Then, a tweezers tops pattern formed (Figure 7.26), indicating strong resistance at 63.65 and that the market would continue its bearish price descent. The dramatic price moves of the three-Buddha top formed a last engulfing bullish line (Figure 7.27) that also formed a tweezers tops pattern. Remember, we're confirming this weekly chart against the daily chart, so we are already aware of the black hangman and engulfing bearish line that started the bearish price movement and created the three-Buddha top in the daily chart. We expect the market to continue in its bearish direction.

On July 17, 1992 (Figure 7.28), another bearish harami line pattern formed, indicating that the bearish price move would continue. On the same day, three-cycle (short-term) and 7-cycle (intermediate-term) moving average values converged with a bearish dead cross (Figure 7.29), indicating that we should see continued bearish price movement. On July 24, 1992 (Figure 7.30), a black inverted hammer formed, telling us that we might see some bullish price movement. We would wait to see if it confirmed with the next candle that formed. The same black inverted hammer confirmed the bearish harami line pattern (Figure 7.31) and issued another sell signal.

The bearish harami line pattern continued for the remainder of this dramatic bearish price move—from 65.00 to 53.50 in three months (Figures 7.32, 7.33, and 7.34). The market eventually reversed after finding support with a white inverted hammer and a renewed entry by the bulls.

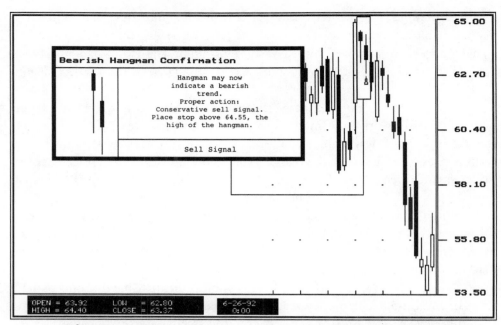

Figure 7.21 Weekly Cotton, December 1992—Bearish Hangman Confirmation (6/26/92)

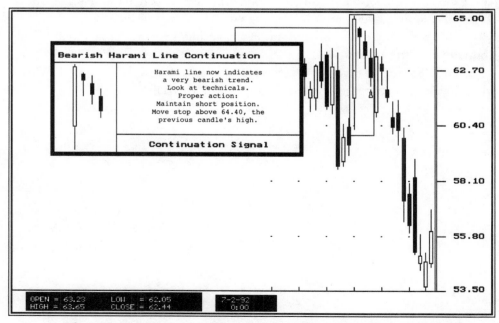

Figure 7.22 Weekly Cotton, December 1992—Bearish Harami Line Continuation (7/2/92)

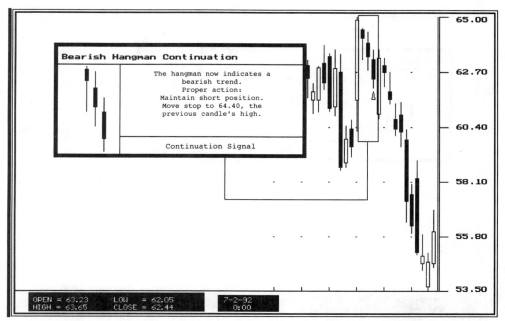

Figure 7.23 Weekly Cotton, December 1992—Bearish Hangman Continuation (7/2/92)

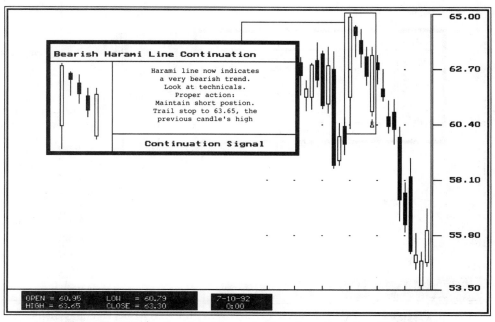

Figure 7.24 Bearish Harami Line Continuation (7/10/92)

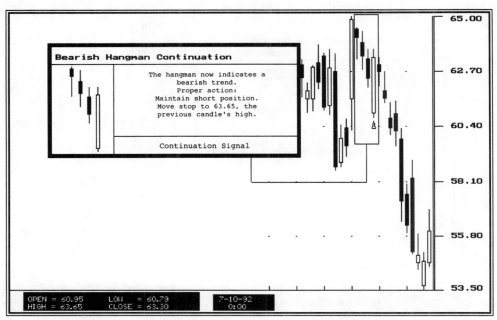

Figure 7.25 Weekly Cotton, December 1992—Bearish Hangman Continuation (7/10/92)

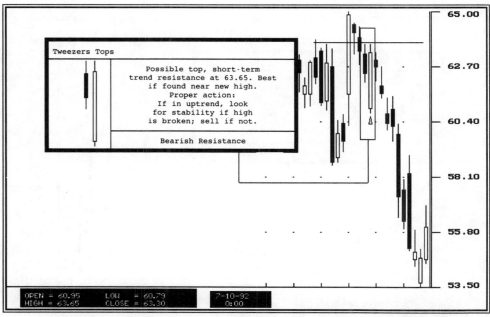

Figure 7.26 Weekly Cotton, December 1992—Tweezers Tops (7/10/92)

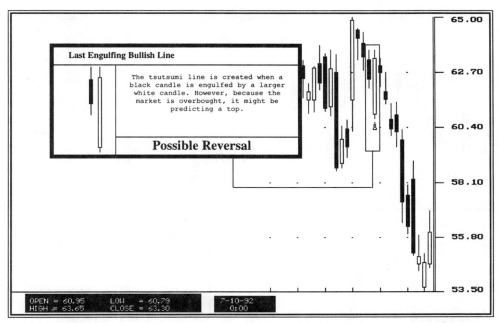

Figure 7.27 Weekly Cotton, December 1992—Last Engulfing Bullish Line (7/10/92)

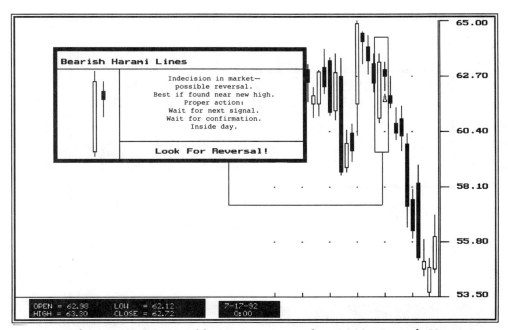

Figure 7.28 Weekly Cotton, December 1992—Bearish Harami Lines (7/17/92)

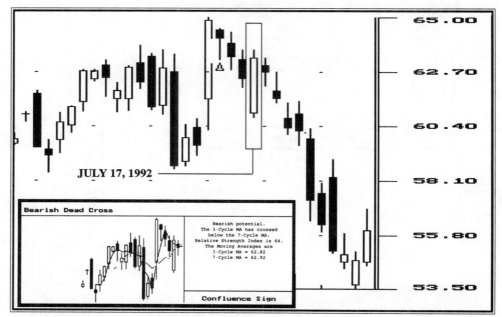

Figure 7.29 Weekly Cotton, December 1992—Bearish Dead Cross (7/17/92)

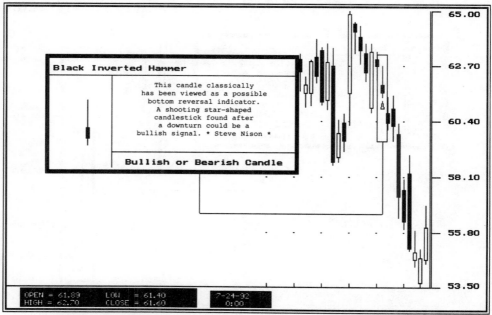

Figure 7.30 Weekly Cotton, December 1992—Black Inverted Hammer (7/24/92)

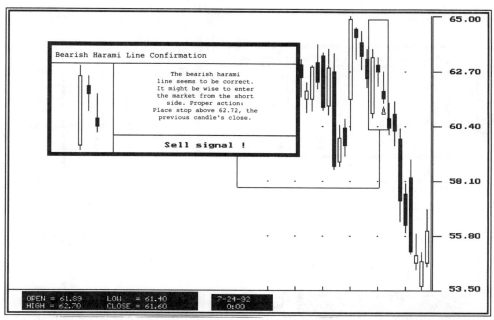

Figure 7.31 Weekly Cotton, December 1992—Bearish Harami Line Confirmation (7/24/92)

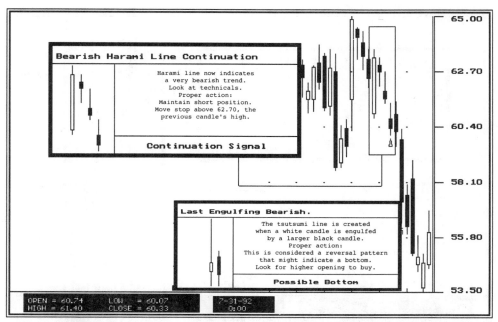

Figure 7.32 Weekly Cotton, December 1992—Bearish Harami Line Continuation and Last Engulfing Bearish (7/31/92)

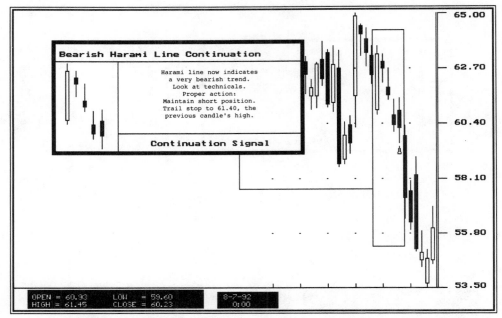

Figure 7.33 Weekly Cotton, December 1992—Bearish Harami Line Continuation (8/7/92)

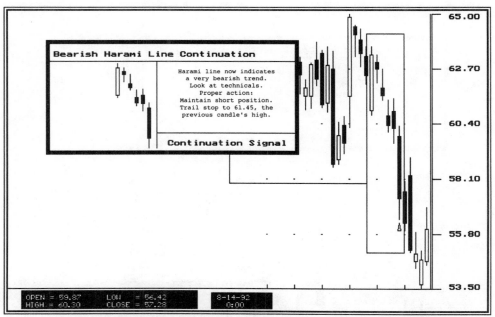

Figure 7.34 Weekly Cotton, December 1992—Bearish Harami Line Continuation (8/14/92)

EIGHT

Energies

Crude Oil

Figure 8.1 is a daily chart for light crude oil during March 1993. The light crude market entered a bearish price trend after a top formed near the end of 1992 (Figure 8.2, Example 1), creating a bearish harami line pattern that was confirmed with a black candle closing lower on the following day. This issued a sell signal. Seven days after the top reversal, an engulfing bearish line pattern was found that issued another sell signal (Figure 8.2, Example 2), indicating that the bears were attempting to continue the market's downward price movement. It is not uncommon to find a series of candlestick patterns within a defined market trend that reissues a signal adding to the confluence of the prior pattern and signaling a continuation of the trend.

After dropping nearly two full points, the market found support near 20.25 and began to consolidate above the support level. Right after support formed, a dark cloud cover pattern appeared (Figure 8.2, Example 3) and issued another sell signal. Even though the bulls were attempting to hold the market price above 20.00, the bears were still very much in control of the market. The next candle confirmed the prior dark cloud cover pattern and began three days of lower prices. A market consolidation is a natural part of any extended market trend, bullish or bearish. At this point, a new support/resistance level formed (Figure 8.2, Example 1). If the bulls were to be successful in holding the market price above support, we would see a bullish price rally. If they were not to be successful, the bearish sentiment would be able to test, and possibly break, a critical support area at 20.00 per barrel.

The price of oil continued downward for over seven days until it found support just below 19.00 per barrel. A tweezers tops and bottoms pattern (Figure 8.2, Example 4, and Figure 8.3) indicated a consolidating market and the possibility of a market breakout at this potential market bottom. With a long-legged doji line as the flagship candle (Figure 8.4), the tweezers tops and bottoms pattern predicted a bullish breakout in the market price. The stochastic indicator also

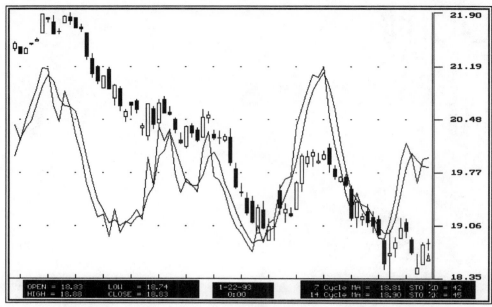

Figure 8.1 Crude Light, March 1993 (1/22/93)—with Stochastic Oscillators Overlaid

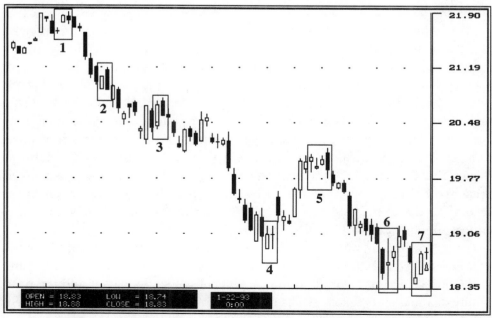

Figure 8.2 Crude Light, March 1993 (1/22/93)—Overall Trend View

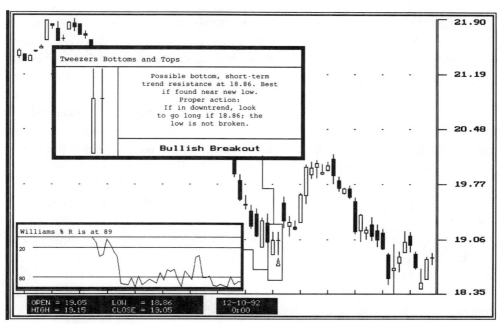

Figure 8.3 Crude Light, March 1993—Tweezers Bottoms and Tops (12/10/92)

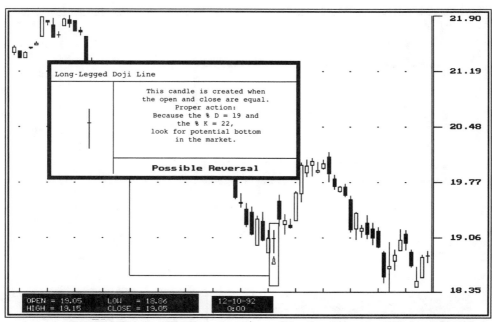

Figure 8.4 Crude Light, March 1993—Long-Legged Doji Line (12/10/92)

confirmed this candlestick pattern by indicating that the market was oversold (Figure 8.1, Example 1). The bullish price reversal initiated by the tweezers tops and bottoms pattern continued for seven trading days until it stalled just below the support/resistance price level indicated by the earlier market consolidation (Figure 8.2, Example 5). We should have expected this stall after the bullish rally because we had already identified the support/resistance level toward which the market price was moving. The presence of the bears in the market and their ability to drive the market price downward, below the support price level, was causing the market to stall and reverse from a bullish trend to a bearish trend. The support price level turned into resistance when the market price fell below it. A white hangman formed first to indicate that the bullish price advance was ending.

Next, a white inverted hammer formed with a higher low price, indicating that the bulls were still attempting to push the market price upward. Notice how each of these new candlesticks was shrinking in size as another indication that the market was consolidating. Then a small white candle formed, followed by a long black candle that engulfed the previous small white line. This engulfing bearish line pattern reinitiated the bearish price move and was pointing out that the bears had reentered the market to push the closing price below the resistance level. This time, the bears were able to drive the market price below 19.00 to a new low of 18.35, where a new support price level had formed (Figure

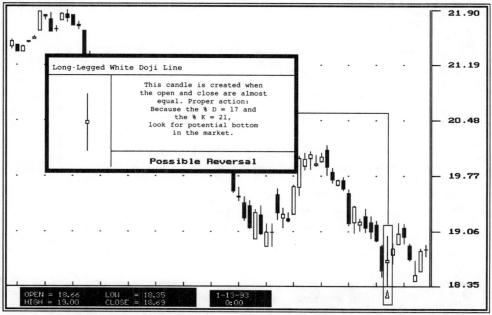

Figure 8.5 Crude Light, March 1993—Long-Legged White Doji Line (1/13/93)

8.2, Example 6). Another long-legged white doji line (Figure 8.5) appeared as a flagship candle to a bullish harami line pattern (Figure 8.6) at the market bottom. Notice that the stochastic oscillator is showing us that the market was, again, oversold and that we should see a bullish price reversal (Figure 8.1, Example 2).

At this time, the market had found support after a long-term bearish price trend. We have isolated three different support and resistance price levels that were defined by market consolidation and the candlestick patterns throughout this bearish price move. With the presence of the bears in the market, we should expect some market consolidation near this new bottom and watch the current market price activity for other signals. Five trading days after the market bottom formed with a doji line, a white inverted hammer formed very near the support level and bottom (Figure 8.7). This inverted hammer prompted a bullish rally that confirmed with a long opening white bozu line and continued upward with a doji line (Figure 8.7, candle under pointer). The doji line is hinting that we might see more market consolidation before another major move happens (Figure 8.8).

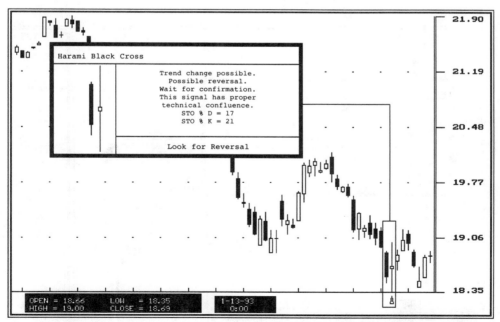

Figure 8.6 Crude Light, March 1993—Harami Black Cross (1/13/93)

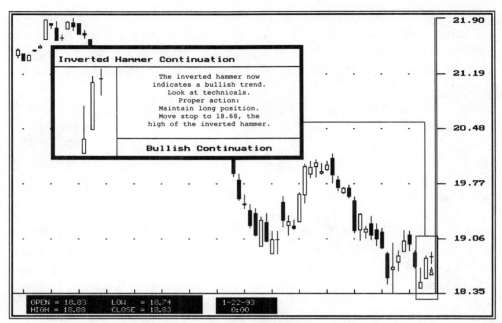

Figure 8.7 Crude Light, March 1993—Inverted Hammer Continuation (1/22/93)

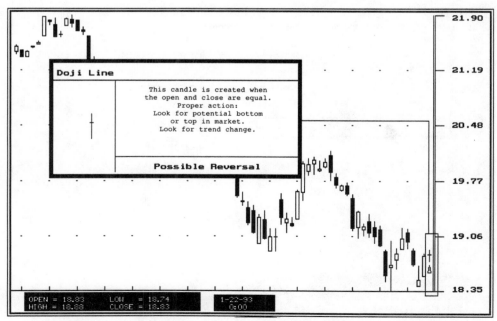

Figure 8.8 Crude Light, March 1993—Doji Line (1/22/93)

Heating Oil and Unleaded Gas

The daily heating oil chart (Figure 8.9) is very similar to the crude light chart (Figure 8.1) and the unleaded gas chart (Figure 8.10). Most of the same candlestick patterns issue similar signals in comparison to the crude light analysis. For this reason, we reintroduce a cross-market analysis technique to maximize potential profit and our understanding of the market's price movement.

All three markets—crude light, heating oil, and unleaded gas—are derivatives of a single natural product, petroleum. Any increase in cost of the refinement, transportation, and extraction of the original product will directly affect the cost of each of the derivative products. Thus, we see very similar price movement in each market. With this fact in mind, we can confirm our interpretation of each market with these other markets. But when we see similar candlestick patterns issuing similar signals in all three markets, we are finding confluence within all three markets that the probability of success is increased.

The initial bearish market price move in crude light started with an engulfing bearish line (Figure 8.11). In unleaded gas, an engulfing bearish line formed (Figure 8.10, Example 1) to issue a strong sell signal. Both of the candlestick patterns were predicting a bearish price reversal. The engulfing bearish line is a stronger pattern formation than the bearish harami line that initiated the bearish price movement in the crude light market. The unleaded gas market's price activity better outlined the market's intention to fall with the candlestick sell signal.

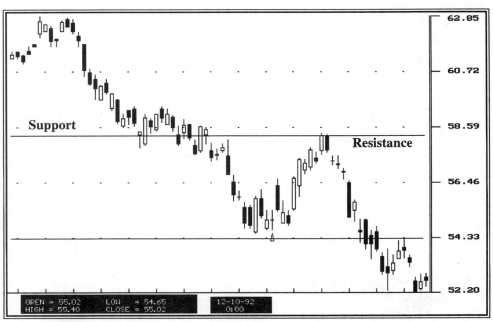

Figure 8.9 Heating Oil—March 1993 (12/10/92)

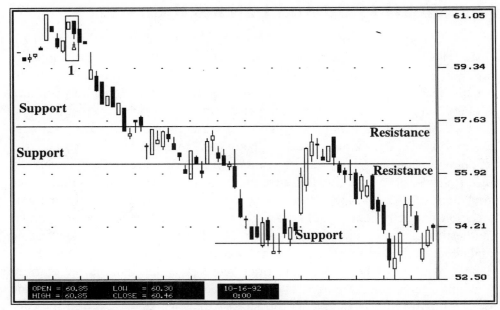

Figure 8.10 Unleaded Gasoline—March 1993 (10/16/92)

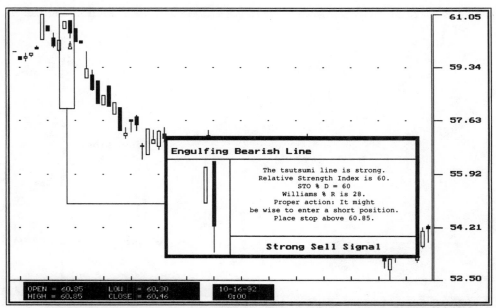

Figure 8.11 Crude Light, March 1993—Engulfing Bearish Line
(10/16/92)

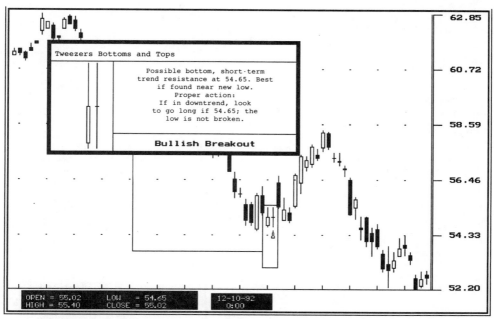

Figure 8.12 Heating Oil, March 1993—Tweezers Bottoms and Tops (12/10/92)

An example of similar markets forming an identical candlestick pattern during the same trading session can be found in the heating oil market and the crude light market. (Figure 8.2, Example 4). After a strong bearish price drop, a tweezers tops and bottoms pattern formed in both markets (Figure 8.12). Due to the candlestick pattern's placement, it issued a signal that the market should attempt a bullish breakout. Now that we have intermarket confirmation between the two markets, we have isolated similar flagship candles and patterns to lead the market price advance.

NINE

Currencies

Australian Dollar

We will begin our analysis with a weekly Australian dollar cash market. In Figure 9.1 a white hammer formed (Example 1) to start a bullish price rally from .7500 to over .7700 a month later. At the market top, a short black line gapped above the previous white candle in an evening position (Example 2). The following three candles failed to take out the resistance created by the close of the star (Example 2) and fell back to a prior support level (Example 3), where we find a last engulfing bearish pattern followed by an engulfing bullish pattern that propelled the market price back up the market channel.

At the top of the channel (Example 4), a dark cloud cover pattern formed (Figure 9.2) and was followed by a shooting star, which retook the prior price advance and closed at a tentative support level near .7500 (Figure 9.1, Example 5). The market fell below support and almost formed a low-price gapping play pattern (Figure 9.1, Example 6), which initiated a bearish price movement to .7100. This pattern was incomplete because it did not fully gap away from the pattern (please refer to figure 3.1f which shows a Bullish Gapping Play).

Intramarket Currency Analysis

The following sections compares price activity on September 2, 1992, in the currencies markets. As we have discussed in earlier cross-market analysis, we sometimes see identical or similar patterns in related markets that predict a similar market move in each. When this type of similar market trait can be identified within different related markets, a common or interrelated price movement can be predicted when similar patterns form in all of the charts.

Initially, the daily December 1992 British pound chart in Figure 9.3 had entered a defined bullish trend and traded within a defined upward price channel for over one month before consolidating into a tight trading range be-

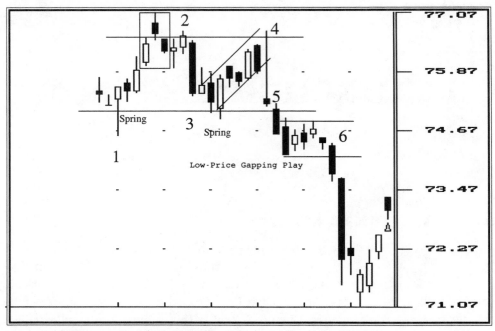

Figure 9.1 Weekly Australian Dollar—Cash 1992

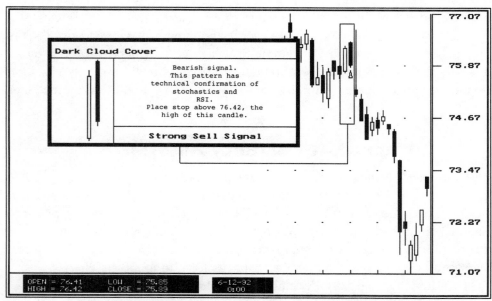

Figure 9.2 Weekly Australian Dollar, Cash 1992—Dark Cloud Cover (6/12/92)

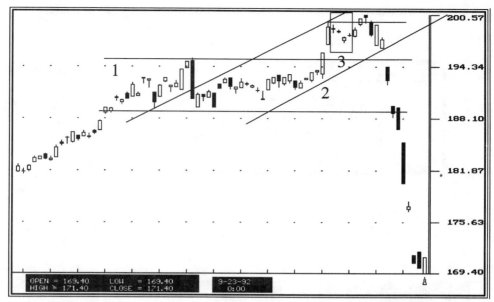

Figure 9.3 Daily British Pound—December 1992 (9/23/92)

tween 189.00 and 194.00 (Example 1). The market price continued to trade in a tight channel until it broke above resistance with a long white closing bozu line (Example 2). This was followed closely with a cluster of doji candles (Example 3) that all traded within the range of the prior white candle's body. The placement of the doji cluster was near these recently formed new highs and pointed to uncertainty in the market. A black hangman formed above the newly formed price channel created by the last long white line to open on a new contract high of 200.57 on September 2, 1992 (Figure 9.4). This hangman indicated that the market might be at a top.

Figure 9.5 highlights the black hangman confirmation received on September 3, 1992, issuing a sell signal. Figures 9.6, 9.7, and 9.8 also contain patterns found in the British pound on September 3, 1992, in both the cash and December 1992 contract months. Figure 9.6 is a three-river black evening star pattern where the black hangman acts as the star and thereby becomes a flagship candle.

A three-river black evening star pattern can be found in Figure 9.8, which depicts the December contract month of the British pound. This pattern is capped with a black doji star. Even more interestingly, a tweezers bottoms pattern (Figure 9.7) formed in the December contract, which created critical support. This critical support level needed to be broken before the accelerated market selloff could begin. The following session, on September 4, 1992, produced a long white opening bozu line in which the market opened below support

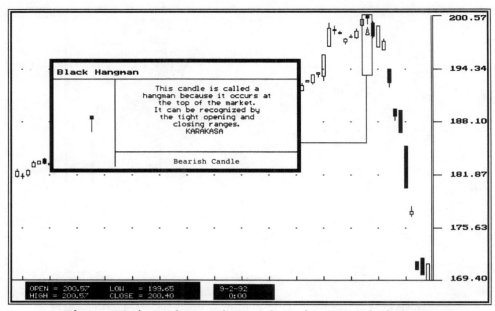

Figure 9.4 Daily British Pound, Cash 1992—Black Hangman (9/2/92)

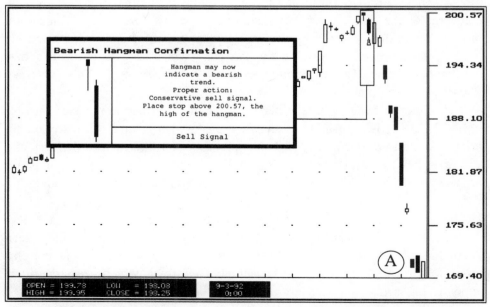

Figure 9.5 Daily British Pound, Cash 1992—Bearish Hangman Confirmation (9/3/92)

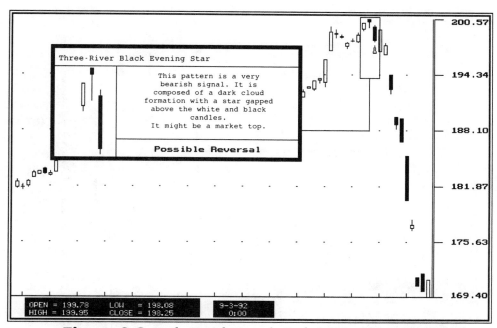

Figure 9.6 Daily British Pound, Cash 1992—Three-River Black Evening Star (9/3/92)

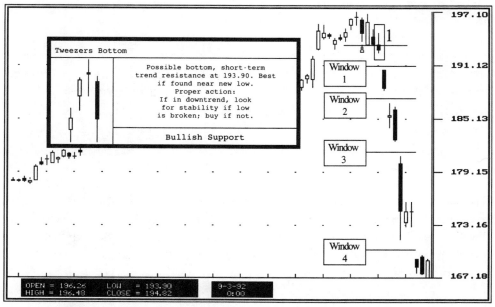

Figure 9.7 Daily British Pound, December 1992—Tweezers Bottom (9/3/92)

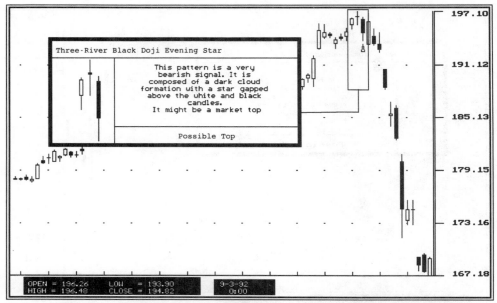

Figure 9.8 Daily British Pound, December 1992—Three-River Black Doji Evening Star (9/3/92)

and closed above the prior low. On September 5, 1992, a short black candle traded lower than the previous white opening bozu candle and closed above its open and low. The next candle is a black candle that opened just below the prior black candle's low, with a lower low and a lower high than the previous candle.

We've now seen four consecutive candles with consecutively lower lows. The next candle gapped below the prior candle, creating the first of a series of four bearish windows. The rest is history. Over the next seven trading sessions, the market dropped to a low of 169.40 (Figure 9.5 at A), a dramatic bearish price move of over 31 points. The British pound, in six short days, devalued over 15 percent, as predicted by the black hangman found on September 2, 1992.

On September 2, 1992, a black hangman candle can be found in both the British pound chart (Figure 9.4) and the German mark chart (Figure 9.9). The black hangman issued a sell signal in the German mark when confirmation occurred (Figure 9.10). It also created an incomplete dark cloud cover pattern (Figure 9.9, Example 2) to issue a sell signal a day prior to its confirmation. Although not as dramatic as the drop seen in the British pound, the price of the German mark was devalued by over 8 percent.

Figure 9.11 is a weekly chart of the German mark. During the same time frame that saw a market top form in the daily chart, a long-legged black doji line formed in the weekly chart. The doji line formed at the market top

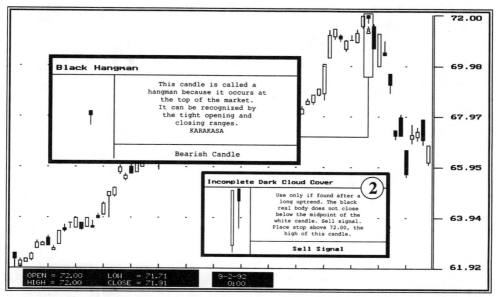

Figure 9.9 Daily German Mark, December 1992—Black Hangman and Incomplete Dark Cloud Cover (9/2/92)

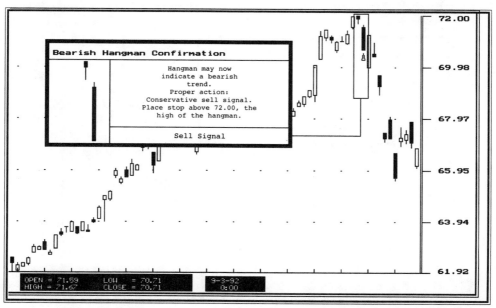

Figure 9.10 Daily German Mark, December 1992—Bearish Hangman Confirmation (9/3/92)

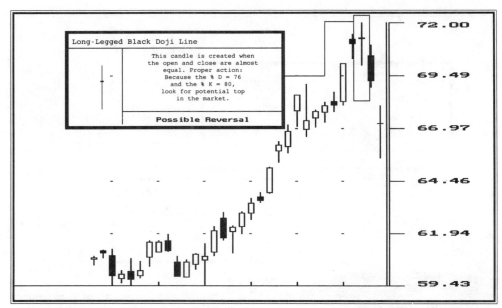

Figure 9.11 Weekly German Mark, Cash 1992—Long-Legged Black Doji Line

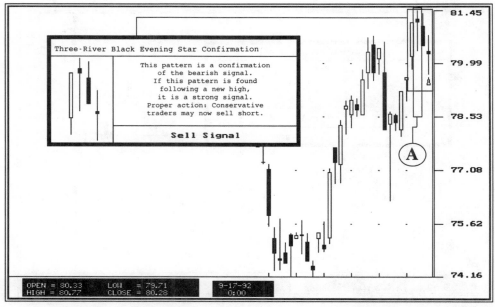

Figure 9.12 Weekly Japanese Yen, Cash 1992—Three-River Black Evening Star Confirmation (9/17/92)

and forewarned of a bearish market reversal. We would have done well to wait for confirmation of the black doji star reversal before entering a short position.

On the week ending September 4, 1992, in the weekly Japanese yen chart (Figure 9.12), a prominent black doji line candle formed (Figure 9.12 at A) at the top of the market at the same time that another doji line appeared in the German mark chart. This black doji line was placed in an evening position and was signaling that we might see a bearish market reversal or market consolidation. Notice that similar candles in related markets had formed, predicting similar price moves. The black doji star found in the Japanese yen chart (Figure 9.12 at A) had not issued a sell signal yet because a confirmation pattern had not formed. The next candle was a long black line that completed a three-river black doji evening star pattern and forewarned of a potential market top. The completed three-river pattern could issue a sell signal because it showed a confirmation of a black doji line that was likely to reverse the market trend. A second black doji line formed next to issue a confirmation of the three-river pattern and reissue the sell signal in this market.

In Figure 9.13, a similar long-legged black doji line formed on September 4, 1992, at the top of the 1992 Swiss franc cash market. The body of the black doji line fell within the body of the prior black candle's body to create a harami line pattern indicating a potential market reversal. The harami line pattern was confirmed on the following week (Figure 9.14) and issued a sell signal. As

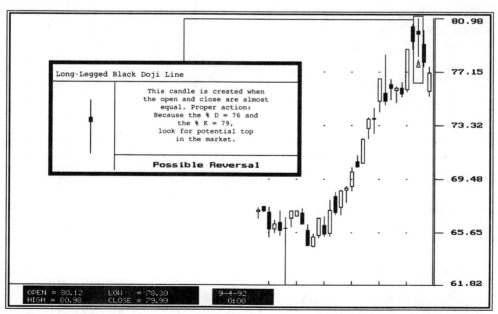

Figure 9.13 Weekly Swiss Franc, Cash 1992—Long-Legged Black Doji Line (9/4/92)

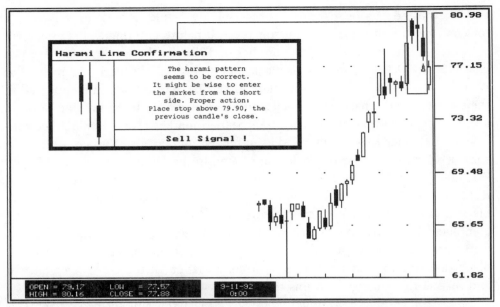

Figure 9.14 Weekly Swiss Franc, Cash 1992—Harami Line Confirmation (9/11/92)

of this writing, on February 27, 1992, the market had fallen to a new contract low of $0.6451.

The last four charts we used for the cross-market comparison are weekly charts. These graph the market's price activity with a slower phase, thereby reducing noise, or short-term price fluctuations—in effect, allowing one to see the long-term defined trend. The daily and intraday charts, on the other hand, are more sensitive to the short-term defined trends, thereby forewarning of market reversals before the weekly chart. In this manner, we confirm the daily chart activity against the weekly chart activity to confirm a short-term market reversal against a potential long-term market reversal.

Once we have identified that a market has entered a long-term trend, a weekly candlestick chart will offer a more distilled view of any prolonged trend. Often, a long-term daily bullish or bearish trend may be depicted as an upward- or downward-stepping market trend and may form a number of short-term price corrections during its long-term price move. The probability of acting improperly during one of these short-term price corrections can be reduced by comparing the daily chart with the weekly chart.

In our cross-market analysis, we've found that similar patterns and candles form in related markets to predict a potential market move. The daily price activity and candlestick patterns found therein forewarn of the potential market top with specific pattern types. The respective weekly charts also forewarn of the market top with similar related candles and advanced patterns. In retrospect, the daily and weekly charts should be used together to confirm any potential major market reversal and to identify critical market support and resistance. In many cases, the candles and patterns found in the daily chart will confirm with the candles and patterns found in the weekly chart, providing stronger evidence of the potential future market move.

For example, Figure 9.15 is a daily December 1992 U.S. dollar index candlestick chart. After over two months of continuous bearish price movement, a small white doji line formed on September 2, 1992, with a new contract low to create a two-day bullish harami line pattern, indicating a potential market reversal. This pattern confirmed on the following day with a long white line to issue a buy signal, and the stochastic oscillator confirmed the buy signal by crossing below 20 percent.

The weekly dollar index chart, a black doji star in a morning position (Figures 9.16 and 9.17), lends confluence to the buy signal issued in the daily index cash market (Figure 9.15) This star was diametrically opposed to the stars found at the top of the market in the Swiss franc (Figure 9.14) and the Japanese yen (Figure 9.12 at A) as well as the black hammers found in both the British pound (Figure 9.4) and the German mark (Figure 9.9).

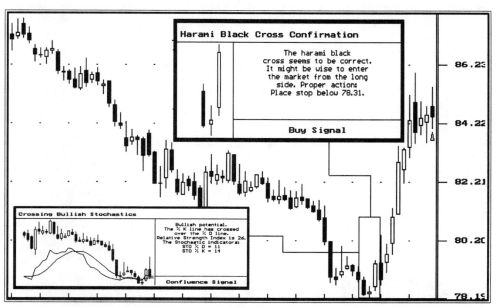

Figure 9.15 Daily Dollar Index, Cash 1992—Harami Black Cross Confirmation and Crossing Bullish Stochastics

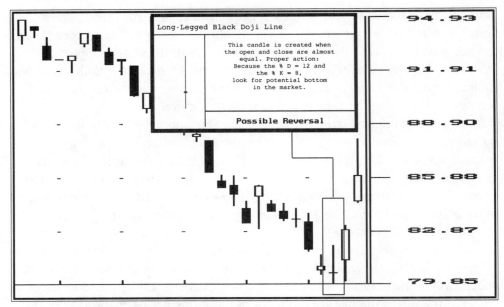

Figure 9.16 Weekly Dollar Index, Cash 1992—Long-Legged Black Doji Line

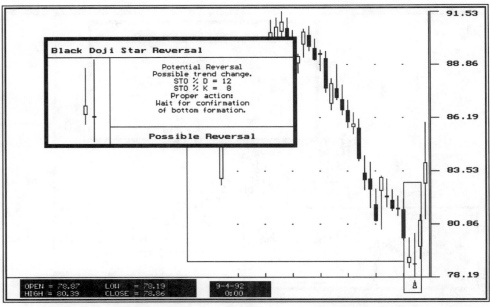

Figure 9.17 Weekly Dollar Index, Cash 1992—Black Doji Star Reversal (9/4/92)

TEN

Financial Interest Markets

30-Year U.S. Bonds

Figures 10.1 through 10.6 are from a daily U.S. bonds chart for March 1993. The time period covered in this chart is from October 1992 to the end of January 1993. Figure 10.1, the primary candlestick chart for this series, illustrates key support and resistance areas that the market will encounter over the next three months.

Figure 10.1 begins in the middle of October with March U.S. bonds trading over 105. The U.S. bonds market remained under bearish pressure through the 1992 presidential elections. Example 1 is a long doji star in a three-river star formation. It is unusual in that three-river patterns typically occur at the top of a market. In this case, it occurred after a short consolidation and also created a Western upthrust pattern. Bonds made four consecutively lower lows during the following four market sessions, but the last of these sessions closed higher on the day, which formed a thrusting pattern (Example 2). For the next two weeks the market traded in a narrow range defined by the prior long black candle. U.S. bonds were now trading below 101, and on November 8, 1992, the March contract made a new contract low of 100⁸/₃₂.

This last black candle would mark the end to the bearish sentiment that had prevailed and finally come to a rest during the next trading session. The following day, a small white spinning top traded inside the prior session. It represented the inability of the bears to continue the price decline, creating a bullish harami pattern (Figure 10.2), on November 9, 1992. Confirmation to the bullish harami came the following day in the form of a white opening bozu line. This was to begin a rally that would last into the following year, propelling U.S. bonds higher and inversely pushing interest rates lower. Figure 10.3 is the continuation pattern of the bullish harami. A white upper shadow gapped above the body of the black opening bozu line.

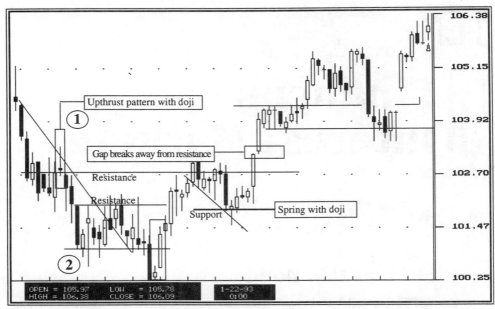

Figure 10.1 Daily U.S. Bonds—March 1993 (1/22/93)

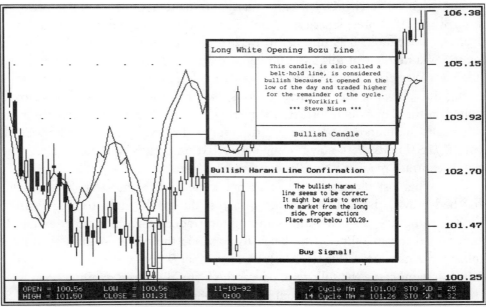

Figure 10.2 Daily U.S. Bonds, March 1993—Long White Opening Bozu Line and Bullish Harami Line Confirmation (11/10/92)

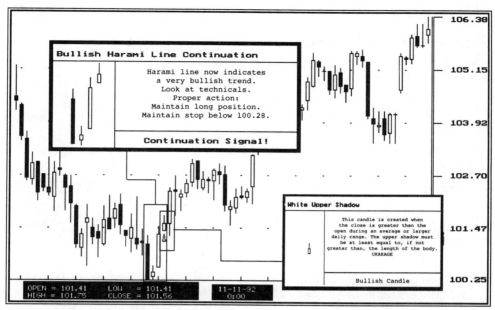

Figure 10.3 Daily U.S. Bonds, March 1993—Bullish Harami Line Continuation and White Upper Shadow (11/11/92)

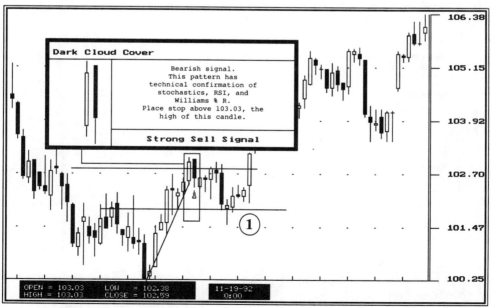

Figure 10.4 Daily U.S. Bonds, March 1993—Dark Cloud Cover (11/19/92)

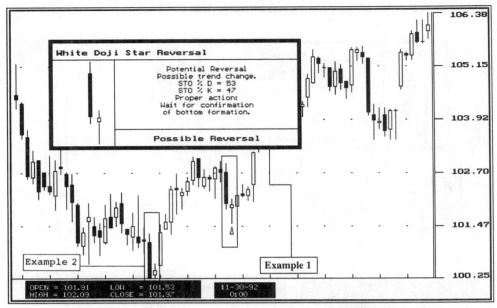

Figure 10.5 Daily U.S. Bonds, March 1993—White Doji Star Reversal (11/30/92)

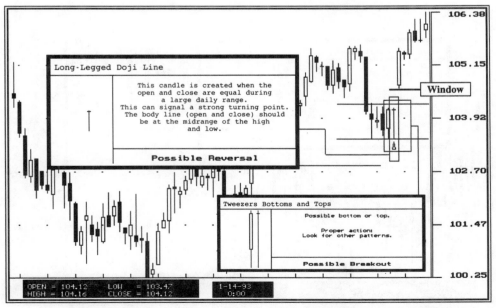

Figure 10.6 Daily U.S. Bonds, March 1993—Long-Legged Doji Line and Tweezers Bottoms and Tops (1/14/93)

At 103.00, after climbing nearly two full points, U.S. bonds entered the first consolidation period since the bottom. On November 19, 1992, a dark cloud cover (Figure 10.4) appeared, and a sell signal was issued. The market once again entered a bearish and narrowly defined range. On November 30, 1992, a white doji star (Figure 10.5) gapped below the former long black candle. This doji acted like a Western spring formation and began the second stage of this dynamic rally. Moreover, this two-day pattern was very similar to the bottom found on November 10, 1992 (Figure 10.5, Example 1). The post-election U.S. bond rally was now in full gear. By the end of December 1992, this rally had moved U.S. bonds back to 105.00, the level that they had back in October 1992.

At the beginning of January 1993, U.S. bonds began a third retracement wave that would drop their price by a full basis point. On January 14, 1993 (Figure 10.6), the market formed a tweezers tops and bottoms pattern that was confirmed on the following day when U.S. bonds gapped above the prior session to challenge the previous highs.

Municipal Bonds

Figure 10.7 is the March 1993 contract of municipal bonds. The time period covered in this chart is from October 1992 to the end of January 1993. It also illustrates key support and resistance areas that the market encountered

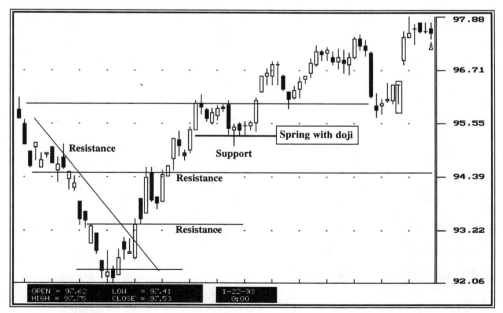

Figure 10.7 Municipal Bonds—March 1993 (1/22/93)

over the following three months. Municipal bonds trade more or less in tandem with U.S. bonds, although divergence in prices does occur. In this example they trade almost identically.

At the end of October 1992, a rare pattern gave early warning of the bottom in the municipal bonds market: an eight to ten–new price low. This pattern contains a minimum of eight candles. As the name suggests, this exhaustion pattern requires that a price have between eight and ten new lows or highs. It does not require consecutive new lows or highs, but they must appear closely together. Figure 10.8 shows an eight to ten–new price low that occurred after a sustained downtrend. Ten consecutive lows had occurred in the market! The following day a white doji line gapped below the eight to ten–new price low (Figure 10.9, Example 1). This doji was in turn surrounded by a large black candle during the next trading session. A last engulfing pattern appeared on the bottom of this market (Figure 10.10, Example 2). Figure 10.10 contains trading bands added to the municipal bonds chart. It is clear from this chart that the eight to ten–new price low that signaled the bottom had broken below the 18-day trading bands. Confirmation of this reversal would have to include a close above this critical price area. Figure 10.10, Example 1, shows that a white opening bozu opened below the lower 18-day trading band and closed above it, signaling the beginning of a two-month rally that would carry the bonds into 1993.

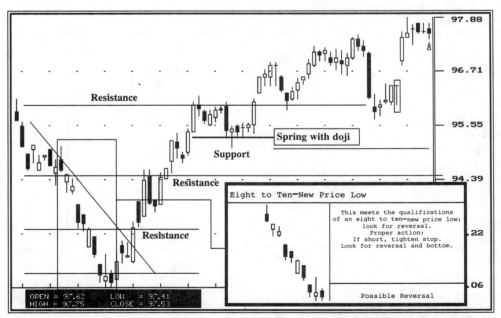

Figure 10.8 Municipal Bonds, March 1993—Eight to Ten–New Price Low

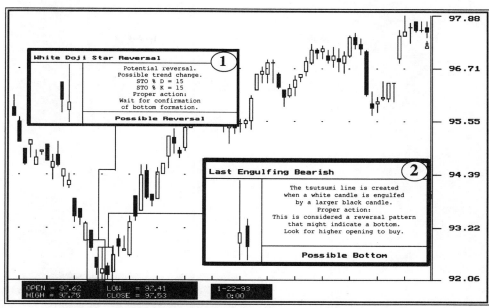

Figure 10.9 Municipal Bonds, March 1993—White Doji Star Reversal and Last Engulfing Bearish (1/22/93)

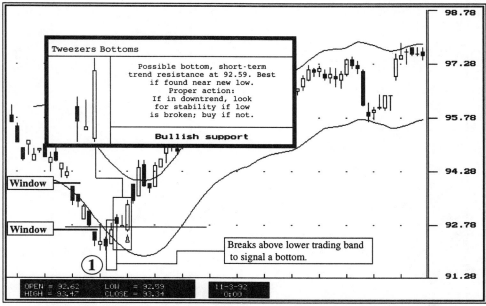

Figure 10.10 Municipal Bonds, March 1993—Tweezers Bottoms (11/3/92)

ELEVEN

Metal Markets

Gold

The doji candle, as mentioned previously, can indicate market reversals. They are significant when found at tops and bottoms. When many dojis are found together, in clusters, they are even more significant and powerful. In this example, a daily December 1992 gold chart (Figure 11.1), we will examine how a common market trait can predict the market's future price movement.

On July 19, 1992, after a considerable bullish price advance, a white doji star formed in an evening position (Figure 11.1, Example 1) after a long white opening bozu line. Its placement forewarned of a top in the market. Next, a black doji line formed with a gap between its body and the prior doji candle's body (Examples 1 and 2) with a minor drop in price, indicating that the market would consolidate. Next, a small white line (Example 3) formed as a last engulfing bullish line and again confirmed that the market was topping. We see quite a number of candlestick patterns, all telling us that the market was topping and that the market was consolidating tightly.

On July 23, 1992, a black candle formed and created a dark cloud cover pattern (Figure 11.1, Example 3, and Figure 11.2, Example 1), which issued a sell signal at the top of the market. Next, a long-legged white doji line formed (Figure 11.1, Example 4, and Figure 11.2, Example 2) and confirmed the dark cloud cover pattern, although it hinted that the market might continue to consolidate before making a move. As leading indicators, Japanese candlesticks were able to forewarn of a market top before the market trend reversed. Each and every one of the different candlestick patterns that predicted a market top were flagship patterns. We should watch for these patterns to form in this market in the future.

We are still short the market from a sell signal issued from the dark cloud pattern found on July 23, 1992. As we're still short the market, we should not expect to see a major bearish price move for a while. The number of doji candles, five in all, points to the market having been very indecisive as it formed

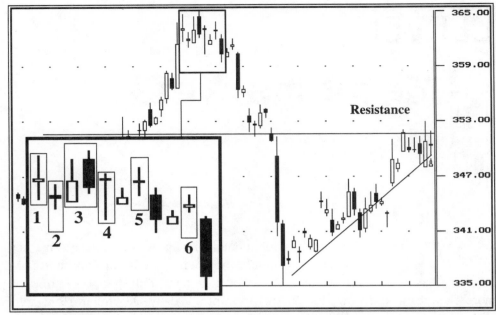

Figure 11.1 Daily Gold—December 1992

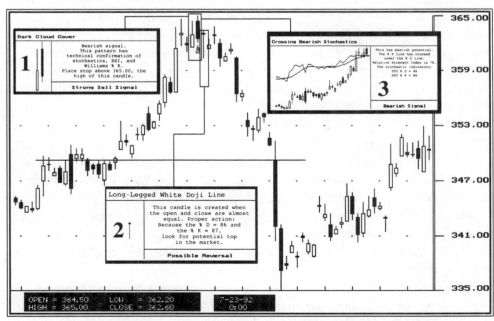

Figure 11.2 Daily Gold, December 1992—Dark Cloud Cover, Long-legged White Doji Line, and Crossing Bearish Stochastics (7/23/92)

its top and likely to consolidate as it reversed direction. Eight trading sessions after our first forewarning of a market top and four sessions after the dark cloud cover pattern, the market began to break sharply downward.

The end of the bearish price move commenced when the market held above 335.00 with the same tight price consolidation that we saw at the top. The doji candles were again indicating that the market was likely to consolidate before making a move and reflecting the uneasiness of the market at that bottom. After eight trading sessions, a high-price gapping play pattern formed (Figure 11.3) and indicated that the market could rally upward. The high-price gapping play pattern results when the market price consolidates between the high and low of a previous long candle's body for four or more sessions. Then the market price must gap upward, above the high of the long candle, causing the price to channel within its body's size for two sessions. It is considered a sign of market exhaustion, predicting a bullish price advance.

In a weekly chart comparison of the December 1992 gold market (Figure 11.4), we find a quite similar market top formation. After an initially slow but continuous bullish price movement, a doji line formed at the top of the market in an evening position; it represents the tightly consolidating market top that we found in the daily gold chart. Notice how the tight market consolidation at both the top and bottom of the market translated into doji lines. The three candles at the top of this weekly chart created a three-river evening doji star

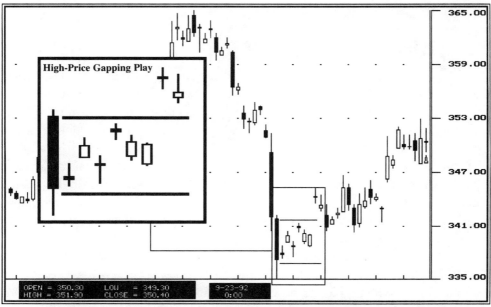

Figure 11.3 Daily Gold, December 1992—High-Price Gapping Play (9/23/92)

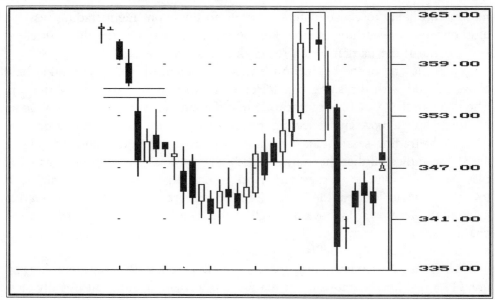

Figure 11.4 Weekly Gold—December 1992

pattern, an excellent market top formation. A bearish market price move would be likely after a pattern formation like this. The three-river doji evening star reversal pattern confirmed with the following candle and continued to a low of 335.00.

Silver

In Figure 11.5, we see a daily silver candlestick chart for December 1992 that ends September 23, 1992. We'll start our analysis at the market top, where an engulfing bullish line pattern (Example 1) initiated a short-term bullish rally that lasted for three days. The two candles that followed the engulfing bullish pattern were white hangman candles (Figure 11.6). These are bearish candles, and they predicted a market top, along with strong bearish resistance near 423.00. Even though a bullish price advance was in full swing, the single candles forewarned that the market was topping. Four days after the white hangman candles formed, an engulfing bearish pattern appeared (Figure 11.5, Example 3) and issued a sell signal at the market's top to start a bearish price move.

As the bearish price move continued, new support was found below 400.00, which caused the market price to climb back up to a resistance level at 405.00. After the market found support, the market price made a slow, deliberate upward movement until two dark cloud cover patterns formed within 5 trading days (Figure 11.5, Example 4). These two dark cloud cover patterns normally

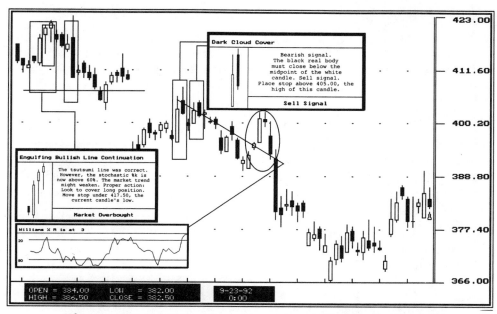

Figure 11.5 Daily Silver, December 1992—Dark Cloud Cover and Engulfing Bullish Line Continuation (9/23/92)

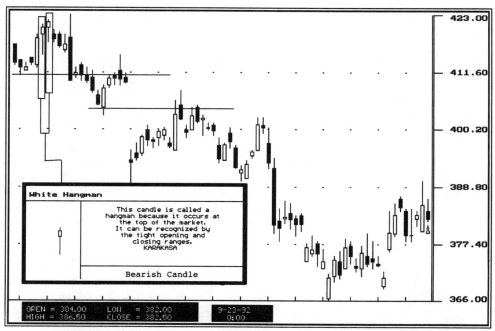

Figure 11.6 Daily Silver, December 1992—White Hangman (9/23/92)

wouldn't form one after another; this was an uncommon pattern formation that strongly predicted a bearish price move in this market future. Keeping a watchful eye on both common and uncommon patterns as they form is essential for gaining a better understanding of the market and the direction of its price movement. Both of the dark cloud cover patterns confirmed, yet the market price didn't start to make a dramatic move until 12 trading days after their initial formation. This is another example of how Japanese candlesticks are a leading indicator and can predict a market's future before it begins to move. The two dark cloud cover patterns started a bearish price move before the bearish harami line pattern (Figure 11.5, Example 5), but the harami line reinitiated the same bearish price move after the market found short-term support at 390.00. Also notice the placement of the harami line pattern. If the small black doji line that created the bearish harami line had opened a little higher, it would have formed a dark cloud cover pattern. By accurately monitoring the placement of each candle, we can learn and associate a great deal of information about the market's future.

Palladium

In Figure 11.7 the market is shown as having begun with an upward climb from 80.00 to near 88.00 a month later. Our analysis starts at the first market top, a very prominent engulfing bullish line pattern (Example 1) indi-

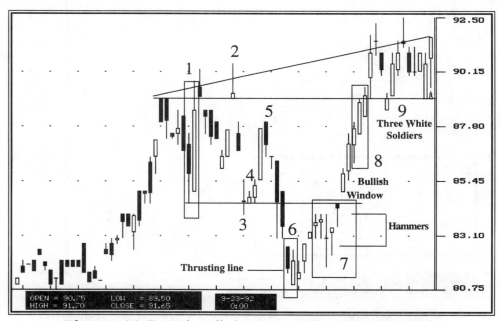

Figure 11.7 Daily Palladium—December 1992 (9/23/92)

cating that a bearish reversal was at hand and the market would move lower. The market began to trade very erratically within the range of the last engulfing pattern. Then a shooting star formed (Example 2) at the top of the last engulfing range. The market gapped lower the following day and closed on its low. Next, a black doji star formed (Example 3) in a morning position, indicating a potential bullish reversal in the market. This was confirmed the following day when the doji was engulfed by a small white upper shadow (Example 4) issuing a buy signal near 85.00. This market move was to be short lived; it was broken three days later when a dark cloud cover pattern formed (Example 5), signaling a bearish market reversal. The dark cloud cover pattern was confirmed when a dragonfly doji line formed at the bottom of the previous black candle. The market broke through the support level indicated by the last engulfing pattern. A striking pattern, bozu three wings, formed on August 14, 1992 (Figure 11.8). This pattern is composed of three bozu lines with progressively lower highs.

At this point a belt-hold pattern formed at the bottom of the market and at support at 81.00. This thrusting pattern could signal a continuation if it appeared in a downtrend because the long white opening bozu line was placed near support at 81.00. We would want to wait for a confirmation on the following day (Figure 11.9). If the market opened lower and broke through support at 81.00, we would have to interpret the thrusting line as a bearish continuation signal. That was not to be the case. On the following day a harami line formed

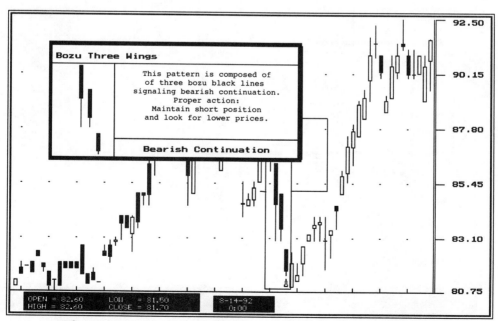

Figure 11.8 Daily Palladium, December 1992—Thrusting Line Confirmation (8/18/92)

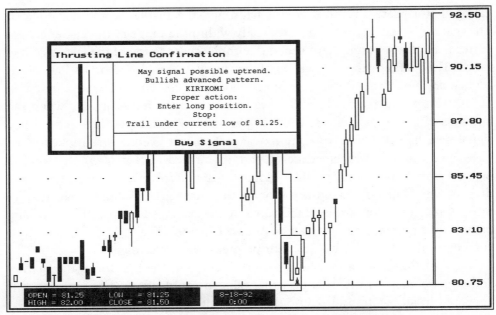

Figure 11.9 Daily Palladium, December 1992—Harami Line (8/18/92)

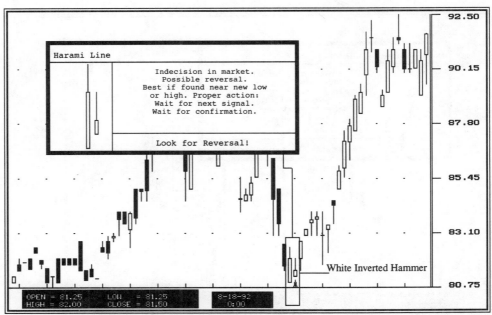

Figure 11.10 Daily Palladium, December 1992—Bozu Three Wings (8/14/92)

with a white inverted hammer as its inside day (Figure 11.10). The white inverted hammer lent support to a bullish market move and confirmed the thrusting line pattern to issue a buy signal (Figure 11.9).

The thrusting pattern initiated a bullish market rally. The market moved higher, and a cluster of hammers (Figure 11.7, Example 7) moved directly under the resistance level created by the low of the last engulfing bullish line pattern (Example 1). A short white line gapped above the prior cluster to form a bullish window (Example 8), which was followed by a bullish continuation pattern known as three white soldiers (Example 9). The last candle of the three white soldiers pattern closed above the prior resistance level, and the market price began to consolidate above 90.00 after this sustained rally had pushed the market over 10.00 points higher.

Platinum

Figure 11.11 is a daily platinum chart for September 1992. Initially, this market began with four individual doji lines (Example 1). These doji lines were present during new contract highs and then consolidated within the initial bullish window. Some bullish price movement took place during the market consolidation, yet the market didn't advance much. Next, a dark cloud cover

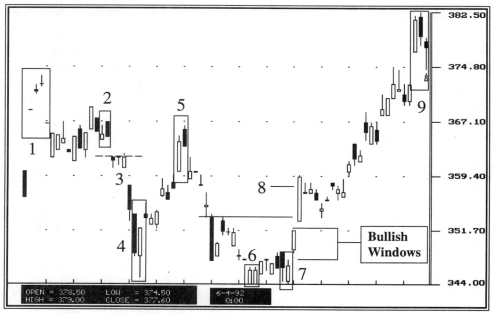

Figure 11.11 Daily Platinum, September 1992—Bullish Windows (6/4/92)

pattern formed (Example 2) and issued a sell signal, indicating that the bears were attempting to drive the market price lower. The next two candles served to confirm the dark cloud cover pattern and create a tweezers tops pattern (Example 3). In this case, the first small black candle formed with a bearish window between the dark cloud cover pattern and itself to confirm the dark cloud cover pattern and show that the bears had taken control of the market trend. The second candle was a small dragonfly doji line with the same high price as the prior candle, showing that the bears had been able to hold the market to this high price and indicating that the market would continue downward.

After three more days of downward price movement and another bearish window, a piercing line pattern (Example 4) formed out of a long black opening bozu line, a strongly bearish candle, and a long white closing bozu line, a strongly bullish candle. This seemingly confusing pattern was actually a very clear indication of the market's future. After seeing a strong bearish price drop ending with a strong bearish candle, an equally strong bullish candle formed and created a buy signal, the piercing line pattern (Example 4). If a weaker bullish candle had formed to create a thrusting pattern or a bullish harami line pattern, we should look for confirmation before entering a market position. With this specific type of candlestick pattern and the type of candles that make up this pattern, we would expect the market to begin a bullish price advance.

As the market completed this bullish price advance, two bullish windows had formed—the same number of windows that were present during the bearish price move. The second bullish window formed right at a support/resistance level of 360.00. As the market price advanced above the resistance level, an incomplete dark cloud cover pattern (Example 5) reversed the market's direction to bearish and issued a sell signal. Next, a bearish window formed again, indicating that the bears had reentered the market in an attempt to drive the market price downward.

When the market drifted leisurely downward to 344.00, a tweezers tops and bottoms pattern formed (Example 6) at what was then the market bottom, suggesting that the market would attempt a bullish breakout. After six trading days and some market consolidation near 345.00, a thrusting line pattern formed (Example 7) at the same market low of 344.00. It confirmed with a bullish window and a long white line to issue a buy signal. Even the next day's trading produced another bullish window with a white opening bozu (Example 8), although the high of the white opening bozu line had reached our prior resistance level. We would want to watch for the market to consolidate at this resistance level before it began another move. Finally, after nearly a 40.00-point price increase, a dark cloud cover pattern formed (Example 9) at a new market high of 382.50 to issue a sell signal. The dark cloud cover pattern had accurately predicted the past bearish price movements in this market, making it a common market trait and the current flagship pattern. It confirmed with a black hangman candle on June 4, 1992, that reconfirmed the market's top formation and reissued a sell signal.

Our second analysis is of a daily February 1993 platinum chart (Figure 11.12). We pick up after the market found support at 350.00 and 352.75 with a series of three tweezers tops and bottoms patterns and hinted at resistance near 362.00 with a black candle gapped above the surrounding white candles (Example 1). The small black candle was in an evening position with a clear window above the other candles, causing the market to reverse and consolidate near our support level. We have defined multiple support and resistance levels within a 20-day trading time frame, and we have seen more white candles than black, all at or near our support level. An engulfing bullish line (Example 2) initiated a short-term, two-day, bullish price rally. Next, an inverted black hammer formed (Example 3) to create a bearish harami line pattern, both predicting a bearish price reversal. The RSI, RMI, and stochastic indicators confirmed (Figure 11.13) that we should expect a market selloff and enter a short position in the market. The bearish harami line confirmed with the following candle, a long black line. The trend continued with another long black line forming a candle pattern called a *bearish window*. The dramatic three-day bearish price movement ended when the market found a prior support level at 345.00.

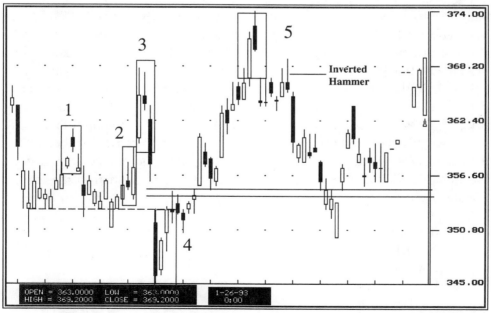

Figure 11.12 Daily Platinum, February 1993—Inverted Hammer (1/26/93)

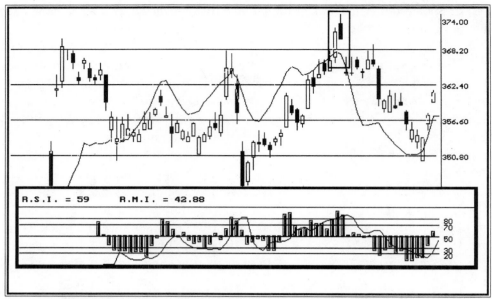

Figure 11.13 Daily Platinum, February 1993—R.S.I., R.M.I. and Stochastic Oscillator confirming dark cloud cover pattern.

The market then reversed with a bullish harami line pattern (Figure 11.12, Example 4) that confirmed with a second long white line and issued a buy signal. We've seen a consolidating market attempt to make a bullish advance, and each time it got slammed back down to its support levels. The bullish harami line pattern was the flagship pattern as it confirmed, indicating that the bulls would attempt to push the market price upward. The bullish harami line prompted a continuous bullish price advance for 16 days to a new high of 374.00 (Example 5). A long black line formed at the market top, created an incomplete dark cloud cover pattern, and issued a sell signal in the market. If the closing price of the long black line had been below the midpoint of the prior long white line, it would have created a complete dark cloud cover pattern. The incomplete dark cloud cover pattern confirmed with the RSI, RMI, and stochastic indicators. We would have done well to reverse and enter a short position in the market (Figure 11.13).

PART THREE

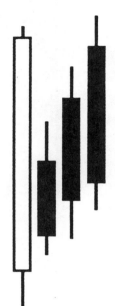

Japanese Candlesticks and the Stock Market

TWELVE

Cross-Market Analysis of Equities

Standard & Poor's 500 and Major Market Blue Chip Index

Our analysis begins December 17, 1992, with a daily Standard & Poor's 500 candlestick chart for March 1993 (Figure 12.1). The first thing we notice is that the market had been in a defined bullish trend. After a short price retracement, the market price found support and rocketed upward, creating a bullish window pattern, or gap, which is a bullish sign. The market continued its price advance, but notice that the white candles began to shrink in size relative to the long white candle that initiated the rally, showing that the bulls might not be able to continue the rally.

On December 22, 1992, a black hangman formed right at the end of the price rally (Figure 12.1, Example 2). This candle is strongly bearish when found at the top of the market, as it is here. It forewarned of a potential bearish reversal by confirming with the following black candle and issuing a sell signal.

In the previous day's Major Market Blue Chip Index, a doji star formed with a gap between its body and the prior candle's body (Figure 12.2). The doji star forewarned of a potential market top, just like the black hangman in the S&P 500 Index. The point is that different yet related markets can confirm one another's price reversals. If one lacks a candlestick pattern, the other usually has one. Another example of this type of analysis can be found in Figure 12.2, Example 2; an engulfing bearish line pattern formed in the Major Market Blue Chip Index, but no patterns were found in the S&P 500.

Figure 12.2, Example 3, is a white hammer that appeared at the bottom of the Major Market Blue Chip Index on January 8, 1993, indicating that the

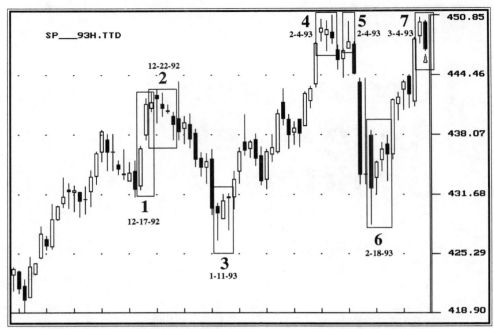

Figure 12.1 Daily Standard and Poor's 500—March 1993

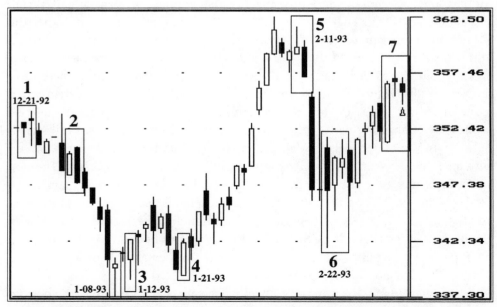

Figure 12.2 Daily Major Market Blue Chip Index—March 1993

market would again begin to rally. All of this activity took place just a few days before the S&P 500 Index formed a bottom with a black hammer and an engulfing bullish line pattern followed by another hammer (Figure 12.1, Example 3). We are beginning to see some consistency between the two markets and the types of candlestick patterns that occur in them. At this point the two markets began to act differently. Whereas the S&P 500 continued the bullish rally, which began on January 11, 1993, the Major Market Blue Chip Index rallied, but then fell to within a few points from its low (Figure 12.2, Example 4). From there, an engulfing bullish pattern began a second price rally on January 21, 1993. The Major Market Blue Chip Index made a dramatic bullish move, with only one short retracement after the second bottom had formed, whereas the S&P 500 Index continued a slower, less dramatic price advance with two defined bearish corrections. This technique of looking at multiple indexes provides us the ability to compare like markets for similar indications of future price movement.

The Major Market Blue Chip Index ended its dramatic price rally near 362.50 (a 7.5 percent increase) with a shooting star–shaped candle (Figure 12.2, Example 5) on February 11, 1993. Coincidentally, another shooting star–shaped candle formed on the same day in the S&P 500 Index (Figure 12.1, Example 5); three days earlier, two small white doji candles had formed, followed by a black inverted hammer that warned of the impending bearish price move. The shooting star–shaped candle in the Major Market Blue Chip Index turned into an engulfing bearish line when the following black candle's body engulfed the body of the shooting star to issue a sell signal (Figure 12.2, Example 5). Within the S&P 500 Index we never really received a sell signal near the top of the market. We did get confirmation of the black inverted hammer with another black candle, although the S&P 500 Index consolidated for four more days before making a move.

Once these markets began this bearish price move, prices fell fast and hard for four days. Notice the similarities between the Major Market Blue Chip Index and the S&P 500 Index after the white shooting star—they almost mirror each other. Figure 12.2, Example 6, and Figure 12.1, Example 6, show a bullish harami pattern that formed three days apart in both indexes to create a market bottom. Again, notice the similarity between the two indexes and their price movements. The bullish harami pattern confirmed with a white candle in both of the markets and issued a buy signal.

On March 4, 1993 (Figures 12.1, Example 7, and Figure 12.2, Example 7), both of the markets had reached a potential top, but their respective candlestick charts represent the situation differently. The S&P 500 Index formed a classic engulfing bearish line pattern just as it reached defined resistance, whereas the Major Market Blue Chip Index formed a three-river black evening star pattern. They both predicted a bearish price reversal but used different patterns to do so.

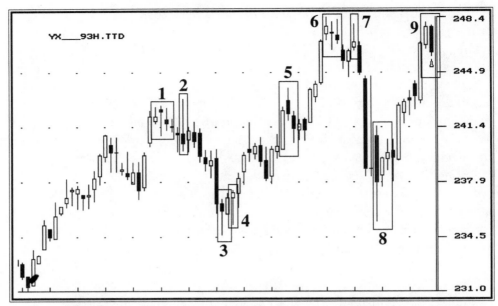

Figure 12.3 Daily New York Composite Index—March 1993

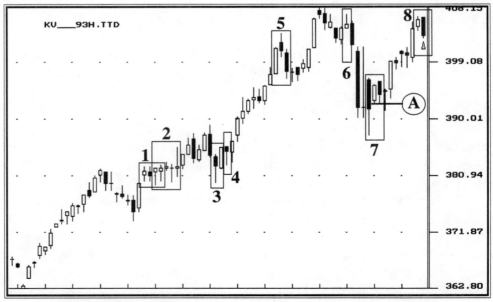

Figure 12.4 Daily Kansas City Value Line—March 1993

Kansas City Value Line and New York Composite Index

We begin our analysis after these markets had entered a bullish trend and begun to consolidate after finding resistance (Figures 12.3 and 12.4). After retracing from resistance to predefined support, both of the markets rallied to points at or above the prior resistance levels. The New York Composite Index was able to establish a new high, albeit a short-lived one (Figure 12.3, Example 1). A black hangman formed after the last bullish rally, indicating a possible bearish price reversal. A series of small doji candles trailed downward, indicating market consolidation, until a long black inverted hammer formed (Figure 12.3, Example 2), which indicated the strong potential for a bearish price move in the future.

At the same time in the Kansas City Value Line, a tweezers tops and bottoms pattern formed after a short price rally (Figure 12.4, Example 1). They were followed by two white hammers and a cluster of doji candles (Figure 12.4, Example 2). Notice the predominance of white candles found during the market consolidation in the Kansas City Value Line after the tweezers tops and bottoms pattern. New support had been formed, then the white hammers appeared after the tweezers top and bottoms pattern near 381.00.

Although the New York Composite Index followed with a bearish price retracement of nearly 50 percent, the Kansas City Value Line Index formed support and held its price. These two indexes exhibited similar candlestick patterns but completely different reactions. Figure 12.3, Examples 3 and 4, shows an engulfing bullish pattern that formed after a black hammer to signal the end of the bearish price retracement. The black hammer indicated a potential market bottom, and the engulfing bullish pattern completed the reversal to issue a buy signal; the white hammer followed the engulfing bullish pattern and confirmed it while also indicating a potential price rally.

Figure 12.4, Examples 3 and 4, presents candlestick patterns that are very similar to those we've seen in the New York Composite Index. First, an engulfing bullish pattern formed after a lower black shadow candle to end a very short bearish retracement. The engulfing bullish pattern was followed by a black hammer, strengthening the likelihood that the market would advance further.

At this point we are again seeing similarities between the two indexes. Because they are similar in composition and somewhat dependent upon one another, we could compare the signals from both to arrive at a more realistic mutual forecast.

After more continued price rallies, both indexes developed another shared pattern on the same day (Figure 12.3, Example 5, and Figure 12.4, Example 5), an incomplete dark cloud cover pattern. Even though both patterns were confirmed with the candle following them, the indexes only retraced a few points before rallying again. The incomplete dark cloud cover patterns that formed were auguring new or existing resistance in both indexes. The Kansas City Value Line Index was still in a defined bullish trend, although the incomplete dark cloud cover pattern had formed at a new market high, indicating that resistance would form above 405.00. The New York Composite Index found predefined resistance from a previous top (Figure 12.3, Example 2) that caused the incomplete dark cloud cover pattern and a short price retracement.

Another six days of price rallies followed until both indexes had reached new market highs. The New York Composite Index was the first to issue a potential top signal and forewarn of the impending price reversal with a doji line that created a bearish harami line pattern at the market top (Figure 12.3, Example 6). The Kansas City Value Line never issued any substantial warning of the bearish price reversal; it just stalled and began to fall after the top had been reached. In this instance we could have predicted the outcome of both indexes with the candlestick patterns from one. Again, notice the resemblance between the candles found in Figure 12.3, Example 7, and Figure 12.4, Example 6. They are both shooting star or inverted hammer candles that portended an impending bearish price reversal.

Both of the indexes dropped after the shooting star– or inverted hammer–shaped candles. The New York Composite Index retraced almost 50 percent, to a previous low of 235.00 (Figure 12.3, Example 8), while the Kansas City Value Line Index fell only 40 percent, to a low of 390.00 (Figure 12.4, Example 7). A bullish harami pattern formed simultaneously in both markets to forewarn of the possibility of a bullish price reversal. A second pattern formed in the Kansas City Value Line Index that seemed to suggest that the market would continue upward when the bullish harami line pattern confirmed with a tweezers bottoms pattern (Figure 12.4, Example 7 at A). The confirmation pattern we received in the New York Composite Index did not create a tweezers bottoms pattern, but it was confirmed nonetheless (Figure 12.3, Example 8).

After both the indexes rallied back to their original market tops, an engulfing bearish pattern formed in both (Figure 12.3, Example 9, and Figure 12.4, Example 8), predicting a classic sell signal. If the engulfing bearish pattern were to have confirmed with the following day of trading, we would have entered a short position.

In short, the similarities between related markets can be identified and used by any trader as a confirming indicator for future market moves. When the candlestick patterns become inconsistent or contradict one another, we should rely on the other indicators and the most predominant candlestick patterns for guidance.

THIRTEEN

Candlesticks and the Equities Markets

Although perceived by most Western technicians as an analytical tool used primarily in the futures markets, candlesticks can provide superb insight in the equities markets as well. The Japanese have been using candlestick technical analysis combined with Western technical indicators to chart equities for some time. They can be used as long- and short-term technical indicators by simply changing the cycle length for each pole line. Traders typically work with both weekly and daily candle lengths to balance their trading styles, but we have found that weekly charts provide an excellent indication of trends and reversals.

Candlesticks have an uncanny knack for finding the key reversal areas of tops and bottoms. When filtered with—that is, used in tandem with—Western technical indicators, these patterns can provide traders with reliable market calls. Our research found that the harami and engulfing patterns are among the most prevalent in these situations, as you will see throughout this chapter.

Jan Bell Marketing

Figure 13.1 is a weekly chart of Jan Bell Marketing; Examples 1 through 10 depict some of its key patterns. Although trading in a choppy price range of five dollars for the better part of a year, reversal patterns can be found at most of the tops and bottoms. Examples 1 and 6 are bearish harami patterns, which can warn of lower market prices. Bullish harami (Examples 2 and 7) formed at the bottom as the bears began losing control over market direction.

Hammers are also excellent bottom indicators. After a month of lower prices, a hammer formed (Example 5) at the bottom of the trading range. Ex-

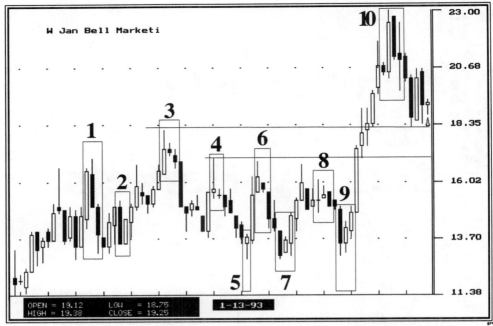

Figure 13.1 Weekly Candlestick Chart for Jan Bell Marketing

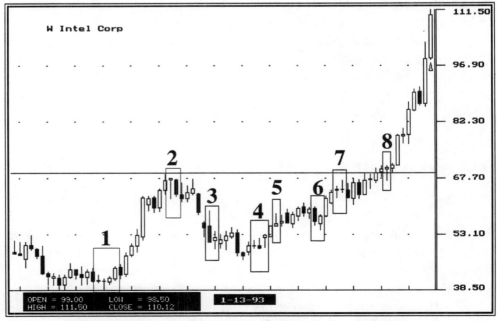

Figure 13.2 Weekly Candlestick Chart for Intel Corporation

amples 4 and 8 are both shooting star and doji combination patterns. Examples 3 and 10 are dark cloud cover patterns; however, Example 3 is incomplete. Example 9 is a piercing line, also an excellent bottom indicator.

Figure 13.2 is a weekly chart of Intel, which was a dynamic stock (to say the least) during 1992. It more than tripled in price in less than three months, rapidly moving higher in the last quarter of that year. Example 1 illustrates a bottom formation consisting of two doji, which were then both engulfed by a short white candle. This began an upward price movement that lasted over two months. Intel stock prices continued to climb until a large hangman formed at the summit (Example 2), which was almost engulfed by a black candle the following week.

In Example 3 we see how the market attempted to find support after selling off for about a month. The stock began to climb higher and continued this uptrend for three weeks until it fell back to its initial support at about $50 per share. An advanced pattern formed again at the bottom of the market; shown in Example 4, it was composed of a doji, an inverted hammer, and a hammer. Remember that inverted hammers are simply shooting star–shaped candles found at the lowest trading point in a market. These three candles were caught in a congestion pattern (or narrow trading range), unable to break above the resistance level or below the support level. The following week a white candle formed to break the resistance line and close above it.

The inverted hammer shown in Example 5 opened the following week above this resistance level, which now became the support level. Once again the market became congested and traded in a very narrow range just above this new support level; attempts to take out the high depicted in Example 3 were ineffective. One last test of the support level can be seen in Example 6, in which a black candle opened just above support and a white candle followed with a lower open. This created a piercing line pattern that signaled a bullish price advance. This rally would move the market to 68.00 (Example 2), where it found resistance. Two doji candles formed at the resistance line (Example 7), creating more consolidation at this significant top. Finally, an inverted hammer pushed through the resistance level and allowed the market to move to higher ground; it traded at new highs for the remainder of the year.

Figure 13.3 is a weekly chart for Kaufman and Broad, which traded to a new high of 25.00 before reversing near the middle of 1992. After more than two months of trading, the market had begun to consolidate above the support level at 12.25 and showed signs of a bullish price advance. Example 1 shows a doji-and-white-inverted-hammer cluster that formed just after the market moved above the support level. This cluster traded above the support level, confirming the potential for a bullish price move, while the two white inverted hammers indicated that the market was more likely to undergo a bullish price reversal than the doji lines alone would suggest. Inverted hammer candles are classic

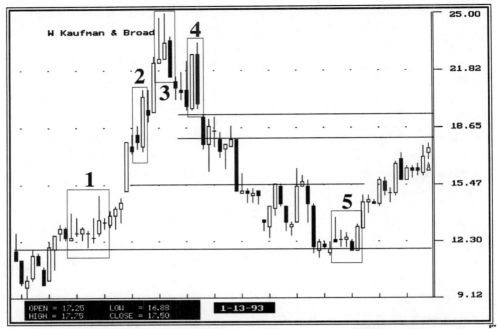

Figure 13.3 Weekly Candlestick Chart for Kaufman & Broad

bottom reversal indicators. Aggressive traders might enter a long position after finding this particular cluster, but conservative traders would wait for a confirmation of the doji lines of white inverted hammers before entering a position. After the last doji line of this cluster, a short white line formed to create an engulfing bullish doji line and issue a buy signal just above the predefined support level.

After the doji-and-white-inverted-hammer cluster, which caused a market consolidation near support, the market price began a bullish price advance from 12.50 to 25.00 in under three months, a 50 percent increase. Along this defined trend, we find a last engulfing bullish line pattern (Example 2) that is often found after a strong bullish rally or near a market top. It was signifying that the bulls were exerting all of their energy to push the market price as high as possible but that they might not have been strong enough to continue the advance. If so, the bears might have reentered the market and taken control, causing a bearish reversal in the market. These candlestick patterns that forewarn of a particular strength or weakness in a market often precede such major reversals. Smart traders would do well to be aware of them.

As the final bullish price rally after the last engulfing bullish line pattern reached a new market high of 25.00, three specific candles formed at this potential market top (Example 3). The first candle to form was a white inverted hammer that opened on the previous candle's close and traded higher during the remainder of the trading session, only to close near the opening price. The inverted hammer represented a shift in power from the bulls to the bears in the market. The bulls were initially able to rally the market upward, but in the end the bears drove it back down. The second candle to form was a long white upper shadow. An upper shadow is similar to a white inverted hammer, except that the former has a much larger tail, at least twice the length of its body with little or no lower shadow. The white upper shadow made a new high yet was unable to hold the high price and fell below the midpoint of the trading session before closing. These patterns are showing us that the bulls were still attempting to push the market price upward but the bears were capable of holding the closing price below the market high. We would expect a bearish pattern to form and a bearish reversal to be initiated soon. Sure enough, the third candle to form was a long black closing bozu line, a very strong, bearish candle that created an engulfing bearish line pattern when its body engulfed the white upper shadow's body. The engulfing bearish pattern was confirmed by Western technical indicators (RSI and stochastic oscillator) and issued a strong sell signal near the market top. It was also confirmed by the following candle, a short black line. Unlike their conservative counterparts, aggressive traders would probably have entered a short position without waiting for confirmation (a lower low than the previous session) of the engulfing bearish pattern. Conservative traders would wait for a confirmation pattern to form before entering a short position.

Four trading days after the market top formed and confirmed, a long white closing bozu line and a long black line formed almost side by side (Example 4). The long white closing bozu line created another last engulfing bullish pattern by engulfing the prior black candle's body and created a tweezers bottoms pattern by having the same low price. Both the last engulfing pattern and the tweezers bottoms pattern were indicating a support level that had formed at or near the low of the long white closing bozu candle. This newly formed support level would need to be broken before a bearish price move could commence. The long black line that formed after the long white bozu line did not indicate bullish support; in fact, it formed a dark cloud cover pattern that reconfirmed the bearish intent of the market and issued a second strong sell signal. The dark cloud cover pattern was itself confirmed by the following black candle that also created a bearish window below the prior support level. This was a clear signal that the market would continue its bearish price move after having broken support.

Example 5, which contains a black inverted hammer followed by two small doji lines, reflects the state of affairs seven months after the engulfing bearish pattern (Example 3) appeared at the market top and the dark cloud cover pattern (Example 4) reinitiated the bearish price move and broke critical support—the market price had fallen back to its original support level of 12.25. During the market selloff, minor support/resistance levels were identified by doji candles, tweezers tops and bottoms patterns, harami line patterns, and others.

It is important to identify as many confirmed support/resistance price levels as possible. This allows us to better determine the direction that the market is likely to take or where it is likely to stall after making a move. The black inverted hammer in Example 5 was created when a session opened near its low, traded higher than the open during the session, and then fell to close at a session low. The bears attempted to hold the market price near the support level, yet the bulls were able to rally the market during the trading session. In the end the bears were able to drive the session's close below its open, thereby creating a black body, yet the entry of the bulls was made obvious with the black inverted hammer. We would look for the market to begin a bullish reversal soon. Next, a small doji cross candle formed with its open and close equal to the black inverted hammer's open. This created a harami line pattern predicting a market reversal. A small white doji line formed after the previous doji cross, but with an even tighter trading range. A reversal pattern was created by two doji lines, indicating that the market would attempt to make a bullish move. A tweezers bottoms pattern forms from the two doji lines when they have the same session low price.

The last two candles to form at this potential market bottom provide concrete evidence of a bullish market reversal. Both the short black line and the short white line that formed fell below the predefined support level and had the same session low, thus creating another tweezers bottoms pattern. These two candles fell below critical support, indicating that the market could begin a bullish rally after retesting support; they also created an engulfing bullish line pattern and issued a buy signal after the appearance of three other bottom reversal patterns. Aggressive traders would probably enter position when the engulfing bullish pattern formed. Conservative traders would wait for the confirmation pattern that was to form with the next long white opening bozu line—a very strong bullish candle.

Kemper Corporation— Yearly Analysis for 1992

The next series of illustrations (Figures 13.4 through 13.20) is of a weekly Kemper Corporation candlestick chart. Figure 13.4 is the master chart for this series, and all the individual candlestick patterns highlighted in it will be viewed in detail throughout this analysis. We will begin by looking at September 20, 1991 (Figure 13.5). Kemper Corporation stock was trading at 32.00 per share when an engulfing bullish line pattern formed, issuing a buy signal. The following week, on September 27, 1991, a white doji line opened above the engulfing bullish with a higher high and a higher low. However, because the

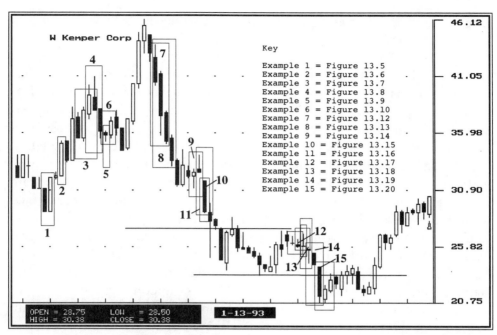

Figure 13.4 Weekly Candlestick Chart for Kemper Corporation

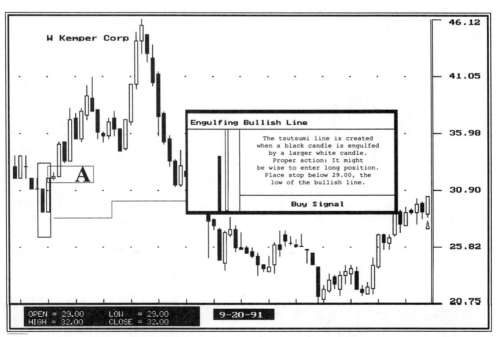

Figure 13.5 Engulfing Bullish Line (9/20/92)

range of the doji line was so small during that week, the bulls were unable to accelerate the initial drive of the engulfing bullish pattern.

The following weekly candle was an opening white bozu line, also known as a belt-hold line (Figure 13.6). A belt-hold line is considered bullish because it opens on the low of the day and trades higher for the duration of the session. As applied to our analysis, this meant that the open of Monday was never tested throughout the week and the closing price on Friday—almost 36.00 per share—was near the high of the entire weekly session. The engulfing bullish pattern that began this rally continued for two months until the market became overbought, as shown in Figure 13.7, which also depicts the bearish harami pattern found on November 15, 1991. This hinted at a potential top or retracement of this rally with a high of 41.00, after gaining 29 percent. Another black candle confirmed the bearish harami pattern (Figure 13.8), issuing a sell signal. On November 29, 1991, the market retraced 50 percent to a low of 35.25. Figure 13.9 shows a black hammer that formed at the bottom of this retracement. Hammers are typically found at market bottoms or interim support levels; they are significant because their lower shadows, in relation to their body size, are indicative of the low range created during that session. When they close near the high of the session, it shows that the bears were unable to maintain the selling pressure that created the low of the session. The black hammer in Figure 13.9 was confirmed on December 6, 1991, with a long white line. The body of the white line engulfed the body of the black hammer and issued a buy signal

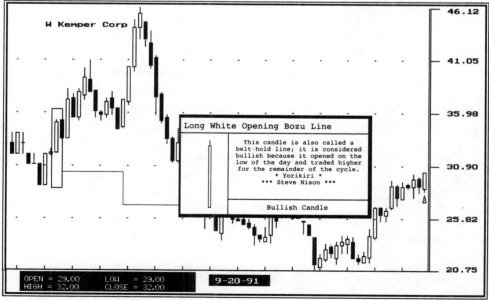

Figure 13.6 Long White Opening Bozu Line (9/20/21)

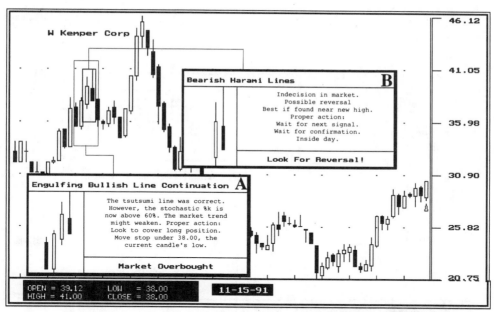

Figure 13.7 Bearish Harami Lines and Engulfing Bullish Line
Continuation (11/15/91)

Figure 13.8 Bearish Harami Line Confirmation (11/22/91)

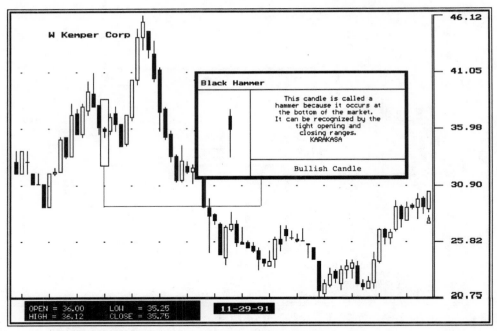

Figure 13.9 Black Hammer (11/29/91)

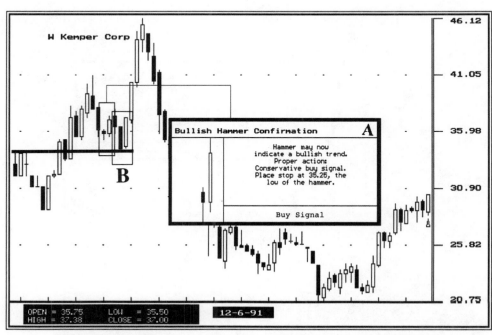

Figure 13.10 Bullish Hammer Confirmation (12/6/91)

by confirming it (Figure 13.10). The bullish rally that resumed with the black hammer was to be short lived. Two weeks after the black hammer formed, a dark cloud cover pattern signaled that the retracement, which had begun with the bearish harami pattern (Figure 13.7), had not yet completed. The market needed to complete its first corrective wave (refer to Chapter 4) before moving higher.

The market found support (Figure 13.10B), but no candlestick patterns were found that signaled the completion of this retracement. The candles in Figure 13.10A almost created an engulfing bullish pattern; however, because the open of the white candle was within the body of the previous black candle, this pattern was unable to form. Using trend lines, we are able to make market assumptions that allow us to use this incomplete pattern. The market then began the second leg of the rally initiated by the engulfing bullish pattern of September 2, 1991, over three months ago. The next four weekly sessions were composed of white candles. The first two were closing bozu candles, which are significant when found within a bullish trend. The third candle was a long white line that opened above the previous session and closed on a new high. The last candle completed a three-candle pattern known as an *advance block* (Figure 13.11B), a bearish variation of a bullish continuation pattern known as three white soldiers. An advance block differs from three white soldiers in that its last two candles point to a diminishing bullish drive. It is indicative of a decreasing buying force

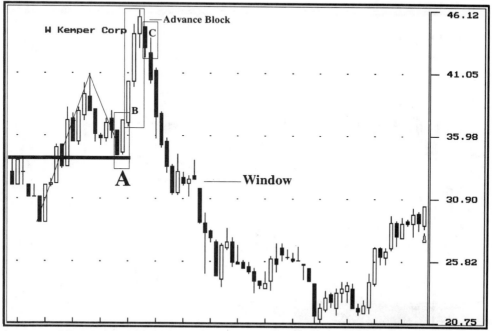

Figure 13.11 Advance Block and Window

or an augmentation in selling pressure. Confirmation is needed to complete the advance block's prediction of a reversal.

A turning point occurred in the market on February 7, 1992, when a black candle, which closed below the previous candle's low, confirmed the market reversal that followed (Figure 13.11C). The bullish drive, which began on September 2, 1991, had finally come to an end with a gain of 17.00, a 36 percent increase. On March 7, 1992, (Figure 13.12) a three-crows pattern was found. This is a bearish continuation pattern composed of three black lines, also known as three-winged crows. Figure 13.13, which covers the following week, contains four black candles, each with lower lows and lower highs. One would think that this pattern should be called "four crows." According to Seiki Shimizu in *The Japanese Chart of Charts,* the Japanese believe that the number three has "divine power that lives within it"; many candlestick patterns are based upon that number. However, the number four is considered bad luck. One Japanese word, *shi,* can mean "four" or "death." For this reason, we have named this pattern "three crows plus one," which, like the three-crows pattern, can be interpreted as a bearish continuation signal.

Within two months after the advance block pattern signaled a market top, the market price had fallen back to the previous support created in September (Figure 13.14). One might assume that the market had found a potential bottom at this support level. However, the following candles would have proved

Figure 13.12 Three Crows (2/14/92)

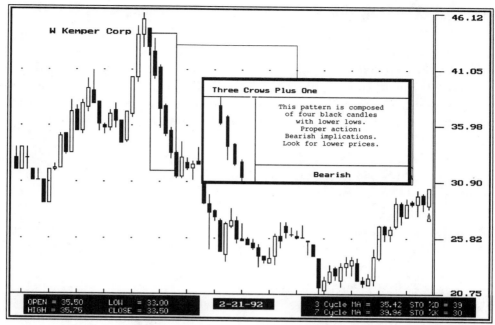

Figure 13.13 Three Crows Plus One (2/21/92)

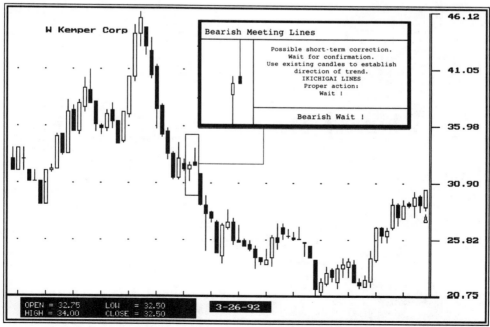

Figure 13.14 Bearish Meeting Lines (3/26/92)

this assumption wrong. Bearish meeting lines appeared after one month of consolidation; these signified a possible short-term correction. Confirmation was needed to act on this signal correctly. The following week, on April 3, 1992, an opening bozu gapped below the previous inverted hammer (Figure 13.15) and the support line to continue the bearish trend that began over two months ago. This gap is called a *black window* (Figure 13.16). The black window is significant when found during a bearish price decline and points to a further price deterioration.

The market continued its downtrend and moved to a new low below 26.00, where it began to consolidate (Figure 13.17). First a doji and a shooting star appeared. This combination of candles is interpreted as a possible market top if found during an uptrend. Because these candles formed within the upper range of the consolidation, they were certainly worth noting. These candles were followed by a gravestone doji line on August 7, 1992 (Figure 13.18). The gravestone doji and the previous inverted hammer had the same session low, creating a tweezers bottoms pattern (Figure 13.19). Tweezers bottoms, if found in a downtrend, signal a continuation of the bearish trend if that low is broken. On August 14, 1992, the weekly candle was a hangman. The combination of a hangman and doji (Figure 13.20) can signal a very volatile reversal; however, because the market was not overbought, we would not look for a significant selloff. The market did fall to a new low and found support at 20.75, where a

Figure 13.15 Long Black Opening Bozu Line (4/3/92)

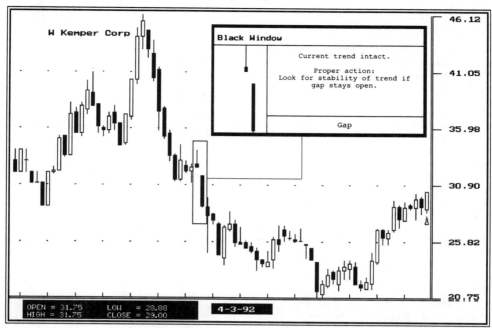

Figure 13.16 Black Window (4/3/92)

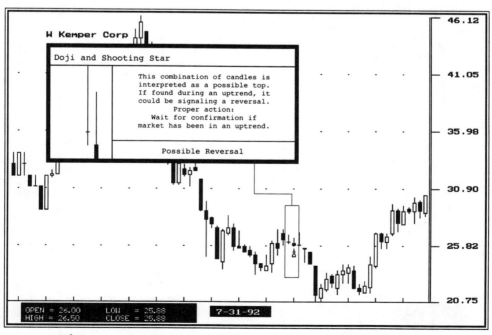

Figure 13.17 Doji and Shooting Star (7/31/92)

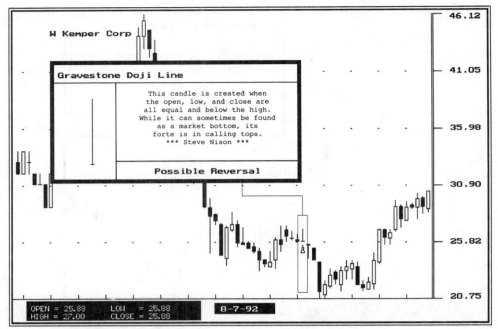

Figure 13.18 Gravestone Doji Line (8/7/92)

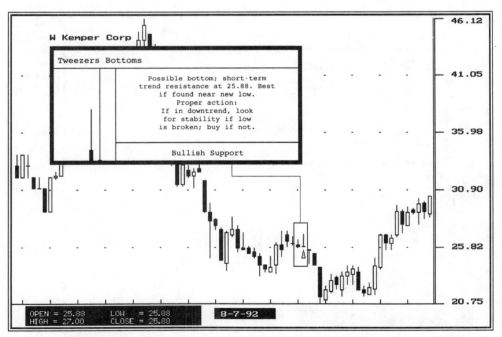

Figure 13.19 Tweezers Bottoms (8/7/92)

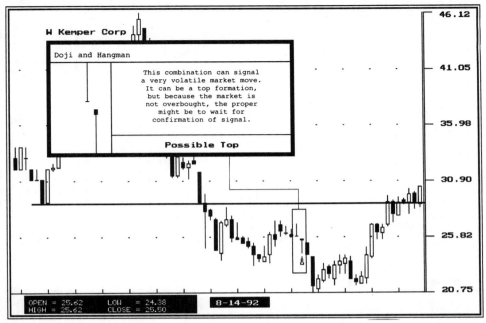

Figure 13.20 Doji and Hangman (8/14/92)

piercing line pattern had formed. This piercing line drove the market, over the remaining four months of 1992, to close just above the support area created by the engulfing bullish that formed on September 2, 1991 (Figure 13.4).

Omnicom Group—Bullish Trend Analysis

Figure 13.21 is a weekly candlestick chart for Omnicom Group from the first quarter of 1992 to the end of that year; as with Figure 13.4, it serves as the template for Figures 13.22–13.29. Initially, the market fell to 32.00 per share price and found support (A). The market began to consolidate between 32.00 and 36.00, a 4.00 range. After a short-lived engulfing bullish pattern at the first market bottom (Figure 13.21, Example A), the market moved up to test resistance at 36.00 (Figure 13.21, Example B) and then began to move back toward the support at 32.00. At this point a bearish harami line appeared that signaled a continuation of the current trend (Figure 13.22). On July 31, 1992, a double bottom was formed at 32.00 when a black hammer was created at a low matching the one found in Figure 13.21.

On August 7, 1992 (Figure 13.23), an opening bozu line (Example 1) formed and opened within the body of the black hammer (Example 2). This combination of candles, the hammer and belt-hold line, and their position sig-

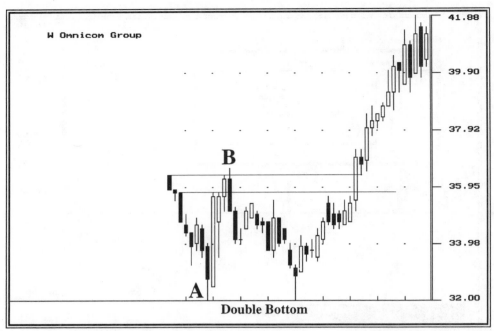

Figure 13.21 Weekly Candlestick Chart for Omnicon Group—
Double Bottom

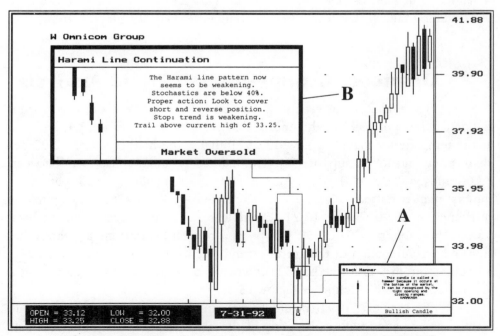

Figure 13.22 Black Hammer and Harami Line (7/31/92)

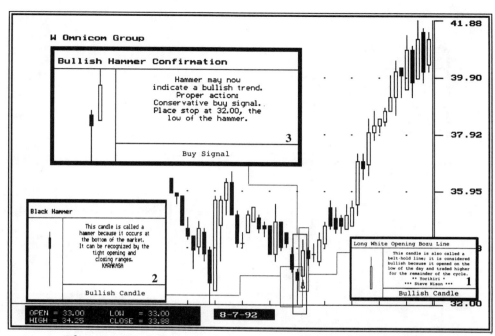

Figure 13.23 Long White Opening Line, Black Hammer, and Bullish Hammer Confirmation (8/7/92)

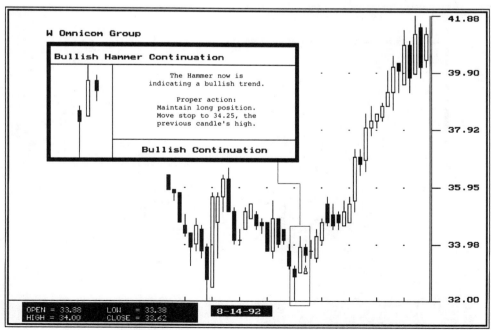

Figure 13.24 Bullish Hammer Continuation (8/14/92)

Figure 13.25　Bullish Hammer Continuation and Doji Line (8/21/92)

Figure 13.26　Tweezers Bottoms (8/28/92)

naled the beginning of a bullish rally (Example 3). Over the next two weeks, although the signal issued by the bullish hammer was still correct, consolidation dominated the trading range. Two small candles formed (Figures 13.24 and 13.25) within the range of the opening bozu candle. The latter of the two candles was a small doji line, which signified the inability of the bulls to push the market above resistance.

Figure 13.26 highlights trading activity on August 28, 1992. The doji candle found in the previous trading session has now been completely engulfed by a large white line. The low of the white line was equal to the low of the small black candle that engulfed the doji line from both directions. The matching lows created a tweezers bottoms pattern, which not only signaled a possible bottom but also defined market support/resistance at 33.38. A month after the double bottom was found, the market had moved up 3.62, a gain in price of more than 10 percent.

The market began to consolidate on September 11, 1992, when a bearish meeting line pattern formed (Figure 13.27) with a high of 35.00. This was just under the resistance found at 36.00. Neither the bulls nor the bears were able to dominate price activity. The market entered a congestion phase, trading narrowly within a tightly defined range inside the bearish meeting lines pattern; it was unable to break resistance. On September 25, 1992 (Figure 13.28), tweezers bottoms defined a new level of support. With a narrower price range than

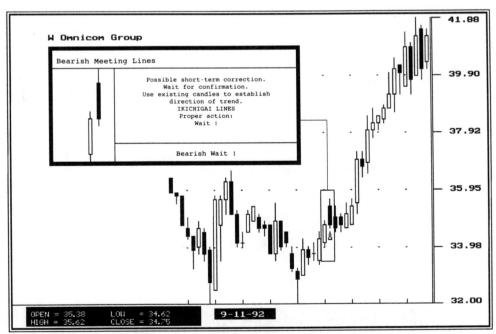

Figure 13.27 Bearish Meeting Lines (9/11/92)

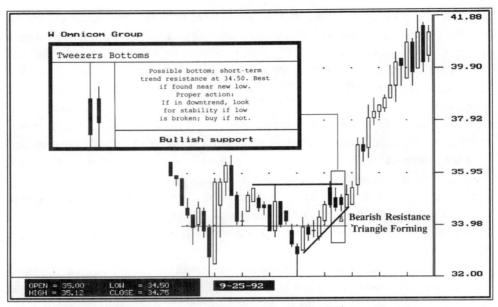

Figure 13.28 Tweezers Bottoms (9/25/92)

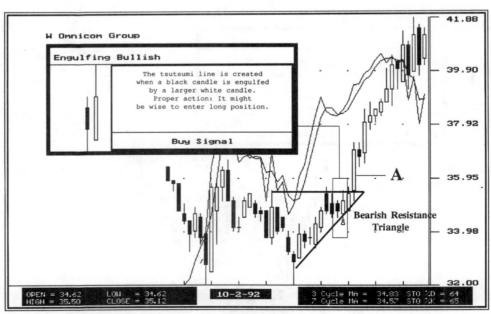

Figure 13.29 Engulfing Bullish (10/2/92)

the previous candle, it formed the beginnings of a *resistance triangle*. A resistance triangle is the end result of a consolidation and congestion period. The line of resistance is located at the top of the triangle.

Normally found during an uptrend, the price unsuccessfully tests that resistance level but maintains a series of higher lows, thereby decreasing the range. If the market breaks above the resistance line, a breakout to the upside usually follows. The resistance triangle found in this chart did not to come to an apex until October 2, 1992, at which time an engulfing bullish pattern issued a buy signal (Figure 13.29). This pattern came two weeks before the market traded above the resistance line, thus signaling a resumption of the bullish trend. The following candle opened with the body of the prior white candle and closed with a higher high.

On October 15, 1992, the resistance triangle was brushed aside as the market began to rally to close on a new high (Figure 13.29).

PART FOUR

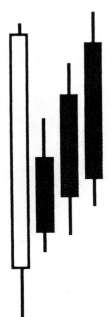

Computer
Analysis of
Candlesticks

FOURTEEN

Computers and Candlesticks

Computers have come a long way in the last ten years. New advances in electronic technology and software development have provided us with an almost unlimited array of computer components and software solutions. Most of these advances have been made in the actual components of the computer, not necessarily in the types of software that have been developed. With these innovations in hand, we, as consumers, can fully exploit the possibilities of the computer and its high-speed problem-solving capabilities. Keep in mind that any computer is only as functional as the application software used to accomplish a specific task. If you have the fastest computer that money can buy and no practical application software with which to do what you want, the computer is worthless.

When computers first hit the market, they were very limited and bulky. Most had little more than 16 kB (kilobytes) of memory—hardly enough to load the operating system. It was difficult for people to find a software program that would exactly meet their needs, so those with enough knowledge and patience usually decided to write their own programs. Upon completion, some of these new software products entered the retail market.

Over the course of the computer's evolution, analytical software applications designed to meet the needs of the trader were few and far between. A good number of traders began using spreadsheets to accumulate data and perform calculations of varying complexity to help them make wise market decisions. These traders had an advantage over other, less technically literate traders because they had learned how to take advantage of the capabilities of the computer. Even in its earliest forms, the computer could process anything much more quickly than any person.

Today, we can get a computer to do almost anything if we have the knowledge and know-how to make it work right. There are now lots of software products on the market for the professional or individual trader, and they offer what was once only available to the institution traders. It was apparent that computers could be used successfully for technical market analysis, yet the successful integration of Japanese candlesticks into an existing technical software product didn't happen for some time. The reason for this is quite simple: Japanese candlesticks require a completely different analytical technique than most Western technical indicators. To build our own software program that could accurately identify single and advanced candlestick patterns, we had to utilize some of the most complex and advanced software techniques ever created: pattern recognition, expert systems development, and neural networking. Each separate technique was utilized to its fullest potential and was integrated with the others so that each contributed equally to the final product.

Many very large software development firms and institutes had been refining these techniques for years, although they were not always willing to share their discoveries openly. Therefore, to accomplish our goal, we needed to use a very structured and defined approach as well as a time-proven method of testing the results—trial and error.

Integrating Japanese candlestick charts into a software program has proven to be very beneficial. The almost instant and accurate identification capabilities of the computer greatly reduce the amount of time necessary to learn and utilize this method of market analysis. The computer can easily identify any candlestick formation on a chart more accurately and much faster than any human, although the lack of subjectivity and intuition in such analyses can be a hindrance. Therefore, we needed to find a way to give the computer more analytical information; in other words, we needed to teach the computer to "think." During the remainder of this chapter, we will walk you down the path we took to this goal.

Computer-aided Pattern Recognition

Computerized pattern recognition might appear to be a simple concept, but there is more to it than you might imagine. For example, how would we build an interpretive process to accurately identify a single candle? Then, how would we build the interpretive process of identifying complex candlestick patterns? Finally, how would we put all of this information together to produce a finished result? This may seem like an overwhelming task to accomplish, but actually we all engage in similar problem-solving processes every day.

Ask yourself this question: How would you begin to identify something? Little kids often provide excellent examples of an identification process being refined on a day-by-day basis. One night, my neighbors' little boy pointed up into the sky and said, "Look at the big ball." I didn't see any balls in the sky; I saw a bunch of stars and a big full moon. We both saw the same thing, although my identification process was more advanced than his at the time. So I informed him that he was looking at the moon. His identification process was functioning, because he could have easily identified over 100 other things, yet without any further information or continued refining of that process, he was unable to accurately identify the moon as what it was.

A computerized pattern recognition system (PRS) uses all of the same principles and techniques that we use to acquire and maintain our knowledge. If we come across something that we have previously encountered, we rely on our knowledge base to identify and rationalize it. If we come across something we have not seen or encountered before, we begin a process of defining the object according to shape, size, and material content and then propose hypothetical assumptions as to its purpose or use (outcome) based on our limited exposure to it. At this point, we begin testing our hypothetical solution to verify that this object is indeed what we assumed it to be. If we are wrong, we must start the whole process over again, but this time we can use the additional information we have acquired through our testing process to reform our hypothetical assumptions until we have identified the object to the best of our abilities. If we have not refined our identification process enough to identify the object after an initial examination, we will continue this defining/testing process until we have made a logically defensible assumption as to its purpose and use. At this point we may look for additional evidence supporting or dismissing our conclusion.

How to Relate Japanese Candlestick Charts to a Computer

A single candle is represented as a simple character, either an empty, full, or doji candle. There are many variations of the basic candles, so our pattern recognition system must be able to identify each of the different types of candles accurately. The candlestick patterns can consist of as many as 30 to 60 single candles, posing an even greater problem for our pattern recognition system. Not only must we accurately identify each of the single candles, but we must also use the single candle identifications in our candlestick pattern identification process.

To overcome these problems of attempting to create a PRS to isolate specific candlestick patterns, we must start at the root of our attempted purpose and continue to expand upon it—namely, the data variables that are required to classify each single candle. Determining which variables are necessary for use when identifying single candles depends upon your level of understanding of the classic definition of each specific candlestick formation and why they form in specific shapes.

To begin accomplishing the task of building the intelligent pattern recognition system, we must first assign classes, or groups, of patterns. This process is similar to building a knowledge base from which to work, as we have all done from the day we were born. We will use this system of classification to recognize single candles and candlestick patterns and link them together correctly. Next, we need to assign the set of data variables used to isolate, or find, the patterns. Japanese candlesticks are composed of four basic data variables: **OPEN, HIGH, LOW,** and **CLOSE.** These define the shape and size of each individual candle. We will need to use other sets of data variables to isolate different types of candlestick patterns after first having identified the single candles. Remember, candlestick patterns consist of single candles in a specific relation to one another. Only after we have accurately identified a series of single candles can we begin to search for patterns.

The knowledge base is critical to making the PRS properly interpret each individual pattern. By incorrectly assigning patterns or groups thereof, the PRS can confuse valid patterns with invalid patterns. Also, incomplete assignment of a pattern will cause mixed or inconsistent recognition of certain related patterns. Imagine that we've incorrectly taught a child how to identify colors, shapes, and objects. Unless that child has the opportunity to interact with other children who have been taught correctly, that child will continue to misinterpret almost everything she came in contact with. She will never know that what she has been taught is wrong and will never be able to correct her identification process. The knowledge base must be structured, complete, and accurate for the finished outcome to be correct. Structure is the foundation of our knowledge base, as even the most complex pattern recognition system, the human brain, incorporates structured association and disassociation to properly identify things.

When defining a computerized candlestick pattern recognition system, the structure must be defined so that we can associate common candlestick formations with other similar candlestick formations and meanings; then, by means of disassociation, we can identify the exact formation of the candle in question.

Practical Example

Assume that we have asked the PRS to locate a long white line. If we assigned its formula (classification) and (**CLOSE > OPEN**), the PRS will associate any candlestick cycle that has a **CLOSE** greater than its **OPEN.** This classification essentially includes any white candle, not just a long white line. The PRS needs to compare the range of this particular white candle against the average range of all the white candles to verify that it has a greater than average range. We add two more data variables, and our formula now looks like this: (**CLOSE > OPEN & CANDLE_RANGE > AVERAGE_CANDLE_RANGE**) Are we done with this pattern assignment? What might the PRS call the examples given in Figure 14.1, given the fact that their range exceeds the **AVERAGE_CANDLE_RANGE?**

Our PRS would interpret all of these candles as long white lines because each of them meets the parameters of our assigned pattern, although only one is a long white line. Our PRS doesn't know that a long white line needs to have a higher degree of classification within our assignment. At this point, we must begin to organize the associations of pattern assignments logically so that the PRS can begin to relate what it knows about the patterns it finds. This is the engine. Its responsibility is to classify all data variables and to provide a basic interpretive structure. The way an expert system is programmed to learn is similar to how we learn the alphabet or how to count to 100. The engine normally consists of all necessary structural formats and data groups assigned to these formats. We've got to analyze the structure of each candle and its relation to the other candles so that the engine can relate this information back to our knowledge base. We'll define the three basic candle types now for our pattern recognition system:

1. **OPEN = CLOSE.** Doji
2. **OPEN > CLOSE.** Black or full
3. **OPEN < CLOSE.** White or empty

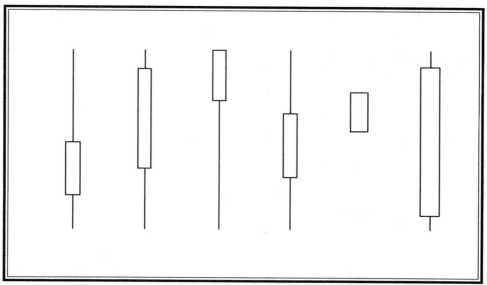

Figure 14.1 White Candles

Based on these three groups of data classifications, we need to define all that we know about each. But to provide a subjective viewpoint for the PRS, we should always consider the relation of the candles to each other. Doji candles are classically defined as OPEN = CLOSE. But doji candles don't always have an equal open and close price. What do we do with these doji? We must teach the PRS about them by assigning a different pattern for each based upon the relationship of the candle body size and placement to the candle shadow.

1. OPEN = CLOSE.
   Doji line
   A. (CANDLE_RANGE > AVERAGE_CANDLE_RANGE)
      Long-legged doji line
   B. (CANDLE_RANGE < AVERAGE_CANDLE_RANGE) Small doji line
   C. (CLOSE = OPEN = LOW) Gravestone doji line
   D. (CLOSE = OPEN = HIGH) Dragonfly doji line
2. OPEN > CLOSE. Black or full
   A. (CANDLE_RANGE > AVERAGE_CANDLE_RANGE &
      CANDLE_BODY_SIZE > AVERAGE_CANDLE_BODY_SIZE)
      Long black line
   B. (CANDLE_RANGE < AVERAGE_CANDLE_RANGE &
      CANDLE_BODY_SIZE < AVERAGE_CANDLE_BODY_SIZE)
      Short black line
   C. (CANDLE_RANGE > AVERAGE_CANDLE_RANGE &
      CANDLE_BODY_SIZE <
      (AVERAGE_CANDLE_BODY_SIZE*BLACK_DOJI_LINE_%))
      Black stars
3. OPEN < CLOSE. White or empty
   A. (CANDLE_RANGE > AVERAGE_CANDLE_RANGE &
      CANDLE_BODY_SIZE >
      AVERAGE_CANDLE_BODY_SIZE)Long white line
   B. (CANDLE_RANGE < AVERAGE_CANDLE_RANGE &
      CANDLE_BODY_SIZE < AVERAGE_CANDLE_BODY_SIZE)
      Short white line
   C. (CANDLE_RANGE > AVERAGE_CANDLE_RANGE &
      CANDLE_BODY_SIZE <
      (AVERAGE_CANDLE_BODY_SIZE*WHITE_DOJI_LINE_%))
      White stars

Our engine will locate patterns based upon their groups and classifications and should return a reference of knowledge to a higher-level PRS. This means that the knowledge gained will be used and then added to the knowledge base of the application. Candlesticks require both levels of PRS, one for single candle identification and a much larger one for candlestick patterns, because the latter are contingent upon the relationship of the individual candles' placement and shape.

At this point, we've begun to create a basic level of knowledge for our PRS. It knows that there are three groups of data classifications and as many assigned single candlestick patterns as we care to define. At this beginning stage, our PRS will return what it knows about a single candle if it finds a pattern matching that candle. Of course, we want our single candlestick interpreter (engine) to be able to identify all of the known single candlestick patters, so we must painstakingly add and test each new pattern classification. Remember that each new candlestick pattern classification must be precise and accurate; otherwise, the interpreter may incorrectly identify the single candles.

We've now developed an interpreter for the basic candle formations, but we still need to consider how single candles relate to each other to form the candlestick patterns. Due to the complexity of the patterns, our high-level PRS needs to be extremely well organized, requires many extra data variables, and must be completely accurate. Many of the fundamentals we learned during the development of the single candle interpreter can be applied with greater structure to the candlestick pattern interpreter.

When applying these techniques, we need to consider the possibility of candlestick pattern variations. Candlestick patterns can often contain a grouping of single candles that deviate from the accepted norm and still retain their classification. This problem is easily overcome by assigning similar candle types a common identification variable or by using Boolean operators (**and, or, nor**) to compensate for minor variations within complex candlestick patterns. This technique is called *computerized pattern recognition subjectivity*. A high-level PRS consists of tightly defined pattern assignments and, again, a reference of knowledge, which uses a structure similar to its companion—the knowledge base. The high-level PRS consists of different groups of patterns and associations to other patterns. We use the data variables and references of knowledge created by the engine to assign each pattern. By combining the information generated from both the engine and the PRS, we can derive a series of conclusions as to which candlestick patterns will appear and the probability of these patterns' accuracy in predicting a future market move.

To begin developing our high-level pattern recognition system, we must also have a complete understanding of the candlestick patterns we wish to identify. For example, let's use the engulfing bullish line candlestick formation and start by defining just one of the many possible candle combinations that could result in this pattern. We'll start by defining a long white line that is engulfing a long black line. The engulfing bullish pattern is classically viewed as a potentially strong buy signal, although there are times when we should consider this pattern a potential top that is showing a weakening bullish trend not initializing the bullish move. For this matter we need to consider filtering the candlestick pattern, which is discussed in Chapter 15. Right now our purpose is to accurately identify the candlestick pattern.

ENGULFING BULLISH LINE CANDLE FORMATION

Formula (Classification)

(CANDLE[-1] = LONG BLACK LINE & CANDLE[0] =
LONG WHITE LINE)

This pattern formula could mean that we are seeing an engulfing bullish line, but it is still incomplete. It does not contain any definition of the relationship between the two candles making up the pattern formation. We have only defined the number of candles, the types of candles, and the order in which they appear. We would need to complete this pattern classification with

... &
CANDLE[0].CLOSE > = CANDLE[-1].OPEN
&
CANDLE[0].OPEN < =CANDLE[-1].CLOSE

We've now assigned a pattern classification that will isolate an engulfing bullish line. This classification will need the following parameters to identify an engulfing bullish pattern: The body of the first candle (CANDLE[0]) must be white and must engulf the prior black candle's body (CANDLE[-1]). Creating the pattern assignment for its opposite, an engulfing bearish pattern, would not be too difficult. Using the data variables and candle assignments generated from our engine, we can easily isolate any candle, regardless of its complexity.

The simplicity of defining pattern assignments is relative to the complexity of the engine. The more associations and assignments we add to our PRS, the more information our PRS is capable of refining and returning as finished outcome (output). We, as market technicians, may rely on as many as ten or more separate technical indicators to accurately predict a market move. A pattern recognition system that identified only certain specific patterns would be rather limited in its capabilities.

Candlestick patterns frequently consist of three or more individual candles, each in specific relation to one another. Sometimes a pattern is simply based on the shapes and locations, not just the color and shape, of the constituent candles. We need to teach our pattern recognition system to associate patterns based on a large number of qualifying factors. Thus, we are left the time-consuming task of teaching our pattern recognition system about each candle and pattern that we want it to remember and continually refining this knowledge base until we have made it as functional and accurate as possible.

FIFTEEN

Computer Filtering of Candlestick Patterns

Candlestick methods, by themselves, are a valuable trading tool. But candlestick techniques become even more powerfully significant if they confirm a Western technical signal.[1]

Japanese candlestick charts, unlike most Western technical indicators, can predict any number of potential market moves by depicting the "personality traits" of the individual candlestick patterns found within the market. Although the engulfing bullish pattern is classically interpreted as a buy signal and the engulfing bearish pattern is viewed as a sell signal, this is true only if the candlestick pattern in question is found at the proper time in the market's current move and if the pattern is confirmed by the Western technical indicators that we choose to use.

Computers are completely unaware of any market rally, top, or bottom unless we define these tendencies so that the computer can test for them. Failing to incorporate this filtering capacity would result in an accurate candlestick pattern interpreter that provided extremely inaccurate predictions for potential future market moves. Thus, we would still not have attained our goal of computerized trading with Japanese candlesticks. Filtering provides the ability to more accurately predict the possibilities of any candlestick pattern or single candlestick that we are analyzing. To properly filter a candlestick or candlestick pattern we need to use logical variables to control what the PRS is able to identify. These are similar to flags or signs that guide the PRS in making the right choice. Using logic variables and organizing your patterns from most critical to least critical ensures proper recognition of the candlestick patterns. Correct use of logic variables is extremely critical to the operation of the PRS. If the PRS is guided illogically, you will obviously end up with false information.

The easiest way to check for any illogical conditions is to test and isolate the current market conditions and then compare them against the supposedly corresponding candlestick pattern and its prediction. By weighing the current market conditions and the candlestick pattern, we can predict the probability of that pattern's accuracy in predicting a market move.

Any custom-developed indicator or oscillator can be filtered into Japanese candlesticks, as long as the indicator or oscillator is a true technical indicator or can be applied to any market and still provide a universally true outcome. The common Western technical indicators we chose to use, such as stochastic oscillators, moving averages, William's percent retracement, and others, can all be exquisitely filtered into Japanese candlesticks. Actually, there are some candlestick symbols for a few market tendencies that directly relate to certain Western technical indicators, mostly the moving averages; however, we'll need to learn how to integrate specialized Western technical indicators into our pre-existing pattern recognition system and define new data variables and classifications to test for the new conditions created by their introduction. Obviously, the types of conditions will vary between markets, so we need to continually refine and build the classifications within our engine to accurately depict current and past market events. We must also realize that even the smallest change to our Western technical oscillators may drastically alter our finished outcome when filtering.

Filtering these Western technical indicators requires some technical expertise and some refining of the actual filter classifications (formulas). Because there are really no set values or conditions under which these indicators will all issue a similar signal, we must develop a variety of data variables and logic control flags to properly ascertain the current market condition derived from the Western technical indicators. We also need to compare the current market conditions against past conditions to help identify the direction, strength, and momentum of trends.

When considering which technical indicators to use as filters, we need to have a complete understanding of each indicator and its returned values in comparison to the actual price movement seen on the candlestick chart. The Western technical indicator should be able to show the defined strengths and weaknesses of the market we are analyzing in relation to past price movements. Some Western technical indicators can be integrated with Japanese candlesticks easily, whereas others may require some extra time to identify exactly what they are saying to us and how they should be integrated with candlesticks and the other Western technical indicators.

Once we understand each of the individual Western technical indicators we intend to use, using them together will provide a clearer picture of current market conditions. By filtering the individual candlestick patterns through a combination of Western technical indicators, we can begin to see what we might expect from any particular market in the future. We are going to concentrate on the following Western technical indicators as filters for Japanese candlestick charts: the stochastic oscillator, moving averages, William's percent retracement, the relative strength index, the relative momentum index, and trading bands.

We've chosen three different markets with completely different trends and completely different current and past market technical conditions. We will explain in detail how each of these Western technical indicators should be integrated into Japanese candlestick charts as filters. The purpose of this section is to illustrate how to properly identify which of the Western technical indicators provide the best evidence of any upcoming market move and to learn how to temporarily omit some that may cause confusion.

We begin by introducing the example markets and outlining their defining characteristics.

December Wheat—1992

October 7, 1992–November 20, 1992 (See Figure 15.1.)

The wheat market had entered what appeared to be a long-term bullish trend that pushed the price from 325.25 to 380.75. This long uptrend actually consisted of a series of short bullish rallies followed by short-term corrective periods. These longer-term trends could be easily identified by viewing a weekly candlestick chart for the same market. From the standpoint of a daily candlestick

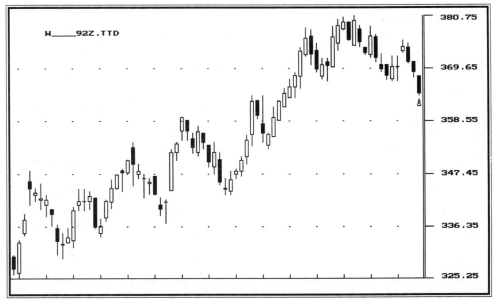

Figure 15.1 Candlestick Chart for December Wheat—1992

chart, this chart could have initiated some very strong short-term moves with a longer-term bullish tendency. It is not uncommon for a market to step up or down in a defined trend until it reaches a point of exhaustion or diminished trend strength. We notice that after a top had formed, the market began to fall slightly, indicating that the bullish rally had lost its drive.

December Sweet Crude Light —1992

October 7, 1992–November 20, 1992 (See Figure 15.2.)

The initial bullish uptrend of this market continued to oscillate between congestion and consolidation before attempting to make a move upward. Again, this should be viewed as a slow upward-stepping market, with the defined steps formed by the consolidation periods. The final attempt to drive this market up to its eventual top was initiated by the candlestick patterns appearing near a defined support level. The top was short lived, however, and the market dropped, retaking all of the upward price movement and more to stop at a support level of 20.00 per gallon. This market could have provided some short-term profit taking, although we would generally attempt to identify the defined trend moves because they are more likely to produce a truly profitable trade. In that case, we could have initially identified a moderately strong bullish trend, followed by congestion, a top, and then a rather strong bearish trend down to a previous support level.

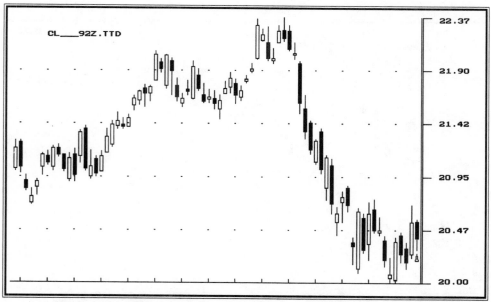

Figure 15.2 Candlestick Chart for December Sweet Crude Light—1992

December U.S. Bonds—1992

(See Figure 15.3.)

The U.S. bond market appeared to be trending rather quickly and with very large dominating black or white candles. The initial trending activity of this market, both bullish and bearish, offered excellent opportunity for profitable trading. Notice that the two distinct tops had very similar doji candles within them; these doji were indicating that the market was consolidating after finding resistance and were a bearish reversal sign, although a defined support level had formed at 103.75. Both of the previous attempts to move the market price upward were initiated after finding this specific support price level. The second top price was lower than the first; this time, the bears took control of the market and drove the price below the initial support level of 103.75 to finally settle near 102.25 before actually bottoming. The inevitable bullish reversal happened after the market found support at 101.41, right at a bottom. The bullish rally after the bottom started with some very positive upward price movement before consolidating at the resistance price level of 103.75 again, at which point it corrected slightly. A second bullish rally broke through the resistance level and drove the market price upward to near 105.00, where the market met its earlier resistance price level, which caused the strong selloff, and began to consolidate again. Overall this market is an excellent example of one that trends dramatically and consolidates near defined support and resistance price levels.

Figure 15.3 Candlestick Chart for December U.S. Bonds—1992

Filtering Candlesticks with the Stochastic Oscillator

sto·chas·tic (sto kas'tik) *adj.* 2. *Math.* designating a process having an infinite progression of jointly distributed random variables.[2]
os·cil·ate *v.* FLUCTUATE 3. to vary above and below a mean value[3]

The stochastic oscillator is an indicator that graphically compares the current market price with the market's trading range over a defined period of time. By graphing its results, we can ascertain where the current price is in relationship to the highs and the lows in the trading range. The stochastic oscillator is used to detect periods when the market is either overbought or oversold by comparing the current close against an average of the highest highs and the lowest lows during a given time period. A market is said to be overbought if the closing price is near the highs of that time period and oversold if the closing price is near the lows of that time period. There are two classifications of this oscillator: slow and fast. However, for the purposes of this book, we will use only the slow variation.

The value derived from the stochastic oscillator will always be from 0% to 100%. A value of 0% means that the current closing price was the lowest price found during that time period. A value of 100% means that the current closing price was the highest price found during that time period. This indicator can be used as both an intermediate and short-term trading oscillator by altering the variables that determine this formula, of which there are four. First is the % K period, which is the number of time intervals used in the calculation. Second is the % K slowing period; this value internally smoothes the % K for a slow stochastic wave. The third value we need to set is the % D period, an average of the % K. Finally we need to determine the type of average to use: simple, weighted, or exponential.

To calculate a slow stochastic % K value, we must first calculate a fast % K value:

$$\% \text{ K FAST} = \frac{(\text{current close}) - (\text{lowest low in \% K periods})}{(\text{highest high in \% K periods}) - (\text{lowest low in \% K period})}$$

$$\% \text{ K SLOW} = \frac{(\% \text{ K FAST 1} + \% \text{ K FAST 2} + \% \text{ K FAST 3})}{3}$$

The % D is calculated as a moving average of the % K. To calculate the % D by a smoothing factor of 3:

$$\% \text{ D} = \frac{(\% \text{ K SLOW 1} + \% \text{ K SLOW 2} + \% \text{ K SLOW 3})}{3}$$

Interpretation of % K and % D Values

When the stochastic oscillator rises above 80%, it is said that the market has entered an overbought condition, and the market now has more sellers than buyers. When the stochastic oscillator falls below 20%, it is said that the market has entered an oversold condition, and the market now has more buyers than sellers. When the % K line rises above the % D line, a bullish reversal is signaled. When the % K line falls below the % D line, a bearish reversal is signaled. When a market is in a defined uptrend, the % K line will lead (be above) the % D line. When a market is in a defined downtrend, the % K line will lead (be below) the % D line. As long as the % K and % D are diverging (separating), the defined trend is gaining intensity. When the two lines begin to converge, the trend is weakening and losing intensity.

December Wheat — 1992

October 7, 1992–November 20, 1992 (See Figure 15.4.)

The stochastic oscillator accurately depicted the short-term reversals of this defined bullish uptrend. The actual bullish trend consisted of an upward stepping motion that the short-term stochastic oscillator would mistakenly show as having more potential for a bearish reversal, rather than showing the continued attempt by the bulls to push the market up. If we had decided to trade the short-

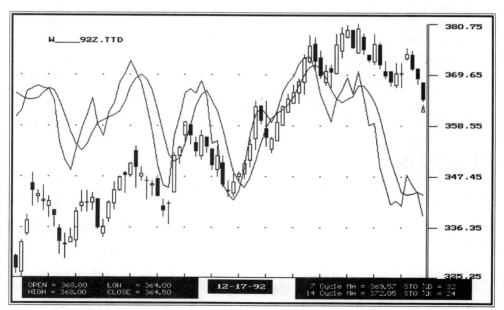

Figure 15.4 Candlestick Chart with Stochastic Oscillators for December Wheat—1992

term reversals instead of the long-term bullish trend, we would rely more intensely on the stochastic oscillator. If we had decided to trade the long-term market trend, we would rely on the stochastic oscillator for signs of bearish intervention. Notice how the stochastic oscillator stayed above the 20% area, indicating that the bears never really gained control of the long-term direction of the market. The stochastic oscillator converged and diverged accurately during the short-term correction periods but always stayed out of the oversold extreme below 20%, the area indicting the continued attempt by the bulls to drive the price higher. The candlestick signals that appeared during this time frame accurately indicated each short-term reversal.

December Sweet Crude Light —1992

August 7, 1992–November 20, 1992 (See Figure 15.5.)

The crude light market had just started a bullish move on August 12, 1992, which was initiated by a three-river morning star pattern. The stochastic oscillator properly indicated the influx of buyers into the market when the % K line crossed above the % D line on August 13, 1992. We saw continued divergence until an incomplete dark cloud cover formed and confirmed, followed by a piercing line; then a second dark cloud pattern formed, followed by an engulfing bearish line from August 18 to August 25, 1992, which intervened and caused

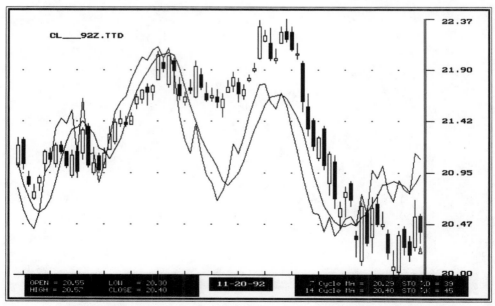

Figure 15.5 Candlestick Chart with Stochastic Oscillators for December Sweet Crude Light—1992

the stochastic oscillator to begin to converge (cross). Next, a thrusting pattern formed on August 26, 1992, paired with its close associate the piercing line on August 20, 1992, which showed renewed interest on the part of the bulls and heralded a second attempt to push the price upward.

At this point, the stochastic oscillator had begun to diverge with a bullish signature. This attempt by the bulls succeeded to push the market price to new highs near 22.00. The stochastic oscillator had moved from near 50% to above 80%, which indicated that the market was overbought and might reverse. The market found a new resistance level when a bearish harami line pattern followed by a last engulfing bullish pattern forewarned of a market top. A second bearish harami line pattern caused the stochastic oscillator to converge with a bearish signature. Although we saw a minor price drop, the stochastic oscillator fell to near 40%. Again, after rebounding off a support level, a piercing line pattern formed on September 30, 1992, which confirmed and issued a buy signal, causing the stochastic oscillator to converge with a bullish signature that indicated a potential for continued bullish price movement. The stochastic oscillator continued to diverge from the piercing line formation until October 8 and October 9, 1992, when two bearish white two-gaps patterns formed one after another, issuing a potential top signal. At this point, the stochastic oscillator had begun to converge, showing the desire of the bears to take control of this market.

On October 14, 1992, a rare on neck piercing line pattern formed, underscoring the intent of the bears to take control of this market, and on October 16, 1992, a dark cloud cover pattern initiated a sell signal at the top of this market, which confirmed and continued with downward price movement. The stochastic oscillator converged with a bearish signature on October 20, 1992, and continued to diverge downward until a prior support level was reached, at which point the market started to consolidate.

December U.S. Bonds — 1992

August 26, 1992–December 17, 1992 (See Figure 15.6.)

The U.S. bond market had just entered a defined bullish trend; the stochastic oscillator started at near 30% after converging and diverging with a bullish signature. As the market began to move upward from the first engulfing bullish line, the stochastic oscillator continued to diverge, showing that the bulls had gained control of the market. The stochastic oscillator moved to almost 80% when the first top formed. As the market began to consolidate after the top, the stochastic oscillator again began to converge, showing us that the bulls were losing their control of the market price direction.

After the stochastic oscillator converged when the long-legged doji candle formed, the % K and % D lines continued diverging downward, indicating that the bears had now entered the market and would drive the market price

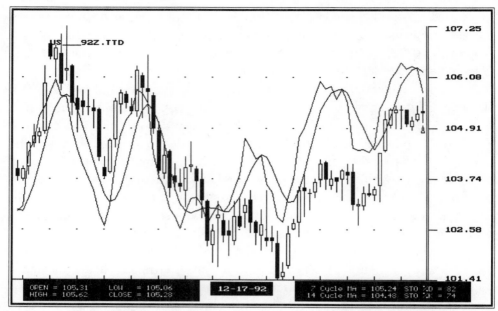

Figure 15.6 Candlestick Chart with Stochastic Oscillators for December U.S. Bonds—1992

down. We would want to look for the % K line to cross and fall below the % D line of above or near 80%, indicating bearish reversal. As the price came down, so did the stochastic oscillator. As the stochastic oscillator neared 20%, a bullish reversal from the defined support level of 103.75 commenced. Remember that when the stochastic oscillator is at or below 20%, the market is oversold, and the bulls should reenter the market to take control. When the stochastic oscillator is at or above 80%, the market is overbought, and the bears should reenter the market to take control. We see the stochastic oscillator converge and diverge with a bullish signature as this bullish reversal happens.

The stochastic oscillator stayed at a value of less than 40% while the remainder of the bearish price move continued. Once the stochastic oscillator reaches a minimum or maximum setting, if the trend continues, it will try to stay near that minimum or maximum instead of reversing with the market price. As new support was found near 102.25, the stochastic oscillator moved to near 50%, indicating that the bulls were entering the market and trying to hold the price level. Again, the bears intervened and drove the market price lower, causing the stochastic oscillator to converge near 50% and drop to nearly 30% as a new bottom formed.

A bullish harami line formed after the bottom and confirmed, causing the stochastic oscillator to once again cross below 30%. Notice that each of the bullish support price levels and bullish reversals occurred when the stochastic oscillator was between 30% and 20%. After the bottom formation, the stochastic oscillator jumped quickly to nearly 80% as the market price went up. Once the stochastic oscillator approached 80%, the market began to consolidate, and the stochastic oscillator fell to 50% —even though the market price only fell 12%. The 50% area of the stochastic oscillator is considered to be uncertain; reversals are likely to happen there. The stochastic oscillator crossed with a bullish signature near 50%, continued to diverge greatly, and reached a new high —85%.

Filtering Candlesticks with Moving Averages

move v. 1a: To go continuously from one point to another[4]
moving adj. 1: marked by or capable of movement[5]
average adj. 5: a ratio of successful tries to total tries . . . the quotient obtained by dividing the sum total by the number of figures.[6]

Moving averages form the foundation for many types of Western market analysis. They allow us to compare the current price against past price movement. A simple moving average of the close is obtained by adding the closing price over a specific time period and then dividing this total by the number of time periods.

This is the formula to calculate a simple three-day moving average value:

$$\text{3-day moving average} = \frac{[\text{price \#1 (high, low, or close)} + \text{price \#2 (high, low or close)} + \text{price \#3 (high, low or close)}]}{3}$$

For example, if the prices for the last three days were 27.00, 45.00, and 42.00, the calculation would look like this: (27.00 + 45.00 + 42.00) / 3 = 38.00. The value of 38.00 would now be plotted for the three-day moving average. To create a moving average, repeat the calculation and plot the new value. This step is then repeated to create a secondary moving average with a slower time period than the last. Using multiple length indicators will detect changes in the momentum of the market.

Born in Japan in 1915, Seiki Shimizu is best known for his trading expertise and knowledge of Japanese technical ayalysis. Awarded the Blue Ribbon Medal by Emperor Hirohito of Japan for his contributions to the commodities markets in Japan, Shimizu is best known for his work, *The Japanese Chart of Charts,* in which he combines both eastern and western trading methodologies. As he notes, ''The average movement line has been in Japan for centuries and if I was to admit to this method originating in the United States, I would be able to say that it has to be one of the most outstanding foreign charts. The change of price direction at crossover points illustrates the value of this chart and its superiority.''[7]

Interpretation of Moving Averages

Comparing a single moving average to the current close

When the closing price rises above (becomes higher in value than) the moving average, it is said that the marker has entered a *bullish trend*. When the closing price falls below (becomes lower in value than) the moving average, it is said that the market has entered a *bearish trend*.

Comparing multiple moving averages

When the short-term moving average rises above the long-term moving average, a bullish reversal is signaled. When the long-term moving average falls below the short-term moving average, a bearish reversal is signaled. When a market is in a defined uptrend, the short-term moving average will lead (be above) the long-term moving average. When a market is in a defined downtrend, the short-term moving average will lead (be below) the long-term moving average. As long as the short-term and long-term moving averages are diverging (separating), the defined trend is gaining intensity. When the two lines begin to converge, the trend is weakening. The moving average indicators will converge and diverge just like the % K and % D lines of the stochastic oscillator, showing the strength or weakness of a trend.

Again, we look for the short-term moving average line to cross above the long-term moving average line, thus indicating that the bulls have gained control of the markets' direction. As the short-term moving average line continues to diverge (separate) from the long-term moving average line, we are seeing a strengthening of the defined market trend. When the short-term moving average line begins to converge with the long-term moving average line, we see that the market is stalling and will likely reverse from its current direction. After the convergence of the short-term and long-term moving average lines, if the reversing party has enough strength to continue the reversal, the short-term moving average line will continue to diverge from the long-term moving average line. If not, the initial controlling party will regain power, and we may see a second convergence in the direction of the initial trend.

December Wheat — 1992

October 7, 1992–November 20, 1992 (See Figure 15.7.)

The continual bullish trend of this market is evident within the moving average lines. Notice that the slower moving average line continually moved upward with the price activity. The only point on this chart where the slower

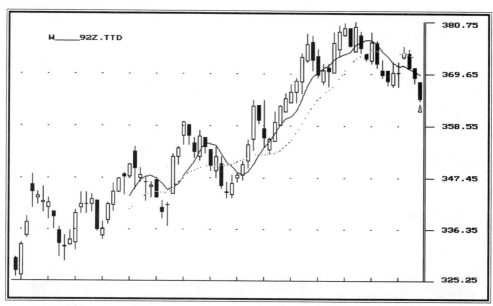

Figure 15.7 Candlestick Chart with Moving Averages for December Wheat—1992

moving average line changed direction was after the actual market top. Even though the market did have some bearish price corrections, the slower moving average line depicted the long-term direction.

The faster moving average line is more sensitive to the market's short-term direction. All of the short-term trend reversals were depicted by the faster moving average line. Every time the market advanced, the faster moving average line moved above the slower line. When the market fell, the faster line fell with it.

The short-term reversals found within the long-term bullish trend are common among other markets. The moving average line helps determine the long- and short-term directional changes in the market price. In this instance, the long-term bullish trend of the wheat market was clearly defined by the slower moving average line. If we had entered a long-term trade, we would have relied on the slower moving average line to indicate the actual market trend. Short-term traders would watch for the faster line to reverse direction and cross the slower line each time the market reversed.

December Sweet Crude Light —1992

August 7, 1992–November 20, 1992 (See Figure 15.8.)

Initially, the moving average lines on this chart were diverging in a bearish manner, signaling a recent bearish reversal, although the three-river

Figure 15.8 Candlestick Chart with Moving Averages for December Sweet Crude Light—1992

bottom reversal pattern had stopped all divergence within the moving average lines and started convergence. As the market began to consolidate, the two moving average values stayed close to each other and tended to converge more than diverge. Notice that during a market consolidation, the moving average values hover near a specific mean price rather than move toward a higher or lower price. We need to be able to identify consolidating trends to learn when to stay out of a market and when to get in.

As the market price began to advance, the short-term moving average line took immediate control by moving above the longer-term moving average line. This was a sign that the bulls had entered the market and were attempting to drive the price higher. The bullish divergence within the two moving average lines continued all the way through the first bullish rally. After the last engulfing bullish line pattern and the bearish harami line pattern at the top, the moving average lines started to converge, showing us that the market was beginning to consolidate again. This time there was more of a bearish price stall than occurred during the first consolidation period. This could mean that the bears were gaining strength and the bulls might not have had control of the market's price direction for long. Again, after finding support at 21.65, the market price began to advance.

The short-term moving average line crossed above the long-term moving average line and continued to diverge bluntly until the market stalled again. This time, a dark cloud pattern caused a bearish price reversal and also caused the short-term moving average value to begin to fall. Throughout the bearish price decline, the market price stayed below the short-term moving average line, indicating that this bearish price trend was strong and would continue downward. After a strong bearish price move, the market price found support at 20.00, and the moving average lines began to converge—as they should.

December U.S. Bonds—1992

August 26, 1992–December 17, 1992 (See Figure 15.9.)

The moving average values were set to 7 and 14 to specify a long-term trend direction, meaning that all of the short-term price corrections would not be as clearly defined by the moving average lines. Initially, the moving average values converged and diverged bluntly, showing that the market had entered a bullish trend. Notice how the shorter-term moving average (7-cycle) line has wide sweeping arches and troughs as compared to the longer-term moving average line (14-cycle). The longer-term moving average line will depict the overall, long-term price movement better, whereas the shorter-term moving average line is more sensitive to short-term price trends and corrections.

Until the second top formation happened, the short-term moving average line trailed the market price accurately. Because the moving average is a lagging indicator, the values it returns can be used for determining a protective

Figure 15.9 Candlestick Chart with Moving Averages for December U.S. Bonds—1992

stop price level. The market price activity converged with the short-term moving average line, crossing above and below; in this manner, the 7-cycle moving average line would be used as a recommended stop price after initiating a market position. After the second top formed, the moving average lines converged with a bearish signature and continued downward until the end of the bearish price move.

Just before the actual bottom of the market, the moving average lines began to converge and came within a few hundredths of a point from each other, indicating that the market had been consolidating during the time that the moving average lines had been converging. Again, notice how well the moving average values could be used to determine a protective stop price level. After the bottom both of the moving average lines changed direction and converged bluntly. Except for the short bearish stall, all of the bullish market price activity stayed above the long- and short-term moving average lines, showing the strength of the two individual bullish rallies.

Filtering Candlesticks with William's Percent Retracement

percent (per-'sent) *adj.* 1. reckoned on the basis of a whole divided into one hundred parts[8]
retrace (re-'tras) *Vt.* 2. to trace again or back[9]

The Williams percent retracement is an oscillator that closely resembles the stochastic oscillator. To calculate the William's percent retracement (% R):

$$\% \text{ R} =$$

$$\frac{\text{(highest high in \% R periods)} - \text{(current close)}}{\text{(highest high in \% R periods)} - \text{(lowest low in \% R period)}}$$

December Wheat–1992

October 7, 1992–November 20, 1992 (See Figure 15.10.)

In this analysis, the William's percent retracement indicator reacted properly by staying out of the 80%-to-100% area, showing us that the bears never really gained control of the market by driving it downward past any support price level until after the market had topped. We would conclude that this wheat market had entered a long-term bullish trend that lasted for nearly 60 days. The bullish trend was not as clearly defined as we might have expected, and because of this we would notice an upward-stepping bullish trend with a few short-term bearish corrections. Now we'll learn how to use the William's percent retracement indicator to verify our market position and the market trend.

The value returned from the William's percent retracement indicator during the upward bullish trend often stayed between 0% and 20%, demon-

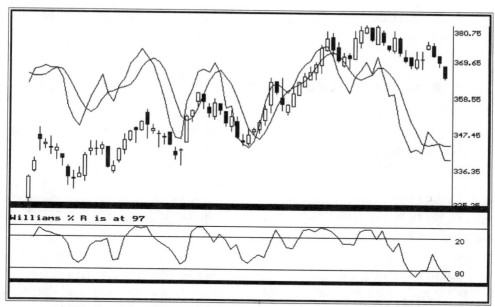

Figure 15.10 Candlestick Chart with William's Percent Retracement for December Wheat—1992

strating the strength and control that the bulls had in the market at that time. When the William's percent retracement indicator dropped into the midrange (between 20% and 80%), it was showing us that the controlling party had temporarily reversed and the bears had entered the market, driving the price down. The fact that the William's percent retracement indicator never moved into the 80%-to-100% area evinced that the bears had never gained enough control of the market to actually reverse its direction for an extended period of time. If the bears had entered the market and gained total control, it would have dropped from below 20% to above 80%, as was evident after the market topped and began to fall. This reversal of the William's percent retracement indicator was the first to occur after the somewhat defined bullish stepping trend.

   In this example, we need to pay close attention to the fact that during the bullish trend the William's percent retracement stayed out of the 80%-to-100% area and continued to try to stay near the 0%-to-20% area, indicating an attempt to continue the bullish trend. The points where it fell below 20% were those points when the bears entered the market and started a short-term bearish correction. The bears were never able to gain total control of the bullish trend move until the market had topped, which was made evident by the fact that the William's percent indicator did not reach 80% or higher. After the market top, the bears entered the market more strongly than they had before. This reversal of controlling parties was evinced by the drop of the William's percent indicator to a point above 80% and its ability to maintain its new value.

December Sweet Crude Light — 1992

August 7, 1992–November 20, 1992 (See Figure 15.11.)

This crude light market was obviously trending, but no short-term reversals or corrections were apparent. This market was more likely to enter a short-term consolidation when a defined trend move finished or stalled. The price action started by forming a three-river morning star reversal pattern after a downward price move, forewarning of a potential bottom formation. The William's percent retracement indicator jumped from above 80% (bearish) to approximately 60% and hovered near the middle of our total range: 0% (bullish) to 100% (bearish). This movement shows us that the bulls had entered the market at this point and were battling the bears for control. The next few days of trading indicated no real evidence of any potential future trend direction, and the William's percent retracement indicator was still hovering at about 50%. At this point some market price consolidation took place, and the William's percent retracement indicator confirmed that there was no actual upward or downward trend direction. Neither the bulls nor the bears had gained control of the market, causing the price to move sideways, or consolidate.

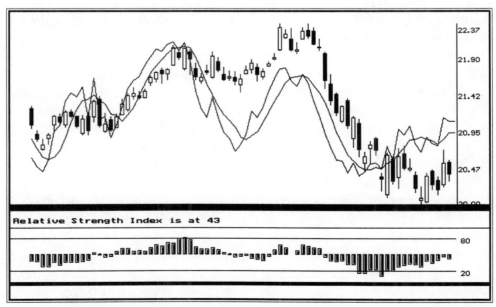

Figure 15.11 Candlestick Chart with Relative Strength Index for December Sweet Crude Light—1992

Next, a piercing line candle pattern formed and confirmed, and the William's percent retracement indicator jumped to 4%, pointing to an attempt by the bulls to regain control of this market. An engulfing bearish pattern followed, showing us that the bears wouldn't give in so easily. The William's percent retracement indicator again fell to about 50%. Then a thrusting pattern (similar to a piercing line) formed to initiate a second attempt by the bulls to drive the market price upward. The market began to stabilize between a defined support and resistance price level. The William's percent retracement indicator had been on the move upward, showing some potential for the potential bottom formation we had seen. The upward spike indicated that the bulls were a stronger force in the market than the bears. We have seen a stronger potential for bullish price movement than bearish price movement by using the William's percent retracement indicator. The thrusting pattern began an upward move from the defined support price level, and the William's percent retracement indicator immediately moved up to just below 20%, indicating that the bulls were attempting to gain control of the market. Notice that while the bulls were in control of the market price movement, the William's percent retracement indicator stayed at or below 20%. The indicator confirmed the fact that the bulls were in control and that the bullish trend move would continue until the indicator fell into the midrange area (20% to 80%)

December U.S. Bonds —1992

August 26, 1992–December 17, 1992 (See Figure 15.12.)

The initial bullish price advance prompted the William's percent retracement indicator to move well above 20%, showing us that the bulls were controlling the market's price activity. As the market's price advance stalled near 107.00 with a long-legged black doji line and began to reverse, the William's percent retracement indicator fell below 20%, indicating that the bulls were unable to maintain the bullish trend. If it had stayed above 20%, then the bullish trend would have been intact. Because it fell below 20%, we should expect a possible bearish reversal.

The William's percent retracement indicator continued to fall towards 80% with each new black candle after the long-legged doji line. Notice that as the market's price activity stalled again with a second doji line, the William's percent retracement indicator stalled near 50%, showing that the bulls and bears were unable to push the market price substantially. After the second doji line, the William's percent retracement indicator fell sharply to near 100% with the market's downward price activity. Again, if the William's percent retracement indicator stays below 80%, then we should consider the bearish trend intact. If not, we should expect a possible bullish reversal.

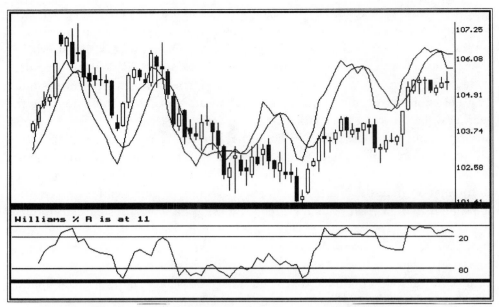

Figure 15.12 Candlestick Chart with William's Percent Retracement for December U.S. Bonds—1992

The William's percent retracement indicator immediately moved back above 80% as the market began another bullish rally. After three bullish white candles, the market price had reached a point near our original resistance area, where the second doji line formed, and began to consolidate again. The William's percent retracement indicator again attempted to stay near 50% as a result of the market's consolidation.

A last engulfing bullish line formed, forewarning of a market top and driving the William's percent retracement indicator to just below 20%. Notice that during defined short-term market trends, the William's percent retracement indicator attempted to reach points within the two extremes (20% and 80%), yet during market consolidation it attempted to stabilize near 50%. From this point on in our analysis, the U.S. bond market entered a more defined long-term trend, and the William's percent retracement indicator began to react differently.

Following the last engulfing bullish line is a bearish harami line that continued to support a market top and caused the William's percent retracement indicator to move downward below 20%. A long-legged black doji line appeared next, informing us that the market was consolidating further with bearish tendencies. This doji line did not have much effect on the William's percent retracement indicator, yet it continued to move downward. After the doji line, the

William's percent retracement indicator fell sharply back to below 80%, where it stayed during this defined bearish price trend.

Remember, the William's percent retracement indicator will attempt to stay above or below the two extremes when the market trend enters a defined long-term price trend. The market found support near 102.50 with a thrusting line pattern and then began to consolidate. The William's percent retracement indicator slowly began to move upward toward 50% yet never moved above that point. Again we are seeing signs of a consolidating market. An engulfing bearish line formed that prompted the William's percent retracement indicator to reverse direction and never attempt to reach 20%, indicating that the bears were still attempting to push the market price lower.

A bullish harami line formed near 101.41 and confirmed with the following long white candle, which caused the William's percent retracement indicator to move upward after again reaching a point near 100%. The continued defined upward movement of the William's percent retracement indicator was an excellent sign that the bullish reversal was intact and strengthening. After reaching a point well above 20%, the William's percent retracement indicator continued to stay there, indicating that the bullish trend was continuing. Even during the short-term bearish correction that caused the William's percent retracement indicator to fall to near 50%, the William's percent retracement indicator never attempted to reach 80%, showing us that the bearish reversal had no long-term strength. The William's percent retracement indicator again rallied back to a point above 20% and stayed there, telling us that the bullish trend had reformed and should continue.

Filtering Candlesticks with the Relative Strength Index

relative ('rel-et-iv) *n.* 5: expressed as the ratio of the specified quantity to the total magnitude or to the mean of all the quantities involved[10]
strength ('stren(k)th) 8: maintenance of or a rising tendency in a price level[11]
index ('in.-deks) *adj.* 2: something that serves as a pointer or indicator 7a: a ratio or other number derived from a series of observations or phenomenon[12]

The relative strength index (RSI), created in 1978 by J. Welles Wilder, is an oscillator that graphically depicts the internal strength of market momentum. Wilder recommends using this formula with a 14-day cycle. The RSI formula follows price movement by looking at the closing price to determine if it has moved higher or lower than the close of the previous trading session. It then compares an average of the higher closes against an average of the lower closes.

This oscillator creates a value between 0% and 100%. The relative strength index requires only one variable to be calculated: the number of cycles.

The way to calculate the RSI indicator is as follows:

$$RSI = 100 \times \frac{100}{[1 + (\text{average upward price change} - \text{average downward price change})]}$$

Interpretation of the Relative Strength Index

J. Welles Wilder, in his book *New Concepts in Trading Systems* (Greensboro, NC: Trend Research, 1978), points out some specific configurations that the RSI is likely to make during certain market conditions. He believes that these configurations or patterns are like fingerprints at the scene of a crime, serving as unquestionable evidence that the market will change in a predictable fashion. For example, look for a divergence in the RSI when trying to identify the internal strength or weakness of a trend. If the commodity or stock reaches a new high but the RSI fails to follow suit, a reversal may be around the corner. In such situations, look for candlestick patterns that also foretell reversal, such as harami and engulfing bullish patterns. Stars, doji, hammers, and hangmen can also be significant reversal indicators.

If this divergence were to continue, it could lead to a market contingency known as a *failure swing*, in which the RSI line turns down (after not taking out its previous high) and falls below its most recent channel. If you are anticipating a bearish reversal in an overbought market, look for candlestick combination patterns such as dark clouds or an engulfing pattern with a doji, hangman, or any long black bozu line (marubozu, opening bozu, and closing bozu). If you are anticipating a bullish reversal in an oversold market, look for candlestick combination patterns such as piercing lines or an engulfing pattern with a doji, hammer, inverted hammer, or any long white bozu line (marubozu, opening bozu, and closing bozu).

The most prevalent use of this indicator is as an oscillator to determine if a stock or commodity is currently overbought or oversold. When the RSI rises above 70%, it signals a top; inversely, when the RSI falls below above 30%, it signals a bottom. The RSI should be used to define support and resistance levels. Also, Wilder suggests looking at the RSI for pattern formations in the same way that you would look at a bar or candlestick chart.

When using the relative strength index, always remember that it is designed to show the relative change of the strength and direction of a trend. As long as the RSI and the underlining market value are moving higher or lower in unison, they have the strength and capability to maintain the rally and make new highs or lows. The RSI will indicate a weakening trend, or exhaustion, when the market might not be able to sustain a bearish or bullish rally. If the RSI is over 70%, look for candlestick patterns such as tweezers tops, anaumes, advance blocks, eight to ten–new price highs, bearish meeting lines, bearish harami (especially harami crosses), doji stars, three-river evening formations, three-winged tops, three-line stars, three-line strikes, dumpling tops, or low-price gapping plays. Also look to see if any of these candles are found in combination with patterns such as hangmen, shooting stars, or belt-hold lines. If the RSI is under 30%, look for candlestick patterns such as bullish harami, three-winged bottoms, eight to ten–new price lows, bullish meeting lines, doji stars, three-river mornings, fry pan bottoms, or high-price gapping plays. Also look for hammers, inverted hammers, and belt-hold lines.

December Wheat—1992

October 7, 1992–November 20, 1992 (See Figure 15.13.)

When a market maintains an extended bullish trend, such as in this example, the RSI indicator will stay slightly above 50%, which indicates that the market's trend and direction are bullish. We would expect the market to continue its bullish price advance until the bears entered the market and caused the RSI indicator to fall below 50%. At this point, we would concentrate on how the RSI indicator continued to move above 50% to indicate the market's trend and di-

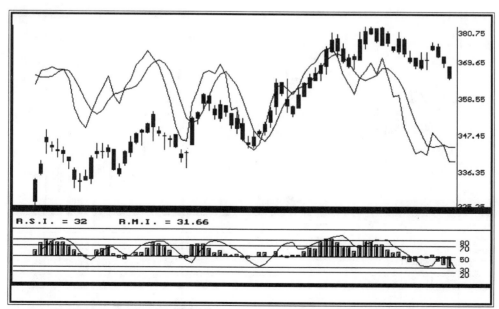

Figure 15.13 Candlestick Chart with Relative Strength Index and Relative Momentum Index for December Wheat—1992

rection. When the RSI value is above 50%, the majority of market strength is bullish; the market price should advance while the RSI indicator remains above that level and can actually increase in value. When the RSI indicator fails to continue to increase in value, it conveys that the bullish trend is weakening, and the extended outlook is for a price decline.

Notice how the RSI indicator continued to rebound from the 50% line and kept attempting to climb with each new bullish rally and that its value fell back to 50% each time the bears entered the market and drove the price back down. The fact that the RSI indicator never fell far below 50% indicated that the market trend was still bullish. After the market top, the RSI indicator began to show signs of weakening bullish strength by decreasing in value. As the RSI value fell to well below 50%, the bears entered the market and took control of its trend and direction, sending them downward. As the top continued and the bears drove the market price down even further, the RSI indicator would continue to fall.

December Sweet Crude Light — 1992

August 7, 1992–November 20, 1992 (See Figure 15.14.)

Because the RSI for this chart was below 50%, we know that the market trend was bearish. When the three-river morning star pattern formed and issued a bottom signal, the RSI indicator decreased in value, showing us that the strength

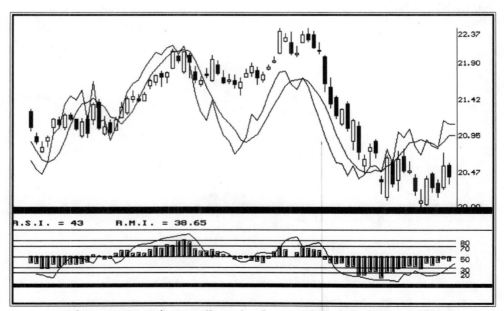

Figure 15.14   Candlestick Chart with Relative Strength Index and Relative Momentum Index for December Sweet Crude Light— 1992

of the bearish trend was increasing. Because the RSI is a lagging indicator that is based on a comparison of closing prices, it accurately showed the drop in price that made up the three-river morning pattern.

After the bottom formation, the market began to consolidate near 21.00. The RSI indicator, on the other hand, was slowly increasing in value; the bulls were pushing their way back into the market and attempting to hold the market price. Their attempt succeeded, and the RSI indicator moved back to 50%. The bulls had retaken half of the market's trend strength and would attempt to gain the majority, thus driving the market price upward.

As the market began to rally upward after a thrusting pattern, the RSI indicator continued to increase above 50%. The bulls had the majority of the market's trend strength and were able to drive the price up. When the RSI indicator climbed above 80%, the bulls had nearly maximized their attempt to move the price up and may have exhausted themselves in that attempt. Whenever the RSI indicator exceeds 80% or is below 20%, we need to watch the market for signs of a reversal. The RSI indicator will reflect the reversal by increasing or decreasing in value. The RSI indicator begins to fall almost immediately after it reaches 80%. Because there is a natural ratio of buyers versus sellers in any market, it is highly unlikely that the RSI value will ever reach 100% or 0%. The market would have to make a very substantial and dramatic move to accomplish this task. The fall in the RSI value is caused by the bears, who are attempting to hold the market price down.

The RSI continued to fall to below 50% as the market consolidated and formed support at 21.60. The bulls made a second attempt move the price up and succeeded, which caused the RSI indicator to jump back above 50%. This short-term bullish rally only moved the RSI indicator above 50%; it never made it to 80% or above. A dark cloud pattern then formed at the top of the market and issued a sell signal. As the market price began to fall after the dark cloud pattern, the RSI indicator slowly turned downward.

The candles predicted the bearish move before the RSI indicator. Remember—the RSI indicator is a lagging indicator. It did, however, show us how strongly the bears controlled the market trend and when they had maximized their efforts. After the bearish price drop, the RSI indicator value fell below 20%. At the same time, the bearish price move began to stall and consolidate. As the market consolidated, the bulls tried to hold the market price at 20.00 and then push it up; this was made evident by the fact that the RSI indicator increased in value.

December U.S. Bonds — 1992

August 26, 1992–December 17, 1992 (See Figure 15.15.)

Initially, the RSI indicator was showing us that the bulls were controlling the market trend and trying to push the market price upward. The bulls were,

Figure 15.15 Candlestick Chart with Relative Strength Index for December U.S. Bonds—1992

at this point, able to hold the market price above 103.75, although the RSI indicator stalled near 65% after the initial bullish rally and fell to below 50% as the market topped a second time. This meant that the bears were gaining the majority of the trend strength and were likely to drive the market price downward. A bearish harami line pattern formed and confirmed at that second top, issuing a sell signal.

As the market price fell after the bearish harami line, the RSI indicator continued to stay below 50% and near the market bottom reached a point below 20%. The fact that the RSI indicator had reached a point less than or equal to 20% meant that the bears might have exhausted their strength and that the bulls would reenter the market to form support or consolidation. After the RSI indicator reached 20%, it began to trail upward as the market continued to consolidate and fall to a new low.

A bullish harami line pattern formed at the bottom of the market and confirmed, issuing a buy signal. At this point the bulls were making an attempt to regain the majority of the trend strength and to push the market price upward. The RSI value moved to a point above 50% within three trading sessions after the harami line confirmed, thus indicating this successful attempt by the bulls.

From this point forward, the bulls remained in control of the majority of the trend's strength and continued to move the market price upward. At one pint, however, the RSI value fell to just above 50%. Again, the reason for this was the change of the market closing price during the market stall and correction before continuing upward. Notice that the RSI indicator value began to fall back toward 50% yet never fell below. The RSI indicator was showing us that the bears had not gained control of the majority of the trend's strength. The following session's trading moved the RSI indicator back above its previous value; it continued to increase as the second bullish rally started.

Filtering Candlesticks with the Relative Momentum Index

relative ('rel-et-iv) *n.* 5. expressed as the ratio of the specified quantity to the total magnitude or to the mean of all the quantities involved[13]
momentum (mo-'ment-em) *n.* property of a body that determines the length of time required to bring it to rest when under the action of a constant force or movement[14]
index ('in.-deks) *adj.* 2: something that serves as a pointer or indicator 7a: a ratio or other number derived from a series of observations or phenomenon[15]

The relative momentum index (RMI) is an indicator that depicts the type of momentum (bullish or bearish) as well as its strength and direction. This indicator is useful for determining when a potential market move is actually going to prompt a defined upward or downward price movement. The relative momentum index is variation of the relative strength index.

The relative momentum index returns a value from 0%, which indicates that the momentum of the defined market trend is bearish, to 100%, which indicates that the momentum of the defined market trend is bullish. Like the William's percent retracement indicator, the RMI will cross from below 20% when the defined market trend and momentum have been bearish to above 80% when the defined market trend and momentum have reversed to form a new defined bullish trend. Of course, the opposite is true when the defined market trend reverses from bullish to bearish; in such cases the RMI will cross from above 80% to below 20%. During market consolidation or congestion, the relative momentum index will not be able move into the extremely bullish or bearish areas (above 80% or below 20%) with ease; instead, it will hover at or near the 50% area, showing the lack of defined bullish or bearish momentum in the market and reflecting the lack of actual upward or downward price movement.

December Wheat—1992

August 7, 1992–November 20, 1992 (See Figure 15.13.)
The RMI indicator was initially above 50% and increasing, showing us that the market was in a bullish trend and, most importantly, that the bullish

momentum was increasing. The continued bullish momentum was being met with constant bearish resistance, which caused the market to advance slowly, accompanied by short-term corrections. Remember that the RMI indicator will rise when the market advances and will fall when the momentum becomes bearish during market corrections.

The RMI indicator is likely to indicate a reversal in market momentum of each of the individual short-term bullish rallies and bearish corrections as a movement to a point above or below 50%. Because the market's long-term direction is bullish, the RMI indicator is likely to stay above 30% and will increase in value toward 80% during bullish rallies.

During the market's defined bullish trend, the RMI indicator stayed near 70% or 80%, showing that the momentum of the market was stable. As the market topped, the RMI indicator reached new highs above 80%. As the top of the market took form and the market price began to fall, notice how the RMI indicator had fallen to below 50 and had not been able to move back up. This simple reaction demonstrated that the market's momentum had become bearish. We would watch for the RMI indicator to continue downward toward 20% if the bearish reversal and top continued.

December Sweet Crude Light—1992

August 7, 1992–November 20, 1992 (See Figure 15.14.)

The bearish price action seen earlier in this market had driven the RMI to a point below 20%. As the market price found support near 21.00, the RMI made a dramatic move to near 50%. This indicated that the bulls were entering the market and attempting to hold the market price up. The RMI had trouble getting above 50% during the market price consolidation that formed support at 21.00. Notice that as the RMI indicator continued to hover between 35% and 50%, the momentum of the market changed from bearish to neutral, meaning that either the bulls or the bears could have regained control of the market's momentum and moved the market price upward or downward. The RMI indicator had been continually increasing in value, which was showing us that the bulls were increasing their control of the market's momentum. If they continued to gain the majority of the market's momentum, they would begin to move the market price upward.

As the market began to rally upward after a thrusting pattern formed, the RMI indicator moved above 50% and then to well above 80% as the bullish rally stalled. The market's momentum had reversed from bearish to bullish during the market consolidation, which was evinced by the fact that the RMI indicator moved from below 20%, showing bearish momentum, to a point above 50%. When the bullish rally began to stall, the RMI indicator fell to nearly 50% even though the market price only fell 0.30, indicating that the bears were attempting to take 50 percent of the market's momentum from the bulls—thus holding the market price at or below 22.00.

The RMI indicator again began to hover around 50%, showing us that neither the bulls nor the bears were able to take the majority of the market's momentum and move the market price upward or downward by very much. As the bulls reentered the market for a second attempt to have their way with it, the RMI indicator moved to a point just above 50%. Before long, after a second, successful bullish rally, the RMI indicator again reached a value of greater than 80%.

This time, the bears reentered the market with a strong intent to drive the market price downward, identified by the dark cloud cover pattern at the market top. Almost as soon as the RMI indicator climbed above 80%, it began to fall back toward 50%, reiterating that the bears were trying to gain control of the market's momentum. As the market price continued to fall, the RMI indicator fell quickly to a point below 20% and stayed there during most of the bearish trend. As the market reached its lowest point, the RMI indicator increased to a value that was greater than 20%, showing that the bulls were entering the market and attempting to push the market price upward. In their attempt, they increased the RMI indicator value and then caused it to fade back to near 50%.

December U.S. Bonds—1992

August 26, 1992–December 17, 1992 (See Figure 15.16.)

The first thing to notice about the RMI indicator here would be that the initial bullish rally that drove the market price to above 106.00 caused the RMI to reach a point above 80%. After doing so, as the market began to form a top, its value fell as the bears took control of the market's momentum and price movement. As the RMI value dropped well below 50%, we would do well to note that the bulls were able to hold the market price above 103.75. At the first sign of a market top and after finding support near 103.75, the RMI indicator reversed direction, showing us that the bulls were attempting to rally the market price again. This time, the RMI indicator was unable to reach 80% and stalled near 70%. This was a sign that the bulls were not able to regain the degree of market momentum they had during their first rally. The bulls had probably exhausted their strength, and the bears would capitalize on the bulls' misfortune by gaining control of the market's momentum.

After the second top formation and a bearish harami line pattern that confirmed, the RMI value fell sharply to a point well below 50% and stayed there for the entire duration of the bearish price move. When the bears have control of the market's momentum, the RMI value is likely to stay below 50%. The

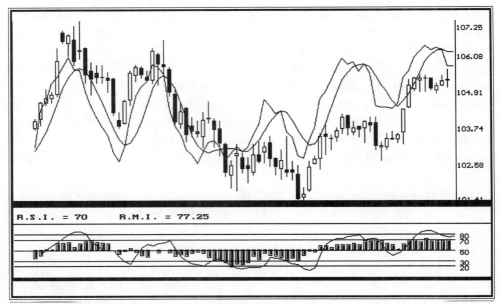

Figure 15.16 Candlestick Chart with Relative Momentum Index for December Wheat—1992

further below 50% the RMI value is, the stronger the bears' control of the market's momentum and the more they will drive the market price down. As the market started to consolidate near the end of the bearish price move, the RMI indicator began to peak at higher and higher values, indicating that the bulls were trying to hold the market price and form support at 101.50.

When the bulls are successful in retaking control of the market's momentum, we should watch for the RMI indicator to climb back above 50% and continue increasing. A bullish harami line formed at the bottom of the market and began a bullish price reversal after it confirmed. With it, the RMI indicator quickly moved back to above 50% and eventually reached a point above 80% during the final attempt by the bulls to push the market price upward. Once the RMI indicator reached 80%, notice that it slipped back but still maintained a value between 70% and 80%. This meant that the bulls were unwilling to release their control of the market's momentum and that continued bullish price movement would be likely. Unless the bears could reenter the market and push the RMI indicator back toward 50%, the bulls would maintain control of the market's momentum.

Filtering Candlesticks with Trading Bands

trade ('trad) *n.* 4b: the business of buying and selling or bartering commodities[16]

band (band) *n.* 5 *specific*: a more or less well defined range of wavelength, frequencies, or energies . . .[17]

Trading bands are used to identify price channels for a particular market. They usually indicate a range of price movement to which the market might try to adhere when making a defined move. Sometimes a market might show enough strength in its defined move to break above or below the trading bands, showing us that the strength of this particular move was greater than expected. When the market does so, we should expect it to correct itself and fall or rise back into our trading band channel. The theory behind trading bands is that the market will move from the lower band to the upper band and then possibly fall back to the lower band during a short-term bullish trend. During a defined long-term bullish trend, we might expect to see the market move repetitively in this manner, forming an upward-stepping motion until either the defined market price move weakens or a top forms. The opposite is true during a bearish trend; in this case the market will move down from the upper band and toward the lower band. During a defined long-term bearish trend, we might expect to see the market move repetitively in this manner, forming a downward-stepping motion until either the defined market price move weakens or a bottom forms.

December Wheat–1992

October 7, 1992–November 20, 1992 (See Figure 15.17.)

The particular type of bullish price movement that we see in this wheat chart is an ideal example of how to apply trading bands to a long-term trending market. Notice how the market price continually advanced to points above the upper trading band. It was never able to fall to a point below the lower band. This type of market activity indicated that the bulls were in control of the market trend and were not permitting the market price to fall to newer lows. Each individual price advance easily moved above the upper band, showing the strength of the bulls. Each time the market price advanced, it established a new high. Finally, after the bulls were able to drive the market price up to a previous resistance level at 380.75, the bears reentered the market and successfully dropped the market price to the lower band. The market might have consolidated and found additional support at 362.00, so we would have needed to watch the market's price activity to see if it continued to fall below the lower trading band.

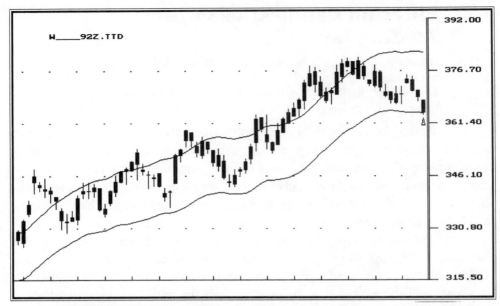

Figure 15.17 Candlestick Chart with Relative Momentum Index for December Sweet Crude Light—1992

Figure 15.18 Candlestick Chart with Relative Momentum Index for December U.S. Bonds—1992

December Sweet Crude Light—1992

October 7, 1992–November 20, 1992 (See Figure 15.18.)

To optimize any trading bands, a technician must change the variables that define the trading bands until the market's tops, bottoms, and defined trends move within the channel created by the trading bands. In this manner, we can visualize the market's activity and trend as the market price moves between the bands.

When the three-river morning star pattern formed below the lower trading band, the market price immediately corrected to above the lower band. This indicated that the market was shifting to the bullish side. If the trading bands are set correctly and the market price is below the lower band, we should look for a bullish reversal. The market price will continue upward until it reaches or exceeds the upper band. Then we should watch for bearish reversal patterns or sell signals to bring the market price back down to the lower band. During extreme market moves, the market price has a tendency to move completely above the upper band or below the lower band.

After finding support at 21.00, the market started a bullish rally that eventually broke above the upper price band. This showed us that the bullish price move was stronger than a common inner-channel move, which is associated with consolidation. (An inner-channel move occurs when a market's price activity never attempts to move toward any trading band.) The first top formation was evident when the market price fell below the upper band. During the consolidation that followed, the bulls never let the bears drive the market price to the lower band, showing that the market had stalled yet had not lost much bullish momentum.

As the market began its second bullish rally, the market price was moving away from the lower band. At the second top, the bulls made a final attempt to drive the market price above the upper band and succeeded. The bears immediately entered the market and pushed the price back to the upper band and below. The bears took control of the market when a dark cloud cover pattern formed and confirmed. Notice how quickly the bears were able to drive the market price below the lower band. It took them three trading sessions, whereas the bulls needed eight or more.

The black doji that appeared after the dark cloud confirmation indicated a significant turning point in the market. It happened to form right at a key supported resistance price level that caused the first market top and provided support for the bulls during the second top. Toward the end of the bearish price move, the market began to find support, and its price activity started to move back above the lower band. If the market price activity were to continue to push upward, we would expect to see the same type of upward-stepping bullish price move that we had seen before. If the market price were to find resistance again at 21.00, we would expect the market price to fall again, possibly breaking below the last support level of 20.00.

December U.S. Bonds—1992

August 26, 1992–December 17, 1992 (See Figure 15.19.)

The first bullish price rally caused the market price to move above the upper trading band and form a black doji star top pattern. Once the market price reached this point, we would want to look for bearish reversal patterns or sell signal patterns to form, causing a bearish reversal of the market price to the lower band. An engulfing bearish pattern formed right as the market price broke below the upper band on its way down—just what we would have expected. After a little market consolidation and some doji, the market price fell to its initial support level of 103.75 and rebounded back from the lower trading band. (This is a common market move.) Often, the market price will approach and test a trading band before attempting to move past it. The market finds support at the lower band, yet it cannot continue to advance to a higher high or the upper band.

The bears had now entered the market and were successfully holding the market price down. A bearish harami line formed and confirmed at the second top, issuing a sell signal, and the bears began to drive the market price

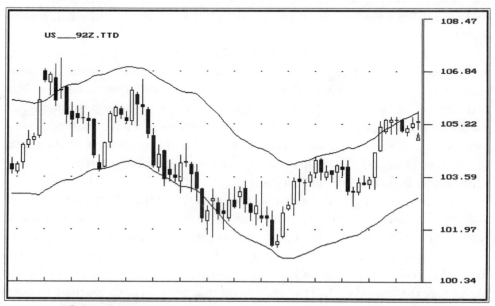

Figure 15.19 December Sweet Crude Light, 1992—Trading Band Overlay

back down to the lower band. The market price moved right to the lower band and stayed there throughout most of the bearish price move. After entering a short position when the bearish harami line pattern formed, we would monitor the price movement with the trading bands to determine where the price move might end. As the market price stayed near the lower band, we would continue our short position and trail our stop price. When the market found support below the lower price band with a thrusting line pattern, we would expect the market to rally and try to either move toward the upper band or consolidate.

Trading bands are very useful in determining key reversal areas. The market price constantly rebounds from one band to another in a continuous attempt to channel. Observe how the bears entered the market a final time to push the market price to a new low before the market reversed to the upside. After the bullish harami line reversal pattern at the market bottom, the market price continued to advance to the upper band where some resistance and consolidation occurred, again at 103.75. The market consolidated to the middle of the price channel and then rallied above the upper band and another pre-existing support/resistance price level. The market price fell back below the upper band, as it should have.

Summary

When we've decided which of the Western technical indicators we are going to use with our candlestick analysis, remember that we, as technicians, have to be able to identify patterns in their movement and assign a scale of relative importance to the indicator's values. Although some Western technical indicators may supersede others in immediate importance during certain market situations, others may simply take longer to react and therefore should be relied upon for determining long-term conditions. To overcome this obstacle, we must learn to constantly summarize the values returned by the Western indicators and weigh them for their strengths and weaknesses. Using this technique, we are better able to determine if the market will continue in this direction or if a reversal is pending. We can also determine the direction and strength of the market trend to ascertain which of the two opposing forces (bulls or bears) has gained or is gaining control of the trend. By combining the Western technical indicators and Japanese candlestick charting techniques, we can ultimately refine our own trading techniques and maximize our trading potential.

Notes

1. Steve Nison, *Japanese Candlestick Charting Techniques* (New York: New York Institute of Finance, 1991).
2. Webster's Dictionary, 862.

3. Ibid., 596.
4. Ibid., 555.
5. Ibid., 555.
6. Ibid., 61.
7. Seiki Shimizu, *The Japanese Chart of Charts* (Tokyo: Tokyo Futures Trading Publishing Co., 1986, 1990).
8. Webster's Dictionary, 625.
9. Ibid., 734.
10. Ibid., 723.
11. Ibid., 868.
12. Ibid., 427.
13. Ibid., 723.
14. Ibid., 546.
15. Ibid., 427.
16. Ibid., 937.
17. Ibid., 67.

SIXTEEN

Artificial Intelligence, Candlesticks, and Western Technical Indicators

Fundamentals of Artificially Intelligent Computers

Japanese candlesticks, as leading technical indicators, can provide insight into any potential market move. Any trader who wishes to use candlestick charts as a primary leading indicator must learn to identify those candlestick patterns that have a greater potential for indicating the direction and strength of a market move. However, we often find that the candlestick patterns that form contradict one another. This is especially true during market consolidation. So, as traders, we must develop a technique to ascertain whether a particular candlestick pattern is capable of prompting a market move in the direction it predicted. Most of the time, we rely on a number of other indicators and oscillators, along with some good old common sense. When we attempt to apply these techniques to a computerized trading system using artificial intelligence techniques, the proposed task becomes more difficult.

The term *artificial intelligence* refers to complex computer programs that have been designed to replicate as closely as possible the cognitive processes of the human brain, including the ability to make and test assumptions. Once the assumptions prove true, the computer program applies them to its knowledge base as truths for future use. Actually, there are a variety of different types and levels of computerized artificial intelligence, and some may produce a more optimum output than others depending on their application.

The foundation of almost all forms of artificial intelligence starts with the definition of rules. The human brain constantly assimilates and develops rules based upon years of continual input from our environment. Our brains develop and maintain these rules until the day we die, helping to guide us through the sometimes complex predicaments of life. Now, consider how the human brain begins to take in, assimilate, and correlate this data to other experiences we might have had in the past or are currently having and finally produces a comprehensive response or answer to the proposed question or situation. It's obvious upon reflection that the human brain is far more complex and efficient than today's computers can ever hope to become.

Another component of the artificially intelligent computer program is the ability to identify and recognize complex patterns. The Japanese candlesticks parallel this component of artificial intelligence because they, too, require pattern recognition to be analyzed correctly. The patterns of Japanese candlesticks are defined and structured, and a trader can always refer to the available literature to identify an unknown candle formation. The artificially intelligent computer program is not allowed this luxury. It must be able to identify, define, and classify any complex pattern that forms for future testing and analysis. This ability to identify new pattern formations as they appear and to make predictions based on them is partially the premise of a learning computer program.

The most common type of artificial intelligence is called an *expert system*. This term implies that the computer software program has been pretrained and refined by its developer or developers (experts) to the point where a minimum accuracy level has been reached and maintained. Because these expert systems are pretrained to accomplish a specific task, they eliminate the possibility of damaging or destroying the integrity of the knowledge base during the course of normal use. In most cases, these types of computerized software programs are more than adequate to accomplish their specific tasks. Of course, the expert system is only going to be as good as the developer who programmed the software application. If this person is truly an expert or has a complete understanding of the task to be accomplished, then the finished software product should encompass the smallest intricacies of the expert's methods of analysis and produce a finished result or series of results that are comprehensible by a nonexpert or novice.

An example of a specially developed expert system is the candlestick pattern recognition system that we developed in Chapter 14. Although it was designed to accomplish only one task—identifying Japanese candlestick patterns—it is a true expert system application because it uses a knowledge base and a series of logical directives (heuristic analysis) to guide the interpreter through the complex candlestick patterns in its knowledge base.

A more complex form of artificial intelligence would be a software program that has the ability to store varying levels of assumptions and then test and refine these assumptions in an attempt to prove which trading paradigms are true, based on past movement. This type of artificial intelligence is called a *neural network*, a trainable computer software application. We, the users, can teach the software program about something or let it learn on its own. These types of artificially intelligent software programs are obviously more complicated and difficult to maintain because they must be capable of making logical assumptions from the information they obtain from their data variables and formulating a solution to a given problem. If, for whatever reason, the software program is trained or structured illogically, the accumulated base of knowledge is unusable, and we must start training it again.

An artificially intelligent computer software program is still rather limited unless we supply it with an almost infinite number of different, complex algorithms and formulas that provide an almost limitless base of reference, or knowledge. But in order for an artificial intelligence (AI) program to be able to discern truth from fiction, we must be certain not to overload (or overtrain) the system with information. As we add new data variables, or elements, to the neural network, the number of possible combinations becomes limitless. This problem is known as *combinatorial explosion*. If the program is overloaded with information, it is likely that the program will not be able to effectively learn anything about the markets (or anything else) that will be of use.

Development of a Neural Network Software Program

In the computer industry today, neural networks are hot. Simply mentioning this term sparks attention, even if the listener had not been very interested in the conversation to begin with. Let's start by defining what we mean by this term. *Neural* refers to the neurological interaction that the human brain uses to process and store information. The individual cells that make up the human brain are called *neurons*. Billions of these neurons are intertwined to form a huge matrix allowing us to process, store, and then recall information that we've previously acquired. The word *network* refers to the intricate web of interrelationships between our input neurons and our output neurons. This interrelationship is vital to the accuracy and efficiency of the combined product—the neural network.

A neural network must have a knowledge base and will employ the same techniques as an expert system to accomplish the dissemination of data before it can begin to learn. The first expert systems were developed in 1965 by scholars at Stanford and MIT. They were designed to accomplish complex mathematical analysis and infer information about chemical structures. Ideally, the neural network must include the following:

1. An extensive base of knowledge from the specific *domain* or *domains* of interest
2. An application of specific *search* techniques
3. Use and support of *heuristic* analysis
4. The capacity to infer new knowledge from pre-existing knowledge
5. The ability of *symbolic* processing
6. The ability to explain its own reasoning in the vernacular (in our case, English)
7. The ability to store, test, and recall any inferred knowledge

The input neurons are responsible for disseminating the raw data as it comes into the neural network. Thus, they break apart the information as it arrives and define common traits or tendencies that are passed to the next layer of neurons. If too many input neurons are defined, the possibility of overloading the neural network increases. The human brain, unlike the computer, has an almost limitless capacity to process extremely large quantities of data. The common computer has a much smaller capacity than the human brain, so a limited number of input neurons should be defined to meet the requirements of the application, thus preventing the computer's neural network from becoming confused (overlooked).

The second layer of neurons is called the *hidden layer*. These neurons associate and correlate the information passed to them from the input neurons and develop their own weighted value corresponding to the input data they have received. After all of the input data has been passed to the hidden layer neurons, they fire a response to the output neurons if their weighted value exceeds a defined minimum. If the hidden layer neurons do not generate a weighted value that is high enough to be passed to the output neurons, that particular data bit is lost or masked because it did not have relevance to producing the finalized presumption. Too many hidden layer neurons may also prevent the neural network from learning to associate the generalized traits or tendencies.

The final layer of neurons is comprised of the *output neurons*. This layer pieces together the returned information to produce a finalized presumption, which should be considered only possibly true at this time. The neural network has not yet begun the testing process to verify if the presumption is true. If the neural network does not have the ability to test its presumptions, then we must train it by providing it with right or wrong answers. Otherwise, the neural network program would continue to make presumptions and would never be able to ascertain which were truthful and which were not.

The structure of the neural network components are illustrated in Figure 16.1. This example is small in comparison to the total number of input neurons, hidden layer neurons, and output neurons that are necessary to properly develop a true neural network program, although this example illustrates the interrelationship between the neurons and how the data is passed from one neuron to another to produce the finalized presumption.

A testing procedure for verifying the truth of a particular presumption may require years of continual training, just as small children acquire knowledge from years of schooling. Sometimes the neural network may have to infer that a truth exists from uncertain knowledge, uncertain data, or incomplete information. This type of uncertainty can be a regular occurrence when developing a neural network to use with markets, because they are constantly changing. Therefore, we can incorporate any of the following techniques to handle these uncertainties:

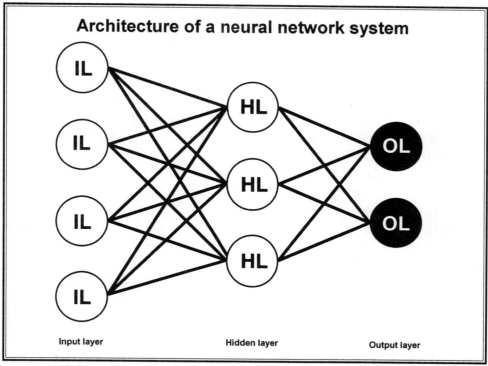

Figure 16.1 Neural Net

1. Monatomic reasoning
2. Nonmonitonic reasoning
3. Truth maintenance system
4. Reasoning based on probability
5. Certainty factors
6. Fuzzy reasoning

Monatomic reasoning is a common technique used to describe a predicate logic system that moves only in one direction, continuously adding additional truth to existing truth.

Nonmonotonic reasoning is more similar to the techniques that we, as humans, use to arrive at a conclusion. It creates tentative beliefs that are commonly based upon default assumptions. For example, when we make the decision to take a vacation and fly to our favorite vacation spot, we will assume that the pilot is competent and that the airplane is airworthy. Unless other evidence presents itself to prove otherwise, we will proceed with our plans.

The *truth maintenance system* (TMS) is an application of the nonmonotonic reasoning system and operates as a management system for the knowledge base. The TMS is called each and every time the reasoning system generates a new truth value. It maintains consistency in the knowledge base by taking any action necessary to modify the dependent beliefs so that they are consistent.

Probability-based reasoning is one of the most widely used techniques to quantify uncertainty. The basis for its appeal is that it has a solidly established mathematical basis and can be applied to many common problems. $P(T)$ is the probability that event T will occur; it represents a quantification of the likelihood of event T's occurrence. Probabilities return a value from 0 to 1. A value of 1 represents the absolute knowledge of T, and 0 represents absolute knowledge that T will not occur. For most applications, the value of $P(T)$ is derived through statistical analysis by calculating the frequency of occurrence of T in a random series of tests.

Certainty factors are informal mechanisms for quantifying the degree to which, based on a set of evidence that is present, we believe or disbelieve in a given conclusion. A certainty factor returns a numerical value that represents the extent to which we should expect a given result, based on a given body of evidence. For example, if a certainty factor returned a value of 1, that would indicate total belief of a given conclusion. A returned value of -1 would indicate total disbelief.

Fuzzy reasoning is the most similar in design to the classifications of knowledge used by humans. Humans commonly group things into classes that have broad boundaries. In fuzzy reasoning we define a set that is a class of elements with loosely defined boundaries. Again, the set should assign a grade of membership to each of the elements, from 0 to 1. A grade of 1 indicates that the element is definitely a member of the set. A grade of 0 indicates that the element is definitely not a member.

The term *back-prop* comes to mind, meaning to pretrain a neural network by feeding it a quantity of historical data to make presumptions and test them. (The actual technical term for this is *feed-forward back propagation.*) We recommend that this method of pretraining a neural network program should only be considered after it has been developed and tested for a period of time to verify that its structure and neuron layers are fully functional.

Before we go much further, let's learn how to develop each of the three layers of a neural network. First of all, we need to begin to define the types of associations, traits, conditions, patterns, theories, and methodologies that we intend to use within the layers of the neural network. This stage of the development of a neural network is similar to the blueprint stage of building a house. Without first defining what it is we want our program to accomplish, it is likely that it won't accomplish anything.

The input layer is the first layer of the neural network, so let's begin with it. This is where the raw data enters the neural network. From there, the input layer extracts and ascertains the preprocessed data groups that we use in the hidden layer. The first four data variables that are going to be passed to the input layer are the price data, which the computer uses to analyze markets and recognize patterns. Of course, if our neural network is going to be integrated with Japanese candlesticks, we would need to include the pattern recognition techniques into the input layer. The candlestick patterns and single candle types need to be defined in the input layer before that information can be used by the hidden layer.

The price data are also an essential part of the Japanese candlesticks, so it becomes logical to include the pattern recognition system in the input layer. Both the engine, to identify as many single candle types as we need, and the pattern recognition library (the series of pattern assignments), to identify any complex candlestick patterns, would need to be included. The responsibility of the engine and the pattern recognition system would be to send an accurate interpretation of any candlestick patterns found to the hidden layer for analysis. Because candlestick analysis can identify more than one pattern in any single trading cycle, the logical way to handle the types of patterns that may be found is with a table.

A table is similar to a spreadsheet. With price data, the pattern recognition system will return a series of values or symbols that accurately identify the types of candlestick patterns that are found. Once a scan for candlestick patterns has been completed, the remaining series of data variables can be prepared for use by the hidden layer.

Our candlestick table might include the following information:

Candle_Title	Candle or Pattern name
Candle_Type	White, Black, or Doji (single candles)
Candle_Signal	Buy, Sell, Bullish, Bearish, Top, Bottom, Reversal, Support, or Resistance
Candle_Date	Date of candle or pattern

As a finished result, after a complete single trading session scan for candlestick patterns, the table might look like Figure 16.2.

We could extend our table further into the past by telling the preprocessor to scan for more than just one session. The information derived from the table above would be passed to the hidden layer after we had completed the preprocessing of the other raw data.

Next, we would we need our preprocessor, or input layer, to prepare data variables for all of the Western technical indicators for use by the hidden layer. The Western technical indicators, individually, make up a composite representation of the current market conditions. Applying these conditions to the hidden layer would greatly increase the accuracy of any presumptions made by the neural network if we trained the input layer to glean accurate information from the Western technical indicators. We would place a definition for each of the characteristics of the different Western technical indicators into the input layer so that it could send a more accurate description of the market to the hidden layer. In much the same way that we assigned pattern definitions, we would assign a particular market condition from its values.

We would want to incorporate all of the information and techniques we learned in Chapters 4 and 15 into the preprocessor to provide it with a solid

Candle_Title	Candle_Type	Candle_Signal	Candle_Date
Long White Line	White	Bullish	1-1-1980
Piercing Line	White	Buy Signal	1-1-1980
Tweezers Bottoms	White	Support formed at low price	1-1-1980

Figure 16.2 Candle Table

foundation for detecting the most accurate current market conditions. The more complicated techniques may require specialized functions or routines that can assimilate the required data and then return the results to the input layer, much like our candlestick pattern recognition system. These specialized functions of a neural net may also be best suited by using a table to return its findings.

Lastly, we may want to include some other common techniques and variables to the input layer such as seasonal trading tendencies, long-term trend definitions, specialized indicators or oscillators, and any other definition we care to make that is relevant to the market's activity. These definitions can be as simple as a market top or bottom or as complex as a statement that the market has a tendency to undergo short-term retracements while within a long-term trend. Just as the human brain would not necessarily center its attention on the obvious, the input layer must be able to identify the most obscure information for its analysis.

We are defining the foundation of how the neural network will begin to interpret its findings. If we limit its ability to reflect the market's tendencies, then our neural network is likely to perform poorly or not at all. Because the analysis of market price movement is based on numbers, almost all types of market conditions can be defined mathematically. This means that anyone who understands math could build an input layer.

An example of how to build a neural input layer based upon the types of criteria we've discussed using as actual raw input data is detailed in Example 1. The functions **Define_Candle** and **Define_Candle_Patterns** are referencing a function call to our pattern recognition system. The pattern recognition system could include some primary Western technical indicators as filters to more accurately identify any candlestick pattern, or it could rely on values returned from the input neurons to filter the candlestick patterns that are found. For this example, we'll assume that the Western technical indicators are separate from the pattern recognition system and that we will have to train our neural network input layer to handle these data variables itself.

Our examples are constructed for the C programming environment. Other environments, such as Prolog, Lisp, Fortran, Pascal, and even BASIC, can be used when applying this example. The variable and function tables and naming classifications on the following pages will help you understand it.

If you understand mathematics but are unfamiliar with computer programming, then this paragraph will better illustrate what a computer program is and what it does. A computer program is simply a series of statements that instructs the computer to complete certain tasks. Most statements are logical or mathematical. The computer executes, or runs, each individual statement in order. The first program, or function, is called **Input_preprocessor()**. This is considered the main program because it is the first to execute and calls to all of the other functions that make up the program. The subsequent functions, detailed further in this chapter, are subfunctions of the main program. This is the wonderful part of programming—we can build complex layers of functions to accomplish almost any task. The three examples that follow are independent functions of one program. Remember to read computer code (the written instructions) as you would a procedure or a map.

Naming Classifications

```
Function name() {
  ...
  ...
}
```
Declares a new function (program) to execute called *name*

```
if (x) {
    y
}
```
If *x* is true, then complete *y*. { indicates the beginning of an if statement and } ends it.

```
for (x = 1;
x < stop_point ;x+1) {
  ...
  ...
}
```
For/next loop to step through records.

`&`

Logical "AND" specifier

`||`

Logical "OR" specifier

`// TEXT`

Note or Reminder Statement to let us know what we are doing

Function Table

`Define_Candle()`	Identifies a single candle type and color
`Define_Candle_Patterns()`	Identified multi-candlestick patterns
`Input_preprocessor()`	Neural Network Input Layer (Main)
`Hidden_Layer()`	Neural Network Hidden Layer
`Write_Conclusion()`	Conclusion maintenance function
`Test_Set()`	Conclusion testing facility

Data Variables

`today`	Today's date or record #
`today-1`	Yesterday
`datafile[today].open`	Open price for today
`datafile[today].high`	High price for today
`datafile[today].low`	Low price for today
`datafile[today].close`	Close price for today
`datafile[today].STO_d`	Stochastic % D value for today
`datafile[today].STO_k`	Stochastic % K value for today
`datafile[today].WILL_R`	William's % R value for today
`datafile[today].RSI`	RSI indicator value for today
`datafile[today].RMI`	RMI indicator value for today
`Closingprice_direction`	"UP" or "DOWN"
`Closingprice_difference`	Today's close — yesterday's close
`STO_Condition`	Overbought, oversold
`STO_Direction`	Converging, diverging, or crossed
`WILL_R_Indication`	Bullish or bearish reversal or bullish or bearish trend
`RSI_Indication`	Increasing bullish strength or increasing bearish strength
`Weighted_value`	Initial weighted value of all indicators' values
`Second_Weighted_Value`	Secondary weighted value for market tendencies and traits
`Number_of_traits`	Number of traits found in market

Example 1 Neural network input layer

```
Function Input_preprocessor()
{
        // process current price data variables through
           candlestick pattern
        // recognition system.
// First define the single candle
     Define_Candle();
```

```
// Now define any and all candlestick patterns
   Define_Candle_Patterns();

      // process current price data variables
      // Check for lower close today
   if (datafile[today].close < datafile[today-1].close &
      datafile[today].close <> datafile[today-1].close)
   {

      Closingprice_direction = "down";
      Closingprice_difference = datafile[today-1]
      .close-datafile[today].close;

   }

      // Check for higher close today
   if (datafile[today].close > datafile[today-1].close &
      datafile[today].close <> datafile[today-1].close)
   {

      Closingprice_direction = "up";
      Closingprice_difference = datafile[today]
      .close-datafile[today-1].close;

   }

      // Check for equal close today
   if (datafile[today].close = datafile[today-1].close)
   {

      Closingprice_direction = "same";
      Closingprice_difference = datafile[today]
      .close-datafile[today-1].close;

   }


//  process current Western Technical data variables
// Check the Stochastic Oscillator
   // Check Stochastic above 80%
   if (datafile[today].STO_d >= .80 &
   datafile[today].STO_k >= .80)
   {

      STO_Condition = "Overbought";

   }

      // Check Stochastic above 60% & below 80%
   if (datafile[today].STO_d >= .60 &
   datafile[today].STO_k >= .60 &
      datafile[today].STO_d <= .80 &
      datafile[today].STO_k <= .80)
   {
```

```
    STO_Condition = "Somewhat Overbought";
}

    // Check Stochastic above 40% & below 60%
if (datafile[today].STO_d >= .40 &
datafile[today].STO_k >= .40 &
    datafile[today].STO_d <= .60 &
    datafile[today].STO_k <= .60)
{
    STO_Condition = "Neutral";
}

    // Check Stochastic above 20% & below 40%
if (datafile[today].STO_d >= .20 &
datafile[today].STO_k >= .20 &
    datafile[today].STO_d <= .40 &
    datafile[today].STO_k <= .40)
{
    STO_Condition = "Somewhat Oversold";
}

    // Check Stochastic below 20%
if (datafile[today].STO_d <= .20 &
    datafile[today].STO_k <= .20)
{
    STO_Condition = "Oversold";
}

    // Check for 2 cycle bearish converging Stochastic
        indicator
if ((datafile[today].STO_d-datafile[today].STO_k) <
    (datafile[today-1].STO_d-datafile[today-1].STO_k))
{
    STO_Direction = "Bearish Converging";
}
    // Check for 3 cycle bearish converging Stochastic
        indicator
if ((datafile[today].STO_d-datafile[today].STO_k) <
    (datafile[today-1].STO_d-datafile[today-1].STO_k) <
    (datafile[today-2].STO_d-datafile[today-2].STO_k))
{
    STO_Direction = "Bearish Converging";
}

    // Check for 2 cycle bullish converging Stochastic
        indicator
if ((datafile[today].STO_k-datafile[today].STO_d) <
```

```
                  (datafile[today-1].STO_k-datafile[today-1].STO_d))
{
    STO_Direction = "Bullish Converging";
}
    // Check for 3 cycle bullish converging Stochastic
       indicator
if ((datafile[today].STO_k-datafile[today].STO_d) <
    (datafile[today-1].STO_k-datafile[today-1].STO_d) <
    (datafile[today-2].STO_k-datafile[today-2].STO_d))
{
    STO_Direction = "Bullish Converging";
}


    // Check for 2 cycle bearish diverging Stochastic
       indicator
if ((datafile[today].STO_d-datafile[today].STO_k) >
    (datafile[today-1].STO_d-datafile[today-1].STO_k))
{
    STO_Direction = "Bearish Diverging";
}
    // Check for 3 cycle bearish diverging Stochastic
       indicator
if ((datafile[today].STO_d-datafile[today].STO_k) >
    (datafile[today-1].STO_d-datafile[today-1].STO_k) >
    (datafile[today-2].STO_d-datafile[today-2].STO_k))
{
    STO_Direction = "Bearish Diverging";
}
    // Check for 2 cycle bullish diverging Stochastic
       indicator
if ((datafile[today].STO_k-datafile[today].STO_d) >
    (datafile[today-1].STO_k-datafile[today-1].STO_d))
{
    STO_Direction = "Bullish Diverging";
}
    // Check for 3 cycle bullish diverging Stochastic
       indicator
if ((datafile[today].STO_k-datafile[today].STO_d) >
    (datafile[today-1].STO_k-datafile[today-1].STO_d) >
    (datafile[today-2].STO_k-datafile[today-2].STO_d))
{
    STO_Direction = "Bullish Diverging";
```

```
    }

        // Check for 2 cycle bullish crossing Stochastic
            indicator
    if (datafile[today].STO_k) >=
    datafile[today].STO_d &
        datafile[today-1].STO_k < datafile[today-1].STO_d)
    {
        STO_Direction = "Bullish Crossing";
    }

        // Check for 2 cycle bearish crossing Stochastic
            indicator
    if (datafile[today].STO_k) <=
    datafile[today].STO_d &
        datafile[today-1].STO_k > datafile[today-1].STO_d)
    {
        STO_Direction = "Bearish Crossing";
    }


// Check Williams Percent Retracement Indicator
        // Check for 2 cycle bearish reversal indication
    if (datafile[today].WILL_R >= 80 & datafile[today-1].
    WILL_R <= 20)
    {
        WILL_R_Indication = "Bearish Reversal";
    }
        // Check for 3 cycle bearish reversal indication
    if (datafile[today].WILL_R >= 80 & datafile[today-2].
    WILL_R <= 20)
    {
        WILL_R_Indication = "Bearish Reversal";
    }
        // Check for 2 cycle bullish reversal indication
    if (datafile[today].WILL_R <= 20 & datafile[today-1].
    WILL_R >= 80)
    {
        WILL_R_Indication = "Bullish Reversal";
    }
        // Check for 3 cycle bullish reversal indication
    if (datafile[today].WILL_R <= 20 & datafile[today-2].
    WILL_R >= 80)
```

```
{
    WILL_R_Indication = "Bullish Reversal";
}

    // Check for 2 cycle bearish trend continuation
if (datafile[today].WILL_R >= 80 & datafile[today-1].
WILL_R >= 80)
{
    WILL_R_Indication = "Bearish Trend";
}

    // Check for 3 cycle bearish trend continuation
if (datafile[today].WILL_R >= 80 & datafile[today-1].
WILL_R >= 80 &
    datafile[today-2].WILL_R >= 80)
{
    WILL_R_Indication = "Bearish Trend";
}

    // Check for 2 cycle bullish trend continuation
if (datafile[today].WILL_R <= 20 & datafile[today-1].
WILL_R <= 20)
{
    WILL_R_Indication = "Bullish Trend";
}

    // Check for 3 cycle bullish trend continuation
if (datafile[today].WILL_R <= 20 & datafile[today-2].
WILL_R <= 20 &
    datafile[today-2].WILL_R <= 20)
{
    WILL_R_Indication = "Bullish Trend";
}
// Check the RSI indicator
    // Check for increasing bullish trend strength in
        the RSI
if (datafile[today].RSI > datafile[today-1].RSI)
{
    RSI_Indication = "Increasing Bullish Trend
    Strength";
}

    // Check for Increasing bearish trend strength in
        the RSI
if (datafile[today].RSI < datafile[today-1].RSI)
{
```

```
        RSI_Indication = "Increasing Bearish Trend
        Strength";
    }


// Check the RMI indicator
        // Check for increasing bullish Momentum
    if (datafile[today].RMI > datafile[today-1].RMI)
    {
        RMI_Indication = "Increasing Bullish Momentum";
    }
        // Check for Increasing Bearish Momentum
    if (datafile[today].RMI < datafile[today-1].RMI)
    {
        RMI_Indication = "Increasing Bearish Momentum";
    }
// Begin hidden layer
Hidden_Layer();
}
```

This example of an input level for a neural network program returns the current market conditions as data variables that will be passed to the hidden layer. Our example, although rather lengthy, shows how to begin the process of preprocessing the necessary raw data to extract conditions that apply to our analysis. Custom functions or algorithms could be placed within this input layer to accomplish more complex tasks if needed. We've chosen to have the data variables return a character string, rather than a numeric value, to indicate the conditions that apply. We could, of course, assign numeric values to the conditions and data variables that apply.

Once the input layer has processed the raw data and passed it to the hidden layer, the hidden layer begins to assimilate the data to produce a completed presumption that will be tested over time for truth. The hidden layer can return more than one presumption if it has been designed to do so. Our hidden layer should produce one presumption for every candle or candlestick pattern found by our interpreter so that we can begin to build a knowledge base to test and rely upon. To accomplish this task, our hidden layer must be able to store the finalized presumptions—and all of their constituent criteria—to a structured data file for future testing.

At this point we need to define a weighted value that will apply to the processed data variables as they are manipulated by the hidden layer. This weighted value will determine if the hidden layer neurons will fire an output layer neuron. In our example, we will use a simple weighted average based upon the Western technical indicators' values to determine the possibility of the candlestick pattern's truth. Assuming that this is the first time any data has been sent through the neural network, these possible truths still need to be tested further before we can rely on its prediction. Still, this example will illustrate the concepts and structure of the neural network's hidden layer.

By assigning a varying weighted value to the Western technical indicators based on their values, we can attain a presumed value indicating the likelihood of the candlestick pattern or candle and its predictions to occur. As time passes and more presumptions are made and tested, the neural network will build and maintain a table of candlestick patterns and their associated market conditions with values returned from the hidden layer's analysis, including refined testing and inferred accuracy rates.

To test the candlestick patterns and the results generated from our neural network, we need to flag, or mark, those presumptions made earlier that still pertain to the market's activity. Ideally, we locate the presumptions that do apply and test them over a varied time frame to see if they become true. If a presumption proves true, we might want to know how many sessions the market moved in the direction predicted by the candlestick pattern and how much price moved during that time frame. The variables derived from the hidden layer and tested results should be stored in the table with the original presumption information. Eventually two tables will be used: one of possible truths, the other of absolute truth.

If the presumption proves untrue this time, the maintenance system of the neural network will store this information in the possible truths table for future reference. If, eventually, the presumption proves completely untrue, the presumption could be marked as false and stored in another table for reference or else discarded completely.

Example 2. Neural network hidden layer

```
Function Hidden_Layer()
{
//  Start at first candlestick pattern in Candle_Table
and continue to last pattern
    for (x = 1; x <= number_of_candles_in_table; x+1)
    {
    Weighted_value = 0;


//  if candlestick pattern predicted a Buy, Bullish,
    Support or Bottom signal
```

```
if (Candle_Table[x].candle_signal = "Buy" or
    Candle_Table[x].candle_signal = "Bullish" or
    Candle_Table[x].candle_signal = "Support" or
    Candle_Table[x].candle_signal = "Bottom")
{
// calculate weighted average of stochastic
   oscillator into Weighted_Value
   Weighted_value = Weighted_value + (100-Average
     (datafile[today].STO_d, datafile[today].STO_k));

// calculate weighted average of RSI Indicator into
   Weighted_Value
   Weighted_value = Weighted_value + (100-
     datafile[today].RSI);

// calculate weighted average of RMI Indicator into
   Weighted_Value
   Weighted_value = Weighted_value + (100-
     datafile[today].RMI);

// calculate weighted average of Williams % R
   Indicator into Weighted_Value
   Weighted_value = Weighted_value +
     datafile[today].WILL_R);
   // Average the total Weighted Value.
Weighted_value = (Weighted_value/4);
}
// if candlestick pattern predicted a Sell, Bearish,
   Resistance or Top signal
   if (Candle_Table[x].candle_signal = "Sell" or
     Candle_Table[x].candle_signal = "Bearish" or
       Candle_Table[x].candle_signal = "Resistance" or
         Candle_Table[x].candle_signal = "Top")
{
// calculate weighted average of stochastic
   oscillator into Weighted_Value
   Weighted_value = Weighted_value + (Average
     (datafile[today].STO_d, datafile[today].STO_k));

// calculate weighted average of RSI Indicator into
   Weighted_Value
```

```
    Weighted_value = Weighted_value +
       datafile[today].RSI;


    // calculate weighted average of RMI Indicator into
       Weighted_Value
    Weighted_value = Weighted_value + 100-
       datafile[today].RMI;


    // calculate weighted average of Williams % R
       Indicator into Weighted_Value
       Weighted_value = Weighted_value + (100-
          datafile[today].WILL_R);


       // Average the total Weighted Value.
    Weighted_value = (Weighted_value/4);
    }


Second_Weighted_Value = 0;
Number_of_traits = 0;
// Now we integrate the other pre-processed values
    if (STO_Direction = "Bullish Crossing") {
       Second_Weighted_Value = Second_Weighted_Value +
          (100-Average(datafile[today].STO_d,
          datafile[today].STO_k)) +
          (datafile[today].STO_k-datafile[today].STO_d);
       Number_of_traits = Number_of_traits+1;
    }
    if (STO_Direction = "Bullish Diverging") {
       Second_Weighted_Value = Second_Weighted_Value +
          (100-Average(datafile[today].STO_d,
          datafile[today].STO_k)) +
          (datafile[today].STO_k-datafile[today].STO_d);
    Number_of_traits = Number_of_traits+1;
    }
    if (STO_Direction =  "Bearish Diverging") {
       Second_Weighted_Value = Second_Weighted_Value +
          (Average(datafile[today].STO_d,
          datafile[today].STO_k)) +
          (datafile[today].STO_d-datafile[today].STO_k);
       Number_of_traits = Number_of_traits+1;
    }
    if (STO_Direction = "Bullish Converging") {
```

```
     Second_Weighted_Value = Second_Weighted_Value +
       (100-Average(datafile[today].STO_d,
       datafile[today].STO_k)) +
       (datafile[today].STO_d-datafile[today].STO_k);
     Number_of_traits = Number_of_traits+1;
  }
  if (STO_Direction = "Bearish Converging") {
     Second_Weighted_Value = Second_Weighted_Value +
       (Average(datafile[today].STO_d,
       datafile[today].STO_k)) +
       (datafile[today].STO_k-datafile[today].STO_d);
     Number_of_traits = Number_of_traits+1;
  }
  if (STO_Direction = "Bearish Crossing") {
     Second_Weighted_Value = Second_Weighted_Value +
       (Average(datafile[today].STO_d,
       datafile[today].STO_k)) +
       (datafile[today].STO_d-datafile[today].STO_k);
     Number_of_traits = Number_of_traits+1;
  }
  if (WILL_R_Indication = "Bearish Reversal") {
     Second_Weighted_Value = Second_Weighted_Value +
       (datafile[today].WILL_R-datafile[today-1].
       WILL_R);
     Number_of_traits = Number_of_traits+1;
  }
  if (WILL_R_Indication = "Bullish Reversal") {
     Second_Weighted_Value = Second_Weighted_Value +
       (datafile[today-1].WILL_R-
       datafile[today].WILL_R);
     Number_of_traits = Number_of_traits+1;
  }
  if (WILL_R_Indication = "Bullish Trend") {
     Second_Weighted_Value = Second_Weighted_Value +
       (100-(Average(datafile[today].WILL_R,
       datafile[today-1].WILL_R, datafile[today-2].
       WILL_R);
     Number_of_traits = Number_of_traits+1;
  }
  if (WILL_R_Indication = "Bearish Trend") {
     Second_Weighted_Value = Second_Weighted_Value +
       (Average (datafile[today].WILL_R,
```

```
        datafile[today-1].WILL_R, datafile[today-2]
        .WILL_R));
    Number_of_traits = Number_of_traits+1;
}
    if (RSI_Indication = "Increasing Bullish Trend
        Strength") {
    Second_Weighted_Value = Second_Weighted_Value +
        (average(datafile[today].RSI, datafile[today-1]
        .RSI) + (datafile[today].RSI-datafile[today-1]
        .RSI );
    Number_of_traits = Number_of_traits+1;
}
if (RSI_Indication = "Increasing Bearish Trend
   Strength") {
    Second_Weighted_Value = Second_Weighted_Value +
        (100-(average(datafile[today].RSI,
        datafile[today-1].RSI) + (datafile[today-1]
        .RSI-datafile[today].RSI);
    Number_of_traits = Number_of_traits+1;
}
if (RMI_Indication = "Increasing Bearish Momentum")  {
    Second_Weighted_Value = Second_Weighted_Value +
        (average(datafile[today].RMI, datafile[today-1]
        .RMI) + (datafile[today-1].RMI-
        datafile[today].RMI);
    Number_of_traits = Number_of_traits+1;
}
if (RMI_Indication = "Increasing Bearish Momentum") {
    Second_Weighted_Value = Second_Weighted_Value +
        (average(datafile[today].RMI, datafile[today-1]
        .RMI) + (datafile[today].RMI-datafile[today-1]
        .RMI);
    Number_of_traits = Number_of_traits+1;

}
if (Number_of_traits > 0) { // if a market trait was
   identified
    Second_Weighted_Value = (Second_Weighted_Value /
        Number_of_traits);
    Weighted_value = average(Weighted_value,
        Second_Weighted_value);
}
```

```
// Initiate presumption maintenance system to store
   and sort proposed conclusions
Write_Conclusion();
// Send output to screen (and user)
Output_Layer();
} // end of FOR/NEXT loop
// Initiate presumption tester to test any pending
   conclusions
Test_Set();
} // end of function
```

This hidden layer returns a value that it believes is the likelihood of truth of the specific candlestick patterns that were found in Figure 16.2. To explain a little further, let's use Tables 16.1 and 16.2 as examples to get a better feel for how the neural network generates its hidden layer values. We'll use two different examples of raw data, excluding the price data. The first table presents data from a bearish-trending market; the second, from a bullish-trending market. Assuming that the candlestick patterns in Figure 16.2 are the patterns found for today, the neural network should represent the differences in the market conditions as different values.

Remember, our hidden layer is taking into account the direction and result of all of the raw input data to determine the proposed likelihood that the piercing line and tweezers bottoms patterns would initiate a bullish price move. As these numeric values change during normal market activity, so will the result generated by the neural network. The results of our neural network hidden layer are as follows.

Using Table 16.1, a finished value of 59.16 is returned. The independent values for the `Weighted_value` and `Second_Weighted_Value` are 76.00 and 42.33, respectively. The reason that the `Second_Weighted_Value` is below 50 is that we did not find a strong confluence within the direction and traits of the Western technical indicators.

Using Table 16.2, a finished value of 47.33 is returned. The independent values for the `Weighted_value` and `Second_Weighted_Value` are 23.625

Table 16.1 Bearish-trending Market

	Today	Today-1	Today-2
STO_k	18	21	24
STO_d	20	25	31
RSI	24	32	38
RMI	31	35	46
WILL_R	78	67	53

Table 16.2 Bullish-trending Market

	Today	Today-1	Today-2
STO_k	71	64	56
STO_d	66	58	50
RSI	72	67	63
RMI	74	63	55
WILL_R	9	18	35

and 71.04, respectively. The reason that the `Second_Weighted_Value` is above 50 is that we found more confluence within the direction and traits of the Western technical indicators than in Table 16.1.

Both the `Weighted_value` and `Second_Weighted_Value` are necessary to counterbalance one another when any uncertainty is derived. If a total confluence of the raw data and the inferred information is found, both of these values should exceed 50, thus providing us with a higher probability that the candlestick pattern will become true. With a lack of confluence, these values should offset one another, causing the returned value to fall below 50.

The returned value from Table 16.1 could be interpreted as a 59 percent chance that the candlestick patterns would, indeed, push the market price upward. We do not know exactly how accurate a neural network is until it has had sufficient time and data to test its conclusions.

The returned value from Table 16.2 indicates that there is less than a 50 percent likelihood that the candlestick patterns would be able to initiate a bullish rally. Because the returned value fell below 50 percent, we might decide to discard this conclusion now or continue testing it to see if the value changes.

The final stage of the neural network is the output layer. Its function is to return any of the values or inferred knowledge generated from the neural network to the user in a comprehensible form. Our example simply returns the finished value in a sentence format. We could include any of the other information that we generated within the neural network as well.

Example 3: Neural network output layer

```
Function Output_Layer()
{
    Printf (''The candlestick patterns found have a
    %4.2f%% probability of being correct.'');
}
```

Sample output:

```
The candlestick patterns found have a 59.16% probability
of being correct.
```

At this point, the concept of how a neural network develops and infers knowledge from raw data should be a little more clear. Other reference books specifically devoted to artificial intelligence and neural networking will provide further assistance.

As we continually expand our thoughts and refine our concepts with the help of a computer and a computer program, we, as traders, can effectively accomplish many complex tasks in far less time than it would take to complete by hand. The computer, and the software programs that we choose to use on it, will define what types of market analysis techniques we are capable of performing. In other words, we could have the fastest computer that money could buy, but if we didn't have a computer program that did everything we want, our efforts would be partially, if not completely, in vain.

If you are at a point where you understand the concepts and methodologies that we've discussed throughout this book and have little or no computer experience, begin to apply these trading techniques to whatever you are using now. Over time, you will attain a more complete understanding of these techniques and of Japanese candlesticks.

Pretrained and Trainable Neural Networks

We should imply no preferences when attempting to generate a computer program while applying the concepts and structures this book details. Computer software programs are designed to accomplish one or more tasks to the best of their abilities. Therefore, we need to develop any given program around the requirements for solving the problem—whatever they may be. We don't need to develop a neural network program to calculate and display the stochastic oscillator or any other common mathematical function. These necessities can be accomplished without the use of a neural network.

As traders and programmers, we need to define the problem, or problems, before we begin any attempt to code a solution. A single problem may be more difficult than it appears at first. Often, principles of logarithmic growth apply to a problem when we find that other, dependent problems stem from the primary one. To avoid a complete restructuring of the software program, apply the following steps to the definition of the problem:

1. Define the problem and dependent problems, to the best of your ability, as they exist.
2. Define the steps necessary to solve the problem, or dependent problems, if you know how to do so.

3. Define the approximate number of possible answers or solutions to the problem and the dependent problems.
4. Does the problem have the need to continuously refine and test its conclusions or not?

Defining the problem ensures that we are completely aware of what we are getting into and also builds a structured "blueprint" of the specific problem from which to work. This blueprint should include a mathematical breakdown of the actual problem and all of its dependent problems.

Defining the steps necessary to solve the problem provides us with a map detailing how to get from point A (a problem) to point B (a solution). This map will help guide us through the development process and make sure we don't stray from our designated goal.

Defining the approximate number of possible answers or solutions allows us to better define the size and complexity of the problem, or problem scope. Again, sometimes seemingly simple problems can produce a vast, almost limitless, number of solutions. For example, the possible number of candlestick patterns and combinations thereof that could form within a 20-candle session is over 140,000.

If the problem requires the ability to learn and test its presumptions before they are found to be true or if the problem scope is too large to handle efficiently, then a neural network application may be the best solution. If the problem scope is rather limited and the ability to learn and test is not needed, then an expert systems application may be the best solution.

A trainable neural network offers a great advantage if the structure and integrity of the neural network is not breached. Its combined ability to learn and test what it has learned produces a greater capacity to acquire and maintain accurate knowledge. The neural network is constantly maintaining its knowledge base with up-to-the-minute analysis for us to reference.

A pretrained system (an expert system) can efficiently accomplish a multitude of tasks and is much more simple to develop. The pretrained system is limited in regards to its knowledge base. But its developers, the experts, can incorporate any technique or indicator in an attempt to maximize the accuracy of its conclusions. Pretrained systems are commonly developed as specialized trading systems because once the system has been taught to understand the trading technique, it can mimic the expert's results without being dependent upon the expert.

Conclusion

synergism (*sin-er-jiz-em*) *n*: cooperative action of discrete agencies such that the total effect is greater than the sum of effects taken independently[1]

The trend toward computerization and globalization in the past two decades have also made a major contribution to expanding our global perspective.[2]

We have come full circle. What began as a journey into the world of Japanese technical analysis has developed into a valid methodology for the twentieth-century trader and technician. The new global technician will have the ability to blend the old with the new, the East with the West, to formulate a new modernistic approach to trading. This synergistic strategy will combine the knowledge of Western technical analysis and the wisdom of Japanese technical analysis with the processing and analytical learning capabilities of the computer. The sum of these components is truly greater than their total taken independently. This synergistic trading philosophy will guide today's trader into the twenty-first century.

An appropriate name for this new style of trading might be *Synergistic Technical Analysis,* or STA. Synergistic Technical Analysis will incorporate elements of Eastern and Western analysis and market relationships (both intra- and inter-) and utilize computers to analyze the data. All technical indicators can be defined in mathematical terms. Computer programmers and market technicians are currently developing applications that are on the frontier of this and related technical research.

E.W.O.L. (Elliot Wave On Line), developed by Tom Joseph, is a software application that has been trained to recognize Elliot waves. The software application that we developed at International Pacific Trading Company, the Candlestick Forecaster, has been trained to recognize over 1,000 patterns and to make judgment calls about its findings based on information provided by Western technical indicators.

Neural networks such as N-TRAIN (produced by Scientific Consultant Services, Inc.) and many others are now commercially available so that the technician can train a neural network to his or her specifications. MetaStock Professional, produced by Equis International, and System Writer, produced by Omega Research, allow the technician to program in mathematical formulas and develop and test trading systems. It's not just the large financial institutions' market analysts who have access to these tools; ten of thousands of traders across the globe are beginning to use them. Any analyst who can imagine an idea can now actualize it. The boundaries of technical analysis will be defined only by the imagination, knowledge, and wisdom of market traders and computer programmers.

Synergistic Technical Analysis will contain the following elements composed on two levels:

Level One

1. Incorporation of Japanese candlestick patterns and Japanese technical analysis into an application library
2. Incorporation of Western technical analysis into the application by mathematically coding rules and parameters based on Western mathematical formulas such as Fibonacci retracement, Gann angles, oscillators, and averages to derive weighted values
3. Incorporation of the symbolic relationship between markets and the addition of this knowledge to the application by mathematically coding rules and parameters based on these relationships to derive weighted values
4. Development of a recognition system based upon the applications library

Level Two

By coding this knowledge base into this software application, an STA expert system will be created. These will be the foundations for neural networks that will become the next generation of AI trading applications. These new applications, with the ability to learn and test what they learn, will produce a tremendous capacity to acquire and maintain accurate new knowledge. These neural networks will continually update their knowledge bases and by so doing will find new connections between all of the variables and additional patterns. This will further the development of technical analysis. This methodology will give the market technician the tools necessary to compete and trade in a global marketplace. As John J. Murphy has so appropriately noted, "One of the most striking lessons of the 1980s is that all markets are interrelated—financial and nonfinancial, domestic and international. . . . As a result, the concept of technical analysis is now evolving to take these intermarket relationships into consideration."[3]

All of us now live in and are a part of a global economy. We work in a universal marketplace. Markets are truly interrelated; traders are no longer limited by continental boundaries, trading methodologies, or national markets. For the first time in the history of the human race, all markets are becoming interconnected, and the global marketplace is rapidly becoming a reality rather than a vision. The tools that are being developed for this ever-expanding marketplace are on the frontiers of software programming and technical research. It is our belief that before the end of this century, Synergistic Technical Analysis will become a part of a definitive trading methodology, a template for a new type of technical market analysis. The challenges ahead for market technicians and traders will be immense, but so will the rewards.

The Candlestick Forecaster

All of the charts found in Parts 2 and 3 of this book were created by a software application called the Candlestick Forecaster, produced by International Pacific Trading Company. This application is the result of years of research into the art of Japanese candlestick analysis and state-of-the-art computer programming. It will guide and teach you about candlestick patterns and charts. Some of its features are

| Instant interpretations of over 750 candlestick patterns
| Detailed information about any pattern found
| BUY and SELL signals and recommended stop placements generated by a copyrighted artificial intelligence neural network pattern recognition library
| Automatic monitoring of stochastic osillators, moving averages, RSI, and William's percent retracement for filtering candlestick patterns

Our most advanced application for end-of-day technical analysis is the Master Edition, which interprets over 1,000 candlestick patterns and was developed for the professional trader. It simplifies all of the essential technical analysis required to actively trade and monitor any number of equities or commodities. It allows you to save custom pages and trend lines, scan candlestick charts for patterns, and print detailed reports. It can also monitor over 400 markets automatically and internally.

If you have a computer and would like this program, you could receive a significant discount (up to the purchase price of this book). Contact International Pacific Trading Company for details. We have also prepared a special version of our demo disk that can be used with this book. It contains all the historical data needed to reproduce and interact with all of the charts contained herein, allowing you to bring this book to life in your computer. If you would like a copy of this special demo disk of the Candlestick Forecaster, send $10.00 plus $5.00 (to cover shipping and handling) with desired disk size to

International Pacific Trading Company
1050 Calle Cordillera Suite 105
San Clemente, CA 92673
(714) 498-4009
(714) 498-5263 FAX

Notes

1. *Webster's Dictionary.*
2. John J Murphy, *Intermarket Technical Analysis.* John Wiley & Sons, Inc., New York, 1991.
3. John J. Murphy, *Intermarket Technical Analysis.* John Wiley & Sons, Inc., New York, 1991.

Bibliography

Bollinger, John. "Bollinger Bands." *Stock & Commodities* (February 1992): 18–25.

Bressert, Walter. *The Power of Oscillator/Cycle Combinations.* Tuscon: Walter Bressert & Associates, 1991.

Burk, Mike. "New High and New Low Indicators." *Stocks & Commodities* (May 1990).

Dobson, Edward D. *Understanding Fibonacci Numbers.* Greenville, SC: Traders Press, 1984.

Hartle, Thom. "Steve Nison On Candlestick Charting." *Stocks & Commodities* (March 1991).

Hurd, Holliston Hill. "Congestion Phase with Candlesticks." *Stocks & Commodities* (February 1993).

Kosar, John J. "Support And Resistance Levels." *Stocks & Commodities* (January 1991).

Murphy, John J. *International Technical Analysis.* New York, NY: John Wiley & Sons, Inc., 1991.

———. *Technical Analysis of the Futures Market.* New York, NY: New York Institute of Finance, 1986.

Nison, Steve. *Japanese Candlestick Charting Techniques.* New York, NY: Simon & Schuster, 1991.

Wilder, J. Welles. *New Concepts in Technical Trading Systems.* Greenboro, NC: Trend Research, 1978.

Shimizu, Seiki. *The Japanese Chart of Charts.* Tokyo: Tokyo Futures Trading Publishing Co., 1986.

Rolston, David W. *Principles of Artificial Intelligence and Expert Systems Development.* New York, NY: McGraw-Hill Inc., 1988.

Glossary of Western Trading Terms

Bar Chart A graphic representation of price activity. The high and the low of the session define the top and bottom of a vertical line. The close for the period is marked with a short horizontal bar attached to the right of the vertical line. The open is marked with a short horizontal bar on the left side of the vertical line. Price is on a vertical scale; time is on a horizontal scale.

Bearish Said of times when traders anticipate market prices to decline.

Bullish Said of times when traders anticipate market prices to advance.

Confirmation When more than one indicator substantiates the action of another.

Congestion Zone or Band A period of lateral price action within a relatively narrow price band.

Consolidation The same as a congestion zone. Consolidation, however, implies that the prior trend should resume.

Continuation Pattern A pattern whose implications are for a continuation of the prior trend.

Divergence When related technical indicators fail to confirm a price move. For instance, if a price reaches new highs and stochastic oscillators do not, this is a negative divergence and is bearish. If prices establish new lows and stochastic oscillators do not, this is a positive divergence and is bullish.

Flag or Pennant A continuation formation comprised of a sharp price move followed by a brief consolidation area. These are continuation patterns.

Gap A price void (that is, no trading) from one price area to another.

Intraday Any period shorter than daily. Thus, a 60-minute intraday chart is based on the high, low, open, and close for a given hour of trading.

Oscillator A momentum line that fluctuates around a zero value line (or between 0 and 100 percent). Oscillators can help measure overbought/ oversold levels, show negative and positive divergence, and be used to measure a price move's velocity.

Overbought Said of times when the market moves up too far, too fast. At this point the market is vulnerable to a downward correction.

Oversold Said of times when the market declines too quickly. The market becomes susceptible to a bounce.

Protective Stop A means of limiting losses if the market moves against your position. If your stop level is reached, your position is automatically offset at the prevailing price.

Relative Strength Index (RSI) An oscillator devloped by J. Welles Wilder. The RSI compares the ratio of up close to down close over a specified time period.

Retracement A price reaction from the prior move in percentage terms. The more common retracement moves are 38, 50, and 62 percent.

Selloff A downward movement in prices.

Stochastic Oscillator An oscillator that measures the relative position of the closing price as compared to its range over a chosen period. It is usually comprised of the faster-moving % K line and the slower-moving % D line.

Support Level An area where buyers are expected to enter.

Trend The market's prevalent price direction.

Uptrend A market that has an increasing price over time.

Index

A

Abandoned Baby, 28, 34
Advance Block With Hangman, 37
Ananume, 36, 38
Artificial Intelligence, 249

B

Bar Chart, 5–8
Bearish Gapping Play, 29
Bearish Harami, 24
Bearish Harami Cross, 26
Bearish Harami Line, 94, 98, 169
Bearish Three Line Breakaway, 37
Bearish Three Line Strike, 65
Bearish White Three-Gaps, 27
Bearish Window, 27, 169
Belt Hold Line, 49, 165
Black Candle, 10
Black Hammer, 94
Black Hangman, 65, 70, 173
Bollinger, John, 48, 49
Bollinger Bands, 48–49
Bonds, 151–55, 155–57
Bozu, 49, 69–70
Bozu Three Wings, 37

Breakaway Three-New Price Top, 27,
 33
Buddha Top, 5, 121
Bullish Black Gap, 106–7
Bullish Black Three-Gap, 33
Bullish Hammer, 94, 98
Bullish Harami, 30
Bullish Harami Cross, 32
Bullish Meeting Lines, 32
Bullish Three-Line Breakaway, 37
Bullish Window, 33

C

Cattle, 75–102
Close-In Line, 37
Closing Bozu, 49
Cocoa, 103–9
Computer Aided Pattern Recognition,
 206–7
Computer Analysis, 203–12,
 213–47, 249–78
Corn, 63–65
Corrective Wave, 43
Cotton, 115–28
Crude Oil, 129–33
Currency Analysis, 139–50

D

Dark Cloud Cover, 24, 98, 107, 165, 166–68
Doji, 12, 13–18, 25, 36, 159, 182
Doji Star, 13–18
Doji Star Reversal, 25, 31
Dojima Rice Exchange, 3
Double Thrusting Pattern, 30
Dumpling Doji, 49

E

Eight to Ten-New Price High, 28
Eight to Ten-New Price Low, 35
Elliot Wave Analysis, 43–47
Empty Baskets, 3
Energies, 129–37
Engulfing Bearish, 24, 94, 98
Engulfing Bullish, 30, 36, 92, 98, 106

F

Failure Swing, 234
Falling Three Method, 36
Fibonacci Retracement Theory, 40–43
Flagship Candle Patterns, 18–20, 169–70

G

Gas, 135–37
Gold, 159–62
Grains, 53–73
Gravestone, 106
Gravestone Doji, 194

H

Hammer, 31, 36, 179–81, 182
Hangman, 25
Harami, 15
Heating Oil, 135–37
Homma, Sokyu, 3–4

I

Impulse Wave, 43
Incomplete Dark Cloud Cover, 72
Inverted Hammer, 31, 36, 169

J

Jan Bell Marketing, 179–84

K

Kansas City Value Line, 177–78
Kemper Corp., 184–95

L

Last Engulfing, 157
Last Engulfing Pattern, 92, 156
Livestock, 75–102
Long Legged Doji Line, 92, 221

M

Major Market Blue Chip Index, 173–76
Marubozu, 49
Metals, 159–70
Mountain Gap, 37

N

New York Composite Index, 177–78

O

Oats, 58–60
Omnicom Group, 195–201
Opening Bozu Line, 49, 118
Orange Juice, 114–15

P

Palladium, 164–67
Paper Umbrellas, 13
Pattern Recognition, 213
Piercing Line, 30, 36, 70
Platinum, 167–70
Pole Line, 5–6
PRS, 169–70, 207–9, 213

R

R.S.I., 169–70, 234–35
Real Body, 5
Resistance and Support Trend Lines,
    47–48
Resistance Triangle, 106, 177
Rising Three Method, 37

S

Seven-Minute Chart, 7
Shadow, 5
Shooting Star, 25
Silver, 162–64
Simultaneous Three Wings, 35
Small Doji, 13–15
Small Doji Line, 78
Southern Evening Cross, 28
Soy Beans, 53–58
Soy Bean Oil, 60–63
Soy Meal, 65–71
Standard & Poor's 500, 173–76
Star Reversal, 25, 31
Stochastic, 169–70
Sugar, 109–14
Support and Resistance Trend Lines,
    47–48

T

Tasuki Downside Gap, 36
Tasuki Upside Gap, 35
Three Crows, 38
Three-Line Star in Deliberation, 38

Three-Line Strike, 35
Three River Doji Star, 5
Three-River Evening Star, 27
Three River Morning Star, 33
Three White Soldiers, 38, 167
Three Winged Top, 35
Thrusting Pattern, 92, 94, 165, 167,
    168
Tower Bottoms, 32, 36
Tower Tops, 26
Tri-Star Bottom, 37
Tri-Star Top, 37
Tweezers Bottoms, 32, 36, 78
Tweezers Pattern, 106
Tweezers Tops, 26
Twin Doji, 106
Two-Mountain Bottom, 34
Two-Mountain Top, 28

U

Unique Three-River Bottom, 35
Upside Gap Two-Crows, 24
Upside Gap Side-By-Side White
    Lines, 36

W

Wheat, 72–73
White Candle, 11
White Doji Star, 156
White Inverted Hammer, 167
Williams Percent Retracement,
    228–33